ROUGH DRAFT

COLD WAR MILITARY MANPOWER POLICY AND THE ORIGINS OF VIETNAM-ERA DRAFT RESISTANCE

AMY J. RUTENBERG

CORNELL UNIVERSITY PRESS

Ithaca and London

Cornell University Press gratefully acknowledges
receipt of a grant from the Iowa State University Publication
Endowment, ISU Foundation, which aided in the
publication of this book.

First published 2019 by Cornell University Press

Library of Congress Cataloging-in-Publication Data

Names: Rutenberg, Amy J., 1977- author.
Title: Rough draft : Cold War military manpower policy
    and the origins of Vietnam-era draft resistance /
    Amy J. Rutenberg.
Description: Ithaca [New York] : Cornell University Press,
    2019. | Includes bibliographical references and index.
Identifiers: LCCN 2018053746 (print) | LCCN 2018054968
    (ebook) | ISBN 9781501739378 (pdf) |
    ISBN 9781501739385 (epub/mobi) |
    ISBN 9781501739361 | ISBN 9781501739361 (cloth:) |
    ISBN 9781501739583 (pbk.)
Subjects: LCSH: Draft—United States—History—20th
    century. | United States—Armed Forces—Recruiting,
    enlistment, etc. | Manpower policy—United States—
    History—20th century.
Classification: LCC UB343 (ebook) | LCC UB343 .R88 2019
    (print) | DDC 355.2/2363097309045—dc23
LC record available at https://lccn.loc.gov/2018053746

For JEREMY and for DAVID
Thank you

CONTENTS

ACKNOWLEDGMENTS

I have a friend who likens writing a book to having a baby. I take issue with a few of the parallels. Gestating any living thing for more than a decade, the length of time it took to write this book, would be wholly unacceptable from any mother's point of view. Like raising a child, however, it definitely takes a village. I have many people to thank.

As an academic, I have been blessed to be part of three wonderful institutions, all of which graciously helped to fund this project. I owe thanks to the Department of History and the Graduate School at the University of Maryland, College Park; the Office of Research at Appalachian State University; and the Department of History, the College of Liberal Arts and Sciences, the Center for Excellence in the Arts and Humanities, and the Office of the Vice President of Research at Iowa State University. This project also received generous research grants from the United States Army Military History Institute, the Marine Corps Heritage Foundation, the Harry S. Truman Library, and the Institute for Political History. I could not have undertaken the travel necessary to do this work without this institutional support.

Once I arrived at my destinations, archivists at the National Archives and Records Administration in College Park, Maryland; the Wisconsin Historical Society in Madison, Wisconsin; the Truman Library in Independence, Missouri; the Dwight D. Eisenhower Library in Abilene, Kansas; the U.S. Army Heritage and Education Center in Carlisle, Pennsylvania; the Swarthmore College Peace Collection in Swarthmore, Pennsylvania; the Library of Congress in Washington, D.C.; and the University of Illinois, Urbana-Champaign offered invaluable help. Megan Harris with the Veteran's History Project at the Library of Congress, David Clark at the Truman Library, Herb Pankratz at the Eisenhower Library, Richard Sommers and David Keough at USAHEC, Wendy Chmielewsky at Swarthmore, and Lee Grady at the Wisconsin Historical Society deserve special mention. I also must thank the unnamed student workers who did so much scut work for me, particularly the poor soul who scanned page after page of the Harold Gauer collection at the WHS. As a graduate student, I worked in two different archives. It's a job that can be both thankless and boring, but it's invaluable from the researcher's point of view. So, thanks to you too.

Research findings, of course, don't interpret themselves. A wonderful community of scholars pointed me in new directions and helped me sharpen my arguments. First and foremost, I must thank Robyn Muncy. As my graduate adviser, she went above and beyond the call of duty. Variously cheerleader, critic, sounding board, and mentor, she played many roles in my life, helping to mold me into the scholar I have become. Her pointed questions helped me make analytical connections that I otherwise never would have. Perhaps even more importantly, she demonstrated by example that academia can be humane. I know of no other adviser who would set up their own office as a safe space for a graduate student to nurse her newborn. Robyn did this for me. I owe Jennifer Mittelstadt a similar debt of gratitude. I'm not sure Jennifer realizes how much I needed her pointed observations and wise counsel. I don't think I would have finished graduate school or stayed in academia afterward without the mentorship of these two wise women.

Along the way, many people read all or part of this manuscript. Thank you to Jeremy Best, Amy Sue Bix, Kristen Baldwin-Deathridge, Stacy Cordery, Gregory Daddis, Allison Fredette, David Freund, Christina Larocco, Clare Lyons, Julie Mancine, Larry McDonnell, Rachel Louise Moran, David Segal, Kimberly Welch, and Timothy Wolters. Thank you also to the unnamed readers from Cornell University Press. At the last minute, three nonhistorians stepped up to help me make sure the introduction made sense to people outside of my little bubble. Julie MacCartee, Michael Hulshof-Schmidt, and Lisa Berkowitz, you rock. I have also benefited from the advice and friendship of Peter Albert, Elizabeth Bellows, Ira Berlin, Andrew Kellett, Melissa Kravetz, Sonya Michel, Helena Iles Papaioannou, Stefan Papaioannou, Chas Reed, Pamela Riney-Kehrberg, Jon Sumida, Dara Wald, and all the scholars who have commented on my work at the various conference panels I have been part of over the years. Emily Andrew and everyone else at Cornell University Press have been immensely helpful in shepherding a newbie through the publishing process. Any errors that remain are mine entirely.

Finally, I would like to thank my family. Not everyone has a parent who supports their child's desire to give up a solid career to embark on the quixotic quest for a PhD and tenure-track job. I was blessed with two. Joel Rutenberg and Rebecca Becker Rutenberg both offered me their love and support when I quit my job as a high school history teacher to return to graduate school. They never complained, even when I did, and for that I am grateful. My father maintained an endless curiosity about the substance of my work and crooked career path, and my mother opened her home to me (and my cat) for extended periods while I was on research trips. I always knew I had a safe place to land. My brothers, Adam Rutenberg and David Rutenberg, were equally supportive. In our quest to be the most overeducated family ever, the three of us engaged in friendly competition to see who would graduate with their terminal degree last. I am thankful that I did not earn that particular title, but I think all three of us won because we each have the others. Gini Tate, Linda Best, Herb Best, Chris Best, Anna Best, Abigail Best, Julie Mac-Cartee, Joan MacCartee, Imogen Rutenberg, and Marissa Conrad all became part of my family along this journey. They are the best circle of in-laws a person could ask for. And, though technically not family, it seems only right to include all of the babysitters, childcare workers, and teachers who made it possible for to me balance the competing demands of scholarly work and parenting.

This brings me to the heart of my support network. Jeremy Best lives up to his name. He is the best husband, co-parent, colleague, scholar, and friend I could have asked for. He is the definition of a full partner, weathering family upheaval, multiple out-of-state moves, many migraines, professional uncertainty, and occasionally unhinged children with grace, love, and many jokes, most of which made me laugh. *Rough Draft*'s title is all him. Our sons, Benjamin and Noah, are the lights of my life. Together, they make me laugh every day. The never-ending exercise in problem solving that is parenthood has made me a more analytical scholar and a better educator. I hope that one day they will think that my professional choices have similarly benefited them. In the meantime, it is a delight to watch them grow. They gave me a reason to complete this project. To all of my men, I love you.

My grandmother, Florence Becker, wanted nothing more from her final years than for me to be happy. I hope that wherever she is, she can see that I am.

Selective Service Classification Chart
(1951–1973)

Classification	Meaning
I-A	Available for military service
I-A-O	Conscientious objector available for noncombatant military service
I-C	Member of the armed forces
I-D	Member of a reserve unit or approved officer procurement program
I-O	Conscientious objector opposed to all military service; available for alternate civilian service
I-S (H)	Student administratively deferred to complete high school
I-S (C)	College student administratively deferred to complete the current academic year
I-W	Conscientious objector assigned to alternate civilian service
I-Y (after 1962)	Unqualified for military service except in times of war or declared national emergency
II-A	Deferred for nonagricultural occupation
II-C	Deferred for agricultural occupation
II-S	Deferred as student to continue higher education
III-A	Deferred for reasons of dependency or hardship
IV-A	Deferred due to previous military service or as the sole surviving son in a family with one or more children who died in military service
IV-B	Deferred government official

IV-C   Deferred foreign national not liable for military service

IV-D   Deferred as minister or divinity student

IV-F   Unfit for military service for physical, mental, or moral
            reasons

Note: Adapted from Ann Yoder, "Military Classifications for Draftees,"
Swarthmore College Peace Collection, http://www.swarthmore.edu/library/
peace/conscientiousobjection/MilitaryClassifications.htm (accessed Feb. 19,
2018).

ROUGH DRAFT

Introduction

In September 1965, Harvey J. Fischer, a fifty-five-year-old man from Largo, Florida, in an act of disgust, mailed a letter to President Lyndon Johnson complaining about America's young men. To bolster his critique, he enclosed a clipping from his local newspaper. The article excoriated the current generation of military-aged men. "Never have so many American boys tried so many ruses to get out of serving their country," it claimed. Without citing any statistics or quoting any government officials, the article accused young men of failing to register, refusing to report for physicals, destroying draft cards, marrying prematurely, taking jobs they did not want, and going back to school for subjects they cared nothing about, all in order to avoid military service. "Those who ask what they can do for their country often seek the answer outside of the armed forces," worried the reporter, who concluded, "Men of draft age . . . simply don't seem to understand the necessity for manning the frontiers of freedom half a world away."[1]

This letter and accompanying article deserve comment for a number of reasons, not least because they were ordinary. The sentiments they expressed were not unique to the people of Florida's Gulf Coast. Rather, the claim that men were shirking their citizenship responsibilities by refusing to serve in the military would become a common refrain in articles, on TV, and around kitchen tables across the nation over the next eight years.

Second, by obliquely referencing President John F. Kennedy's 1961 inaugural speech, the reporter acknowledged an evolving definition of service to the state. What constituted service, who was responsible for it, and how those responsibilities could or should be carried out had been subjects of national discussion for years but had gained new salience with the commitment of ground forces to Vietnam. By 1965, Fischer, like most Americans, had already constructed the nebulous past, particularly World War II, as a time when male citizens had not questioned their duty to serve in the armed forces during times of national emergency. His generation, later branded the "greatest generation," understood the importance of military service, or so he believed. But, as Fischer's letter pointed out, men of the younger generation, those who would become the Vietnam generation, simply did not have the same understanding of service, which, incidentally, was why Fischer was writing the president. He wished to prove himself a good citizen by enlisting to fight in Vietnam at age fifty-five, but the armed forces kept rejecting him.

The most striking reason why the article is remarkable, however, is its timing. In the month it was published—September 1965—American combat troops had been in Vietnam for less than six months. Draft calls had started rising slowly after the Gulf of Tonkin Resolution the previous year, but the machinery for inducting men was only just creaking into high gear. Antiwar protest, though a frequent news item, was still a fairly marginal phenomenon when Fischer wrote the president. Rather, the timing of the article proves that patterns of draft avoidance behavior that later came to be associated with the Vietnam era draft—marrying young, entering particular occupations, going back to school—existed well before the war heated up.

The reporter of Fischer's article may have been correct that more men than usual were managing to avoid military service during a time of war, but Fischer was wrong in his letter to characterize American youth in the mid-1960s as lazy, unpatriotic, or different from previous generations. Instead, men during the Vietnam era were doing what American men had done during every one of America's earlier wars: they were taking advantage of the legal loopholes in the draft available to them. By 1965, those loopholes were wide enough to drive a bus through, but such expansion did not happen by accident. It was the result of twenty years' worth of pragmatic manpower decisions combined with planners' assumptions about men's proper role as citizens in a Cold War environment. The Vietnam War, with its heightened draft calls, exacerbated points of friction caused by the policies, but it did not cause them.

Prior to the Cold War, defense officials argued that conscription was warranted based on military need. During World War II, the American government and most of the populace defined total victory over the Axis powers as the primary shared war aim. Although the process of determining *how* that objective would be met was fraught, ultimately most citizens supported deferring those civilians who would keep the country's arsenal and food pantry stocked. The Selective Service grudgingly granted deferments and exemptions from military service to those with unique skills or characteristics, but only under duress. Although draft officials had to contend with competing civilian desires and political demands—which often privileged social values of importance, like fathers as the moral center of the family—Selective Service officers ultimately framed deferments as wartime expedients designed to support a military endeavor.

Between 1948 and 1965, however, Congress, the Selective Service, and the Department of Defense justified both the draft and deferments differently. During these years, they explicitly used the draft to support a prolonged ideological, technological, and economic struggle against communism in which the home front itself was a crucial site of defense operations. The Cold War draft was expected to be an indefinite addition to American society. Because there was no immediate military emergency through most of these years, there was no "for the duration." Conscription became the new normal. As they shifted their focus from externally oriented national defense to internally oriented national security, military manpower policy planners across federal agencies defined men's domestic choices as appropriate concerns for themselves. In particular, the Selective Service System took license to use deferments from the draft as a tool of social engineering. The agency openly used them to coerce men to matriculate and enter occupations defined as in the national interest. It also implicitly encouraged men to marry and have children. This policy, known as manpower channeling, specifically defined these pursuits as service to the state and granted them the equivalency of military service.

In the process, policymakers privileged a particular version of breadwinner masculinity, first by offering deferments to those men who could most easily access the specialized training of higher education and who could meet the Selective Service's stringent requirements for supporting dependents, and then by targeting poor and minority men for specialized training to help them meet those requirements through military channels. Policies normalized deferments for middle-class men, whose status as heads of household was viewed by policymakers as essential to national security, and targeted poor men for military service in order to teach them middle-class masculine values. Ultimately, manpower policy not only *protected* men who became students, who entered privileged occupational fields, and who married and became fathers, but it *encouraged* them to do so by defining what they did as service to the state, and it did this in a particularly race-based and class-oriented way.

These policies, though formulated to meet specific military needs, had two unintended consequences. First, reframing the rationale for military manpower policy in the 1950s and early 1960s unintentionally fortified American men's already existent ambivalence toward military service, culminating in men's widespread draft avoidance behavior during the Vietnam War. Military manpower policies weakened the relationship between service in the armed forces and masculine citizenship obligations so thoroughly by the mid-1960s that neither the rhetoric of protecting home and hearth through military service nor the threat of government reprisals could save the draft. Too many men did not feel it was their responsibility to serve, especially in a war many placed somewhere on the continuum between misguided and immoral. Second, defining civilian pursuits as service to the state using the civic republican language of obligation, ironically, fueled the arguments of activists and politicians who focused on individual citizens' rights in a classically liberal mold. Left-leaning antiwar activists, including draft counselors, and right-leaning civil libertarians both used the waning relationship between military service and male citizenship obligations to argue that men had the right to decide if they wished to serve in the armed forces rather than subject themselves to conscription. In a significant departure from the trends of earlier wars, American men, especially white, middle-class men, continued to look for ways to avoid service even after Congress and the Selective Service tightened draft regulations during the Vietnam War. They did not see it as their responsibility to serve.

Citizenship in the United States has never been predicated on military service.[2] Nevertheless, the ideal of the citizen-soldier has functioned as a potent symbol of American manhood. Idealized expectations for men have centered heavily on their responsibility to defend the nation through the use of force during times of emergency. Because military service, for the most part, was available only to men and only men could be drafted, serving as a member of the armed forces became uniquely associated with a particularly masculine form of citizenship.[3] A type of masculinity that emphasized duty, honor, patriotism, and strength consistently infused cultural representations of military service from the mid-1800s up through the modern era.[4] From pamphlets to propaganda posters to characters portrayed by John Wayne, those images, in turn, consciously were used to encourage men to enlist.[5] The feminized social position of conscientious objectors, who were branded as sissies, weaklings, cowards, and traitors during the Civil War and both

World Wars, underscores this point. Additionally, veterans, who until the very late twentieth century were overwhelmingly male, earned special benefits, including pensions, preferential hiring status, health care, low-interest loans, and access to education, that remained unavailable to Americans who did not—or could not—enter the armed forces, a phenomenon historian Patrick J. Kelly has termed "martial citizenship."[6]

World War II marked the high point of mass citizen participation in the American military and of martial citizenship in the United States. Approximately sixteen million men—including 80 percent of those born in the 1920s—served in the armed forces during the war.[7] The majority were drafted. But whether each individual enlisted or was conscripted, military service was, for that generation, a common experience. The passage of the Servicemen's Readjustment Act of 1944, more popularly known as the GI Bill, allowed almost an entire generation of American men access to the benefits of martial citizenship. Volunteers and draftees alike—citizen-soldiers all—gained special status through their military service.

Moreover, just as had been the case throughout the era of modern warfare, the majority of eligible men who received draft notices during World War II served without protesting publicly. Within their circles of family and friends, inductees grumbled and complained, but if they were drafted they served. Their reasons for doing so were complex, but they tended to boil down to a combination of public pressure, legal coercion, economic benefit, and a sense of personal responsibility.[8] Men who willfully failed to answer the call to arms faced the possibility of jail time, which for most was an adequate deterrent to resistance. Others chose not to seek legal deferments for fear of social ridicule. For them, the benefits of the masculine, martial citizenship that accompanied military service outweighed the sacrifice of that service. Many enlistees and draftees, therefore, felt some obligation as citizens and as men to defend their homes, their communities, their comrades-in-arms, and their nation. They may not have volunteered for military service, but if their country called them, they served.

And yet, despite the benefits of martial citizenship and strong social pressure to serve during times of war, the process of induction was never seamless. By pairing the promise of bonuses and benefits with the threat of jail time, the US military has been able to fill its ranks during every American war that has utilized the draft, but only after massive expenditures of time, effort, and money. The draft was a major source of contention during the Civil War in both the South and the North, as the 1863 New York draft riots most famously reflected, and during World War I.[9] Men of all stripes have tried to avoid military service in each of America's wars.

Many men who refused to bear arms opposed America's wars on the basis of conscience. Whether religious or secular, opposed to all wars or solely the one at hand, absolutist or willing to perform noncombatant service in the military or alternate service in a civilian capacity, conscientious objectors (COs) have confounded authorities. Legal definitions of conscientious objection and the regulations governing COs changed within and during each American war, but regardless of wording, laws invariably excluded some men who considered themselves conscientious objectors. During World War I, the law allowed only men from historic peace churches—Quakers, Brethren, and Mennonites—to legally object to war. Legislators during World War II expanded the definition of a CO to incorporate men from mainline religious faiths, but left out thousands of others. Approximately five thousand men, including Jehovah's Witnesses and members of the Nation of Islam, whose claims to CO status were routinely rejected by local and appeal boards, went to prison between 1940 and 1947.[10] Further, some small percentage of men outright resisted induction during each war in which the US (and Confederate) government utilized conscription. War resisters, as a loosely defined group, objected variously to the political rationales for war, the moral implications of violence, the level of government compulsion inherent in a draft, the sacrifice military service demanded, and the threat of death on the battlefield. They refused even to register with authorities, claiming that any cooperation with a militarized system enabled the prosecution of war. War resisters and most COs, therefore, were activists. They actively campaigned against war, conscription, and, at times, the federal government itself.[11] Their commitment to activism historically tied them together as they advocated both for an end to hostilities and for what they perceived as their right not to fight.

This book, however, is generally not about war resisters or COs, although such activists do factor into the story at times. Rather, it focuses on the much larger number of men, the nonactivists, who sought legal means to avoid induction between World War II and the Vietnam War. These men have always been present, finding ways to slip between the cracks, frequently by angling for deferments. Even during World War II, a historical moment when the military, the state, and the American populace were more tightly connected than ever before, the Selective Service and War Department had to fight vicious political battles in order to tighten deferment criteria. Lobbying organizations and individual men alike emphasized the importance of men's civilian roles, even in the depths of total war, in large part because the sacrifices of military service were simply too great.

In the aggregate, American men have been consistent in their reluctance to perform military service. Most tellingly, conscription during wartime has been necessary because men have rarely been eager to leave their families or put themselves in mortal danger, regardless of the cause. As early as the nation's founding, Thomas Paine praised the men who remained at the continental army's 1776 encampment at Valley Forge because so many "summer soldier[s]" and "sunshine patriot[s]" had simply walked away from the battlefield.[12] Over the years, those who received draft notices tended to serve, but men used all manner of strategies to avoid qualifying for Uncle Sam's greetings. Those who sought methods to avoid induction through much of American history tended to do so quietly and as individuals rather than through social movements or public activism.

And this is why the Vietnam War was different. Once again, most men who were drafted served, but a much higher proportion of eligible men, including those who would not define themselves as political in nature or as social activists, did not, frequently because they *actively* and *publicly* sought legal means to avoid military service.[13] Men shared information with one another about how to escape military service. They sought help from organizations. They consulted manuals published to help them. They visited draft counselors. New Left and pacifist organizations with nationwide followings such as Students for a Democratic Society and the Central Committee for Conscientious Objectors along with hundreds of smaller, local antiwar groups and organizations, helped foment "a massive campaign of public disobedience."[14] One survey of 1,586 men found that 60 percent of draft-eligible men took some sort of action to escape conscription during the conflict.[15] According to another study, 26 percent of draft-age men altered their educational plans in order to gain a student deferment, 21 percent spoke to a doctor to learn how to qualify for a medical deferment, 11 percent allowed their desire to avoid the draft to influence their career choice, and four percent chose to alter their bodies in some way to avoid military service.[16] This public expansion of draft avoidance behavior was possible during the Vietnam War because military manpower policies during the 1950s and early 1960s, especially manpower channeling, made it possible. They provided individual men with multiple legal avenues by which they could escape military service.

Individual men who sought to avoid the draft did not do so because they consciously recognized a government message that their civilian pursuits counted as service to the nation. They did not justify their own deferments by claiming patriotism in engineering or fatherhood. Rather, by the time of the Vietnam War, many men with means viewed military service as a choice, even when faced with conscription. However individual men chose to define their own masculinity and citizenship, policies and practices conveyed the message that more affluent men did not need to serve in the armed forces to prove themselves responsible men or good Americans, a message that antiwar draft counselors reinforced. Moreover, as military service became a less common experience, especially for middle-class men, draft avoiders were much less likely than during previous conflicts to have their masculinity questioned, which in turn may have encouraged more men to seek deferments.[17] Policies, therefore, weakened the masculine citizen-soldier ideal, especially within white, middle-class communities.

This book joins a growing body of literature that highlights how assumptions about gender, race, sexuality, and social class shaped public policy and how, in turn, public policy shaped identities and social relations.[18] It argues that debates over men's proper role in society influenced military manpower policy. Different constituencies, including defense officials, members of Congress, civic and professional organizations, and activists of all types, created a rich discourse as they debated who should offer service to the nation, what form that service should take, and what those who served—and the country itself—should gain as a result of that service. As they discussed which men should serve in the armed forces and which should not, politicians, military officials, and ordinary Americans betrayed strong attachments to competing ideals of masculinity. They asked questions about whether men could better protect their families as breadwinners or as soldiers and they tied their disparate answers to assumptions about the rights and responsibilities of male citizens, the only constituency subject to the draft.

Rough Draft, therefore, uses the lens of military manpower policy to shed light on the contested relationships between choice and compulsion, rights and responsibilities in a democracy. During the 1940s and 1950s, the law— and most Americans—agreed that men had a responsibility to bear arms in the name of national defense. By the mid-1960s, however, Selective Service policies and practices, combined with a changing political, social, and diplomatic landscape, significantly undermined that consensus, even as the agency continued to use the language of civic republican obligation. Public debates over military service were intimately tied to ideas of the responsibilities of masculine citizenship. This book shows how and why military manpower policy specifically targeted underprivileged men for the draft and men from privileged backgrounds for deferments in the years before 1965. Working-class men often did not want to serve in the armed forces any more than middle-class men, but manpower policies that stressed middle-class standards of education, family structure, and earnings potential offered them fewer options to avoid induction.

From these class-based policies flow an additional use of the scholarly term "economic citizenship." Recent historians have used the term to signify the system of benefits workers earned from the state through their employment, including the right to Social Security's old age pensions, unemployment compensation, and disability insurance. Such benefits offered workers a measure of economic stability and marked them as full participants in the political economy.[19] Entitlements also afforded them the ability to consume, a fact evident even on US military bases in Vietnam, where soldiers demanded the right to consumer goods, including American steak and Coca-Cola.[20] Historians have also used the term as shorthand for the right to earn a living.[21] This work pushes the term further. It uses "economic citizenship" to refer to a set of responsibilities citizens owed to the state in addition to the benefits workers expected from it.

Economic markers, including a high gross national product, full employment, and a consumerist lifestyle, became, in the minds of some, weapons of the Cold War in the 1950s and 1960s. Men's ability to earn a living for their families not only earned them the right to federal entitlements but also became a matter of national security in the minds of significant policymakers. A democratic, capitalist system could not prove its superiority if a significant segment of the population lived in poverty and was therefore dependent on handouts.[22] Breadwinning fathers kept families off the dole and earned the federal benefits they gained. But their labor—and therefore their economic independence—was also defined by the Selective Service as a contribution to the nation's defense. Self-sufficient workers strengthened the United States. Deferments in the 1950s and Department of Defense initiatives in the 1960s designed to locate and "rehabilitate" poor and minority men were designed to encourage and train men to enter the civilian workforce. These programs sent the message that military service was only one way for men to defend and serve the nation. Supporting their families was another. For certain defense planners, helping men earn full economic citizenship eclipsed the masculine obligation of military service.

This connection has important implications for the historiography of militarization in the United States. Military manpower policies that defined nonmilitary pursuits as essential to national security clearly served to militarize the civilian sector, as certain occupations and domestic arrangements were portrayed as aiding the country's national defense against communism. Civilian scientists conducted the research necessary to build a better bomb. Fathers financially supported their families, which helped Americans achieve the consumerist lifestyle that was supposed to characterize a capitalist democracy. Public education campaigns encouraged fathers to lead their families' civil defense efforts.[23] Manpower policies helped militarize huge swaths of civilian life by associating national security with civilian pursuits.

Such militarization had some odd effects. The defense establishment, in using deferments to encourage middle-class men to stay in the civilian world, unintentionally undermined its own manpower procurement system. Planners militarized civilian masculinity even as they de-emphasized military masculinity as a citizenship obligation. Policies harnessed civilian men's professions and parenthood to the state in the name of national security and oddly downplayed their duty to serve as soldiers. Military manpower policies weakened the citizen-soldier ideal and ensured that a shrinking proportion of men would serve in the military.

And here lies the difference between militarization and militarism in American history. Both terms have slippery definitions. At times, scholars, journalists, and the public have used them interchangeably. Others, as I will, make distinctions between them. Following Lisa M. Mundey, this book defines "militarism" as Americans did in the immediate wake of World War II. Following their experience fighting fascism, Americans tended to understand militarism as "the aggressive use of a military force; the military's possession of power outside of civil authority or constitutional limits," and the "regimentation" of society.[24] Even as they maintained a military draft and mobilized for the Cold War, most people in the United States saw themselves as antimilitarist. They believed that the nation's insistence on civilian control of the military and the glorification of democratic individualism separated their society from the militarist totalitarianism of Nazi Germany, Imperial Japan, or the Soviet Union. In the words of Richard H. Kohn, America's "institutions, policies, behaviors, thought, and values" absolutely were militarized as they became "devoted to military power and shaped by war."[25] Or as Michael Sherry put it, "war and national security" certainly became "consuming anxieties" that "provided the memories, models, and metaphors that shaped broad areas of national life," but militarism did not take hold.[26] "War and military power" did not become "dominant . . . or defining values" or "ends in themselves."[27] The United States did not turn into a "garrison state."[28]

More concretely, most little boys during the Cold War grew up steeped in the glorification and heroism of military service. They played cowboys and Indians, Americans vs. "Japs," and, later, G.I. Joe. They watched war movie after war movie and television programs funded by the American military. Some internalized the connection between military service and masculinity.

They romanticized service in the armed forces as an opportunity to build their own manhood and develop heroism.[29] But the connection was not universal. Cold War America offered many different models of how to be a man, and even popular war stories offered ambivalent and contradictory messages about military service.[30] A militarized America did not necessarily translate into universal martial manhood, particularly when manpower policies themselves encouraged middle-class men to stay out of the active duty military. Policymakers militarized civilian, breadwinning forms of masculinity by coopting them into to the national security state, even as their policies undercut ideals of martial masculinity.

Military manpower policies, therefore, affected the life choices of men and their families, what historian Anne Deighton has called "the lived Cold War."[31] As deferments from military service became normalized through the 1950s and 1960s, they became significantly easier to obtain and excuse. This in turn influenced the career choices of some men, when they married, and the circumstances under which they decided to have children. For a few, the availability of deferments affected how they treated their bodies, including whether they sought treatment for medical conditions. These men directly reacted to laws and regulations that governed deferments and that had evolved in response to America's foreign policy and defense needs. *Rough Draft* explicitly illustrates how policies shaped in reaction to Cold War strategy directly impacted individual lives.

And the draft impacted almost all American men in one way or another between 1940 and 1973. Therefore, a note explaining the process by which men entered the military is in order. Between 1948 and 1973, men became soldiers in one of two ways. The first was by volunteering. If a man chose to enlist, either because he genuinely wanted to serve or under pressure from the draft, he signed up for the service branch and program of his choice through local recruiting stations. He would then undergo a physical exam, aptitude testing, and an interview at an Armed Forces Examining Station (AFES) in his home state.[32] If he met the entrance requirements for his desired service branch, he was sent to basic training, upon the satisfactory completion of which he would be a soldier, sailor, airman, or marine. College men could also volunteer for the Reserve Officer Training Corps (ROTC), which, if successfully completed, would lead to a commission in the reserves or active duty forces.

The second option for entering the military was to wait to be drafted through the Selective Service System. Most men registered at their local Selective Service boards in person upon their eighteenth birthdays. Through the 1950s and early 1960s, as deferment standards became more lenient, those who could demonstrate physical disabilities with a note from a physician could be classified as IV-F, or ineligible for military service, upon their initial contact with the Selective Service. Everyone else received a questionnaire designed to provide local board members with information about the registrant's dependents, educational status, occupation, and religion. Based on the man's answers, members of the man's local board—unpaid volunteers who were overwhelmingly veterans and who were all men—would provisionally classify the man as I-A, eligible for service, or begin proceedings to determine if he was eligible for a deferment according to current Selective Service regulations. Those who received deferments would have their files reviewed once per year to determine if the mitigating factor remained. If a man graduated from college, lost his job, or experienced some change in his dependency status—if an elderly parent whom he supported died, for example—he would be provisionally reclassified as I-A.

Those whom local boards provisionally classified as I-A eventually would be called to their nearest AFES for their preinduction exam, a procedure identical to the induction exam taken by volunteers. Men were asked to strip down to their underwear and move from station to station to have various parts of their bodies examined. After the physical exam was completed, men would dress and move on for what the Army described as a mental test, an aptitude test designed to measure a potential recruit's ability to absorb military training.[33] After a full day, men returned home to wait. If and when the military needed them, they would receive an induction notice and be returned to the AFES for an induction exam. If a man passed muster, he would be sworn into a particular service branch—the army for most of the period under study—and be sent to basic training. Between 1948 and 1973, the preinduction exam was a common and nerve-wracking process for almost all American men.

Rough Draft, then, analyzes trends to make an argument about Americans' attitudes toward military service over time. It moves chronologically from the outset of World War II through postwar debates over universal military training, the Cold War development of manpower channeling, and attempts by manpower planners to yoke the War on Poverty to military service. Along the way, it examines how race and class became part of planners' calculations over who should be drafted and who should remain civilians. It ends with the death of the draft during the Vietnam War, arguing that in working to avoid the draft, men during the Vietnam War did not behave terribly differently from men during World War II or the Korean War. Rather, it was the context of their actions that changed. The historical conditions of the Vietnam War made it easier for men to engage in draft avoidance behavior.

This book cannot and does not represent every individual's experience of the time period under study. Americans' experiences were diverse. Men have served—and men and women continue to serve—for a variety of reasons. During the period the book covers, individual men enlisted or accepted their inductions out of a sense of duty and patriotism. They sought to defend their homes, defeat the threats of fascism and communism, support their families, or better themselves as individuals. Nevertheless, in the aggregate, midcentury military manpower policies weakened the relationship between military service and the responsibilities of masculine citizenship. In so doing, they opened the door to the antidraft protest of the Vietnam era.

In many ways, this book is a story of unintended consequences. The Selective Service grounded its deferment policies during the 1950s and 1960s in the language of masculine responsibility. Officials explicitly defined nonmilitary pursuits as essential to the national defense against communism. Ironically, the rhetoric of civic republicanism planners used to justify otherwise pragmatic manpower procurement decisions aided the ascendance of a rights-based conception of citizenship and helped usher in the era of the All-Volunteer Force.

Chapter 1

"Digging for Deferments"

World War II, 1940–1945

Just weeks before the Japanese attack at Pearl Harbor, Gen. J. O. Donovan, the state director of Selective Service for California, wrote the agency's central headquarters in Washington, D.C., asking for advice. It seemed that a particular registrant had requested a deferment from induction because, he stated, his wife was pregnant. The man's local board, however, had reason to question the legitimacy of the registrant's claim and wished to submit the man's wife to a pregnancy test at the state's expense. Donovan wanted to know if the national office would reimburse the California office for the cost of the test. Col. Carlton S. Dargusch, the deputy director of Selective Service, responded promptly. Yes, he replied, Donovan could authorize the test at government expense after "due examination" had established its necessity.[1] This case was not unique. The Selective Service tried to make clear to the states and to local boards that it was the responsibility of individual men to pay any costs associated with proving dependency claims, but there are other examples of the agency reimbursing states for pregnancy tests.[2]

Asking women, who were theoretically outside of the purview of the Selective Service, to submit to medical exams was perhaps the most invasive example of the Selective Service digging into the private lives of registrants and their families during what became the World War II draft, but it was not the only one. Many local boards spent considerable time and resources investigating individual families to determine whether and to what extent the men materially contributed to family resources and when children had been conceived before granting draft classifications.[3] By 1943, the Selective Service had a detailed policy on determining the date of a baby's conception that included discussion of a woman's menstrual cycle and methods of counting forward from the first day of her last period or the baby's quickening and backward from its delivery date.[4]

As this example illustrates, the issue of deferments bedeviled the Selective Service throughout the war. It was an agency that justified its mission based on the idea that all able-bodied men within a given age range had an equal obligation to serve in the military but that not all of these men could be spared equally from the civilian economy. America's "arsenal of democracy" had to be supplied and fed, and many men otherwise qualified for military service could not be replaced easily if conscripted because they possessed skills needed in the civilian world. The key was developing the criteria on which decisions could be made about which men should remain civilians and which could be spared for military service.

By 1945, the Selective Service had classified most men between the ages of eighteen and twenty-five as eligible for military service. The diversity of men classified as available undeniably made the American military of World War II a citizen army. Just under 16 million men served in the armed forces between 1940 and 1945 out of a total population of 130 million, including women, children, and the aged. In other words, approximately 12 percent of the entire American population performed some type of military service during the war years, and scholars have estimated that a full 80 percent of the men born in the 1920s served in uniform.[5] These men came from all walks of life, all races, all socioeconomic levels, and all levels of educational attainment. They were from all regions of the country and had ancestry from all over the globe. The vast majority never considered military service until the war began and did not envision staying in the military afterward. The military was racially segregated, but, taken as a whole institution, it was diverse and filled with men oriented more toward the civilian world than toward professional soldiering.

But what is frequently lost in this statistical picture is that many, many individual men were more than happy to take advantage of the legal deferments offered them by the Selective Service during the early years of the war, and they resisted the loss of those deferments as the war progressed. Military service was not a given for a large proportion of the American male population. Although they tended not to call attention to their actions, many men sought any legal avenue they could find to avoid military service. In so doing, they took advantage of the mechanisms for deferment created by the Selective Service, much to the chagrin of Selective Service officials.

Determining the dividing line between draftable and nondraftable men provides the central tension of any system of selective military service. What is striking, however, is that through at least 1943, the calculus over which men should serve and which men should remain civilians was not solely related to how a man's job supported the war effort. Instead, laws passed by Congress, Selective Service regulations, and the on-the-ground practice of individual local draft boards reflected a national belief in the importance of men as the financial and moral center of the household. Cultural values about the domestic responsibilities of husbands and fathers suffused the entire system, and whether it wanted to or not, during World War II—as during previous American wars—the Selective Service had to grapple with these cultural values. Dependency deferments, which were created to support alternate visions of male responsibility, including breadwinner and father, created loopholes in the draft, which is precisely why the Selective Service found itself ordering pregnancy tests.

As the war deepened and manpower needs increased, procuring enough men to expand the armed services became more important. After significant political and public debate, Congress and the Selective Service rescinded deferments that protected husbands and fathers. Occupational deferments, the major remaining category of deferments, continued to shelter men who held jobs in essential industries and in agriculture, but this classification was defined specifically as supporting the military effort in Europe and Asia rather than protecting domestic morality. It was based purely on national defense considerations, as the needs of a total war effort ultimately trumped the needs of individual families. The resultant wide net that put so many men into uniform made it appear in retrospect that men's patriotism and deeply felt responsibility to defeat the Axis powers had driven America's victory against fascism. Certainly that is the narrative created by the myth of the "greatest generation," but such widespread participation in the armed forces was far from automatic. Uniformed service was contested during World War II—not to the scale it would be in later years—but in a more significant way than is generally acknowledged. Even during the so-called "Good War," the links between masculine forms of citizenship and military service were not as strong as many Americans believe.

When Americans of the early twenty-first century reflect back on World War II, the image that most conjure is some version of the myth of the "Good War." They envision the era as one of unity and consensus, when their forebears came together to beat truly evil enemies. The cause was just, the people patriotic, and the soldiers brave. There was no moral ambiguity. The sacrifices war required were difficult, but they were shared and bore dividends in the form of good jobs during the war and prosperity afterward that few could have dreamt of during the prior decade of depression.[6]

Special attention is lavished on the men who served in the military. According to the common narrative, men, regardless of how they ended up in the armed forces, fulfilled their responsibilities as citizens through military service, and—through their manly sacrifice and the GI Bill—earned the educational and economic opportunities that allowed them to become successful masculine breadwinners after the war. Military service more than any other factor defined the so-called greatest generation. Male veterans of this generation have been described as daring, brave, uncomplaining, innovative, persistent, and humble.[7] They "spread the lesson of tolerance throughout the country."[8] In American cultural memory, widespread military service during World War II turned hyphenated Americans into full Americans, boys into men, and the United States into a world power.[9]

Scholars have debunked most of these myths, describing them as incomplete at best. While Americans *did* come together in ways they rarely had before or since, they did so kicking and screaming. Political parties squabbled over the best way to finance and run the war, military officials disagreed with civilian ones, government agencies jockeyed for power, labor clashed with management, race riots erupted in cities like Detroit and Los Angeles, Japanese Americans were incarcerated in camps without the right of due process, lynchings and more subtle forms of racism continued unabated, women struggled to gain respect in the workforce, children faced upheaval as parents left home for work and the front.[10] Even in 1944, three years after the start of the war, polls indicated that up to 40 percent of the population did not know why the United States was fighting.[11] For families who lost loved ones, the notion of a "good war" would have seemed strange indeed.

In fact, the popular linking of the World War II generation with these characteristics—fearlessness, strength, selflessness, manliness—was the result of careful and conscious image production both during and after the war. This was particularly true with regard to military service. Prior to World War II, military service was a profession viewed with suspicion.[12] In the colorful words of one observer, the popular perception of the American soldier in 1942 was "still a national guard jag staggering drunkenly down the street at two a.m."[13] During the war, however, government and civilian sources alike used images of soldiers to embody a renewed American muscularity after the impotent years of the Great Depression. They were used as a symbol of masculine patriotism through which all Americans could confirm their citizenship.[14] They became "the personification of the cause" that gave "America a beautiful personal stake—emotional stake—in [the war's] success."[15] Such imagery became necessary because neither the federal government nor private interests were able to persuade Americans that they should fight out of political obligation.

Instead, media—from both public and private sources—purposely connected the ideas of manhood and moral responsibility. Organizations, groups, and companies from the War Department to the American Red Cross, from Coca-Cola to Community Silverplate, which manufactured silverware, encouraged men to join the military and risk their lives because it was their manly responsibility to protect their loved ones.[16]

FIGURE 1.1. "O'er the Ramparts." This poster, created by Jes Wilhelm Schlaikjer in 1945, advertised the valor of American soldiers serving in the Army Air Forces. It used a number of masculine tropes common to American patriotic imagery during World War II. Note the figure's strong hands, broad shoulders, chiseled jaw, and determined yet wistful expression. Photo courtesy of Northwestern University Library, https://images.northwestern.edu/multiresimages/inu:dil-4d5f2160-973b-46f3-938c-3310031e8816.

Historian Christian Appy has termed this type of imagery "sentimental militarism," a media trope that constructed the GI as a peace-loving American reluctantly fulfilling his citizenship obligations in order to protect his loved ones, proving his patriotism and manhood in the process.[17]

Informational campaigns reminded the public that men in essential war industries "fought" the enemy and were therefore necessary to the war effort. They, too, could be protectors.

Yet the dominant cultural message of the war years clearly elevated those who served in the military as the "real" men. Over and over, cultural

FIGURE 1.2.   "We Can't All Go—But We Can All Help!" This 1942 poster, created by the US Department of the Treasury, tapped into World War II's brand of sentimental militarism. It used the viewer's knowledge that the soldier was willing to leave his child to help save his nation as a mechanism to encourage civilians to purchase war bonds. Photo courtesy of Northwestern University Library, https://images.northwestern.edu/multiresimages/inu:dil-c4229910-ece1-4031-bd10-84814d8ee0f5

FIGURE 1.3.   "Give 'Em Both Barrels." This 1941 poster by Jean Carll for the US Office for Emergency Management reminded industrial workers that their civilian tools, too, could be weapons of war. Photo courtesy of Northwestern University Library, https://images. northwestern.edu/multiresimages/inu:dil-4481ed9c-cd51-4485-b5a3-92ba6e709ce1

productions of the war years, especially Hollywood movies, portrayed worthy men as soldiers, sailors, and marines. Male characters who sought to avoid the draft saw the error of their ways, while those in production work, supposedly vital to American victory, schemed and scraped to enter the service or be shipped overseas.[18] Songs like 1943's "4-F Charlie," which depicted a man deferred for physical reasons as "a complete physical wreck" who could "never be a father," implied that a man who did not enter the armed forces could never be useful or worthy of love. Women would not "praise [the] martial daring" of—or even date—a man who never wore a uniform.[19]

Americans responded to these cues. They tied themselves tightly to the expansion of the state in an effort to win the war through their home front activities. They grew victory gardens and collected scrap metal at government urging. They submitted to rationing. They took war jobs. Eighty-five million people out of 130 million invested in the government's war effort by buying war bonds. Yet no matter how much civilians contributed, "everything they did was measured against the idealized sacrifice of the combat soldier," who was always equated with the best American manhood had to offer.[20]

Men of military age internalized the messages that connected manhood with military service. Veterans who have given oral histories repeatedly return to the theme of joining up to become "men." In the iconic oral history, "The Good War," by Studs Terkel, rifleman Robert Rasmus explained that he wanted to "forever be liberated" from the "sense of inferiority that [he] wasn't rugged."[21] Roger Tuttrup wanted "to be a hero."[22] Ted Allenby, a gay marine, chose the marines, "the toughest outfit," because, as he put it, "being a homosexual, I had that constant compelling need to prove how virile I was."[23] In his interview for the Library of Congress' Veteran's History Project, Robert McClure of western Kentucky explained that he enlisted because he was worried that people would think he was afraid to go.[24] Ralph Chase of Connecticut similarly believed that he would be "blackballed" as a coward if he did not join up.[25]

Yet this type of narrative, no matter how ubiquitous during and since the war, was not universal. Countless other men either outright rejected the connection between manhood and military service or simply failed to let it dictate their decisions. Close to twelve thousand conscientious objectors chose alternate service in Civilian Public Service camps rather than be drafted into the armed forces, and another six thousand went straight to federal prison in their desire to avoid cooperating with the warfare state. These men found meaning in principled resistance to military service, and many consciously connected their activism to the masculine qualities of bravery and courage.[26]

Other men simply tried to avoid induction in any way they could. Arkansan John L. McRee, after getting married in a double ceremony to one of two sisters, took his I-A classification to appeal in order to challenge inconsistencies between local draft boards after his new brother-in-law received a marriage deferment from the next board over. It was not that McRee wanted the other man to be drafted, it was that he himself wanted to remain with his new wife.[27] Joe Paul Monte of Jefferson County, Alabama, applied for a dependency deferment because, he claimed, he conducted all the business transactions for his widowed mother's grocery store. His application explained that his mother needed help because she only spoke Italian, Joe's brother was busy running his own business, and his sisters were married. In other words, although the other Monte siblings were theoretically available, Joe felt he was needed to support his mother while the others fulfilled their gendered responsibilities to their families. Military service, he believed, would cause him to fail in his filial duties, or at least this was the account he gave to the Selective Service.[28] Photographer and public relations man Harold Gauer and his friend Robert Bloch, who later went on to write *Psycho*, spent much of 1942 scheming about how to keep Gauer from being

FIGURE. 1.4. "Portrait of Group in Costume: Result of the Draft." This tableau, staged by Harold Gauer, was supposed to illustrate the probable result of being drafted to fight World War II. Gauer and his friend Robert Bloch both took positive action to avoid conscription for the duration of the war. Photo courtesy of the Wisconsin Historical Society, WHS-64493.

conscripted.[29] Bloch himself likely married as a way to disqualify himself from the draft.[30]

Even the United States Military Academy at West Point developed a reputation as a haven from combat. In fact, once World War II ended, more than 20 percent of cadets left their training before being commissioned.[31] These stories have been glossed over in the years since World War II in an effort "to recast the war" into a "Good War."[32]

The terms of the Selective Training and Service Act of 1940 were contested from their first inception. In the spring of 1940, as Europe's "phony war" came to an end, those with an interest in American preparedness for war began to gain political ground.[33] Supporters of universal military training, led by New York attorney Grenville Clark, used the crisis caused by the fall of France to convince Republican senator James Wadsworth of New York and Democratic senator Edward Burke of Nebraska to introduce a bill asking for a reinstatement of the draft. Clark, Burke, and Wadsworth hoped to use the draft as a first step toward universal military training. The War Department, under the new leadership of Secretary of War Henry Stimson, lent support to the idea of renewing conscription, but took issue with the intent of the Burke-Wadsworth bill. Since 1926, a Joint Army-Navy Selective Service Committee (JANSSC) had been working on a plan to efficiently reinstate Selective Service should it ever be needed again, and the War Department preferred a more narrow focus on manpower procurement.

Despite growing public support for an expanded military, it took three months of quiet negotiation and public wrangling to get the bill through Congress. Pacifists vigorously protested a departure from the American peacetime tradition of a small standing army filled solely through voluntary enlistment. They saw a rapid and compulsory expansion of the military as a scant step from the militarism of America's enemies.[34] Among those who supported conscription, the age of the men who should be liable for service, the length of that service, and how it should be compensated created major legislative obstacles. Finally, on September 16, 1940, President Roosevelt signed a substantially modified Burke-Wadsworth bill into law.[35]

The law, as passed in 1940, required all men between the ages of twenty-one and thirty-six to register with the Selective Service. Inductees would be liable for twelve months of active-duty training and service followed by not more than ten years of reserve obligation. As a nod to the peacetime nature of the draft, the law limited the total number of draftees to 900,000 and forbade them from being deployed outside of the western hemisphere, except to American territorial possessions, unless a state of emergency were declared. It also gave the president the authority to re-establish the Selective Service, which had lapsed at the end of World War I, appoint a director of the agency, and authorize those regulations the Selective Service needed to function properly.

The Selective Service System of 1940 was modeled on that of 1917, which, in response to problems encountered by the Union during the Civil War draft, had been created as a highly decentralized, civilian agency.[36] In this vein, the director of Selective Service, a presidential appointee, reported directly to the chief executive rather than the War Department or any individual service branch. Roosevelt initially appointed a civilian, Clarence A. Dykstra, the president of the University of Wisconsin, to the position in an attempt to downplay the agency's military connections. After Dykstra resigned in April 1941, however, the job fell to newly promoted Maj. Gen. Lewis B. Hershey, a World War I artillery officer, who had decided to make the military his career. He had been assigned to the JANSSC in 1936 and appointed as the deputy director of Selective Service in 1940. His extensive knowledge of conscription in America and his ability to navigate the halls of power made him ideal for the job in 1941. He would remain in the position until 1970.

Over his almost thirty-year tenure, Hershey molded the Selective Service System to match his own civic republican political ideology. He grew up on a small Indiana farm, worked his way through college, and entered the military through the National Guard. By all accounts, his worldview was based on a Jeffersonian understanding of virtue and responsibility.[37] He believed that the nation's greatest asset was the strength of its local communities, and throughout his tenure as director of Selective Service, he fought to keep the system decentralized. He argued that small, "little groups of neighbors" would know the needs of their own communities better than would any bureaucrat in Washington or elsewhere.[38] They would understand who could be spared for military service, the requirements of the local economy, and for whom military service would be a true hardship. For this reason, Hershey always treated regulations governing deferments as guidelines rather than hard-and-fast rules. Board members were expected to use their local expertise to make their best judgments. Theoretically, their personal connections to the communities they served would also put a human face on the system and, by virtue of their presence, encourage men to register and serve. Shame and a sense of duty would prevent prospective inductees from doing otherwise, since everyone, especially local board members, would know if a particular man was medically disqualified, performing an essential job, or a slacker.

To this end, National Headquarters in Washington, D.C., was kept relatively small—with just over 1,300 employees at its height in 1943—so that the bulk of the work of registering, classifying, and calling men could be done at the local level.[39] During the war, close to 6,500 local boards with support from nearly 4,000 advisory, medical, and appeal boards, all of which were staffed almost exclusively by unpaid volunteers, classified approximately 49 million men.[40] As of August 31, 1945, 183,451 volunteers manned—and except for female secretarial clerks, all of the volunteers *were* men—the Selective Service System throughout the United States and its territories.[41]

Congressional legislation provided the broad outlines of the system of conscription, but it was up to the president, through executive orders, to define the system further, while the director developed the regulations necessary for the agency's day-to-day operations. These included regulations related to deferments, a subject on which the Selective Training and Service Act was purposely vague. The law authorized the president to defer any individual engaged in essential war work, whose status as the supporter of dependents rendered him more useful on the home front than in uniform, whose religious beliefs caused him to be "conscientiously opposed to participation in war in any form," or who was "found to be physically, mentally, or morally deficient or defective."[42] Except for those incapable of or religiously opposed to military service, the law offered deferments to those who could perform service to the country in some other manner.

The question of how to define civilian service to the country during wartime, however, proved almost impossible to answer. What was an essential job? How important was it to keep husbands and fathers home with their families when the country faced grave peril? Was an eighteen-year-old more valuable as a farm hand or as a soldier? Throughout the war, the Selective Service struggled mightily with these questions. But at the outset of the draft, while the United States was technically at peace, officials had the luxury of establishing broad criteria for eligibility under the umbrella of four basic categories. Class I was for men available for service, with most placed in subclass I-A, meaning that registrants had no special restrictions on that service. Class II was for those deferred by reason of occupation, including in war industries (II-B) and eventually agriculture (II-C). Class III was for men deferred for dependency reasons, and Class IV was for men deferred by the law itself, including veterans (IV-A), government officials (IV-B), nondeclarant aliens (IV-C), and those deemed unfit (IV-F).[43]

These broad categories of deferments made practical sense. They assured equity of national service, if not equality; left enough skilled workers to equip the military; and protected the interests of society's most vulnerable. The armed forces could not expect to draw their personnel haphazardly from the young male populace without ramifications in the civilian sector. Factories and hospitals could only operate when fully staffed with skilled employees; the nation needed farmers and agricultural workers to maintain its food supplies and feed its allies; schools required teachers to educate children; and many families could not afford to lose their primary breadwinners and caregivers to the low pay of the army.

It was also a system with precedent. Though contested, targeted short-term deferments and permanent exemptions from military service had been used during each of the United States' previous experiences with conscription.[44] Most recently, the Selective Draft Act of 1917 had authorized the president to exempt federal, state, and local officials and men working in vital fields, especially agriculture and war industries, that were defined by the law as "necessary to the national health, safety, or interest," language that carried over into the 1940 law.[45]

But military manpower policy supported dominant social values as well. At the outset of World War II, for example, the majority of white Americans, including policymakers, deemed the maintenance of a racially segregated military more important than the full use of American manpower.

In their eyes, staving off domestic unrest from disgruntled whites and maintaining the existing power structure ensured force effectiveness in wartime.[46] In terms of deferments, both the 1917 and 1940 acts protected the beliefs of those men who could prove they were religious conscientious objectors. Although it was a heavily debated issue, the majority of Americans agreed that compelling a man to compromise his sincerely held religious ideals, even in the name of national defense, undermined the nation's foundational principle of religious freedom.[47] Ministers and divinity students were exempted from military obligations for similar reasons.

Deferments were essential, militarily, economically, and socially, even as these three types of interests competed with one another. Primarily, it was left to the Selective Service to decide how to balance the needs of the armed forces with those of civilian society. As dissatisfaction with deferment regulations waxed and waned throughout the war, the questions of whom to defer and why became political. Congress, the War Department, and civilian advocacy organizations frequently came into conflict with one another over Selective Service practice and policy. The independent nature of local boards exacerbated the situation. In the absence of central authority, board members had a tendency to bend regulations to their will or to ignore them entirely. This left the fates of individual men in limbo, a situation that the men and their families protested. Disputes over dependency and occupational deferments raged through most of the war years.

The deferment for dependency was arguably the one most clearly divorced from military necessity and most strongly connected to domestic values. In part, this deferment assumed that the father (or occasionally another male family member) was the main source of income within the family. Since the base pay of the enlisted grades outside of wartime was low and military allowances for dependents of soldiers and sailors were not automatic until the Korean War, many families did, in fact, face hardship when the male head of household was conscripted. But the application of the dependency deferment historically went far beyond cases of individual hardship.

How and when the federal government, local boards, and particular men chose to use the deferment illustrates the complex interplays among military service, economic need, competing value systems, and the obligations of masculine citizenship. The Selective Draft Act of 1917, for example, allowed the president to "exclude or discharge . . . those in a status with respect to persons dependent upon them for support which renders their exclusion or discharge advisable."[48] This vague language granted local draft boards wide latitude in classifying individual men and has led to disagreement among scholars over how to interpret men's behavior.

Historian Christopher Capozzola has argued that more men preferred to volunteer for service or allow themselves to be conscripted than apply for an exemption.[49] For some, the promise of three square meals, a regular paycheck, and a roof over their heads may have been enough to spur enlistment. But others likely felt that their obligations to the state trumped their responsibilities to their families or believed that they *were* meeting their familial obligations *through* their service to the state.[50] Jeannette Keith and Dorit Geva, on the other hand, have shown that in some localities up to 80 percent of eligible men applied for dependency or occupational exemptions, indicating that the majority of registrants had little inclination to fight.[51] In some cases, wives, elderly parents, and children who depended on would-be soldiers appeared before local draft boards to request the exemptions their loved ones would not.[52] In other cases, these same dependents begged local boards to conscript their men in order to guarantee the military's thirty-dollar-per-month family allotment or divest them of abusive spouses.[53] In all cases, the experience of conscription during World War I brought the state—in the form of the local draft board—into personal family relationships, allowing draft board members to evaluate the relative importance of military service versus service to the family.[54] That draft board members applied their personal value systems to each individual case in the absence of centralized guidance made this a particularly fraught process.

Congress, the Selective Service System's national office, and local board members again tried to protect fathers from the draft during World War II. The 1940 draft law repeated the language of the 1917 act with respect to dependency. Local boards interpreted this throughout 1940 and 1941 to mean that all married men should receive a deferment, including those whose wives worked. More than ten million of the seventeen million men who registered in 1940 and 1941 were classified as deferred for reason of dependency.[55] After Pearl Harbor and especially as the war deepened in 1942 and 1943, the practice of deferring all married men and then of deferring fathers became untenable.

At issue was the role of the man within his family. Public and political debate focused on whether a man's main importance was as financial support or as something deeper. Prior to Pearl Harbor, when there was virtually no strain on the nation's system of manpower procurement, it was relatively easy to focus on men as the moral center of their families. Local boards generally interpreted Selective Service regulations to mean that families' dependency was based on "more than dollars and cents," in the words of Eleanor Roosevelt. Men without children, men whose wives worked, and even men who were independently wealthy regularly received Class III deferments. The first lady defended the practice at a press conference by quoting Maj. Gordon Shaw of the Selective Service, who had stated, "to say that a man is to be called because his wife and children would not starve is to deny that the wife and children depend upon him for more than his pocketbook. It is to deny his moral leadership and protection."[56] Col. John Langston, the chairman of the Selective Service's Planning Council, further clarified the agency's position when he explained that taking a man's guidance from his family was to make the home the "potential prey of the philanderer," since "the forces of evil and greed" did not "hesitate to war upon the weak and helpless." To him, drafting married men away from their homes before it was absolutely necessary undermined the very "source of the nation's strength."[57] Roosevelt and the Selective Service assumed that a husband and father provided a moral compass for his family. To draft a man away from his home would leave his dependents directionless and would do more harm than good.

Even so, local boards did not automatically confer dependency deferments. Many balked, especially as marriage rates climbed, seemingly overnight, after the passage of the Selective Training and Service Act.[58] Early numbers provided to the Selective Service indicated as much as a 25 percent increase in marriages for draft-aged young men between 1940 and 1941.[59] Local studies occasionally showed even greater increases. Between July 1939 and 1941, for example, applications for marriage licenses in Cook County, Illinois, which encompasses Chicago, increased by 42 percent, and rates skyrocketed by 58.5 percent in the southern part of the state.[60] In response, national headquarters instructed local boards to "scrutinize" cases of late marriages "carefully and considerately," but to avoid either blanket rejections or blanket deferments based on the date of marriage.[61] Understandably, this directive led to significant confusion for those board members without a strong ideological stance on the issue.[62] To those boards seeking guidance, Hershey merely answered that there was no universal rule on the matter and that "each case must be considered on its own merits."[63]

As inconsistencies grew, officials within the Selective Service became increasingly concerned over negative public opinion. Stories of families complaining that they had been wronged by their local draft boards began appearing in newspapers, congressional offices, and at the Selective Service. One West Virginia wife, for instance, wrote to syndicated columnist Helen Essary to complain that her husband had been conscripted into an Army training camp full of beautiful "Camp Hostesses" and "stream-lined cuties" simply because his wife, the letter writer, worked in a lunchroom.[64]

Complaints like these frustrated officials, who worried that such inconsistencies "penalize[d] thrift and [led] . . . to poverty."[65] New York City's local boards were reminded that the system could not function without public support. Even if a wife could live comfortably on her salary, members were told, drafting her husband away from her and forcing her to give up her home, put her furniture into storage, and "move into a hall-bedroom in a boarding house" was "unreasonable and unjustified."[66] Memos began to circulate within national headquarters as officers sought a solution. Langston held strongly to the opinion that all married men, except the "riff-raff who have never made homes even though living in houses," should be deferred. Nevertheless, he suggested, national headquarters should not become overly concerned if a few boards "got a little hard-boiled." If the purpose of local control was to ensure that men were drafted by neighbors who understood the needs of the local community, then it was incumbent upon the Selective Service to let those communities work out their own needs. "Aggregate justice is vastly more important than complete equalization," he wrote.[67] Other officers disagreed. Deputy Director Dargusch tried to convince the Operations Group that economic need should be the only valid criterion for a Class III deferment. If a dependent absolutely required the presence and salary of a registrant to put food on the table and keep a roof over his or her head, then it made economic sense to keep the man at home. Otherwise, Dargusch argued, there should be no debate. The man should be eligible for the draft.[68]

America's official declaration of war forced Congress to take up the issue. Members acknowledged that it was logistically impossible for the American military to expand sufficiently to meet its war-hardened opponent when 65 percent of all registrants held dependency deferments.[69] In an effort to forestall hasty marriages and war babies conceived as a tactic to avoid military service, members of Congress amended the Selective Service Act of 1940 to allow only those dependents acquired or conceived before December 8, 1941, to be considered as part of a man's draft eligibility.[70] In terms of fatherhood, this functionally meant that a child needed to be born before September 15, 1942, in order for its father to receive a deferment. In June 1942, Congress passed the Pay Readjustment Act and the Servicemen's Dependents Allowance Act, both of which provided needed financial support for military personnel, especially in the enlisted grades.

In anticipation of the passage of these laws, the Selective Service reclassified men with dependents to indicate those who had children and those who did not, as well as men who worked in war-related jobs and men who did not. Although the agency was not yet ready to draft men with dependents, this effort was designed to encourage men with dependents to bolster their deferred status by taking a job in the national interest as insurance against a time when Selective Service would have to draft them. National headquarters instructed local boards to begin calling married men without children once their supply of eligible single men had been exhausted.[71] After the passage of the two laws in June, board members were also told to weigh families' financial need particularly heavily when deciding whether or not to grant a dependency deferment.[72] In essence, as a result of wartime exigencies, married men without children lost their preferred status. The Selective Service continued to protect the social role of fatherhood in its classification system, but in disaggregating those fathers who held war-related jobs from those without and by rescinding guaranteed protection for men who became fathers after Pearl Harbor, the agency set the stage for a time when manpower needs would trump men's familial responsibilities.

As the war deepened, deferments had to be tightened to meet the manpower needs of the growing military, but the debate continued over whether men were more important as the heads of their households or as soldiers. Families themselves certainly did not wish to see husbands and fathers drafted. Following the regulatory and statutory changes of mid-1942, an estimated 500,000 wives quit their own jobs in order to bolster their husbands' claims to Class III status.[73] More strikingly, the national birth rate spiked, from 17.9 per thousand in 1940 to 21.5 per thousand in 1943, with an especially significant increase among women aged twenty to twenty-nine, whose partners would have been extremely vulnerable to the draft.[74] While there are many possible reasons for this rapid increase, it is not unreasonable to attribute at least some of these babies to couples trying to keep the male partner out of the military, since almost no fathers, even those whose children had been conceived after Pearl Harbor, were being called at that point.

Letters continued to pour into Congress and newspapers complaining about inconsistencies in draft board practices. Writers protested older men being taken before younger men, married men before single ones, the drafting of men married before Pearl Harbor or the passage of conscription in 1940, and so on.[75] Others wondered why athletes, especially baseball players, were not being drafted.[76]

Under significant public pressure, Congress again took up the issue. In November 1942, in the context of the Allied invasion of North Africa, Congress amended the Selective Training and Service Act to allow men between the ages of eighteen and twenty to be conscripted. Members passed this measure specifically to grant the military access to a wider manpower pool without rescinding those protections enjoyed by married men and fathers. A Gallup Poll showed that 77 percent of Americans favored the conscription of eighteen- and nineteen-year-olds before men with children, but the amendment was not without controversy. Poll respondents split as to whether young men should be taken before married men without children. Only 43 percent chose to draft eighteen- and nineteen-year-olds before childless married men.[77] College presidents, who already faced severely declining enrollments, worried that higher education would suffer if undergraduates were drafted away from their studies.[78] Some psychologists and psychiatrists argued that taking teenagers would irreparably harm the younger men, who, they worried, might develop an undue dependency on the military rather than the independence that characterized mature manhood.[79] Despite these protests, President Roosevelt signed the amendment into law on November 13, 1942, freeing up approximately sixty thousand younger men each month for military service.

And yet it still was not enough. Through 1942 and 1943, officials at the War Department, Selective Service, and War Manpower Commission (WMC), as well as agricultural lobbyists and industrialists, all warned of an impending manpower crisis. Each constituency argued with the others in an effort to ensure manpower policies that met its individual needs. The War Department projected a combined armed force of 10.9 million men by the end of 1943, necessitating an average of just over 327,000 call-ups per month to yield enough physically fit men.[80] Representatives of industry, especially in war-related trades like aircraft and munitions manufacture and shipbuilding, predicted dire circumstances if workers were drafted away from their positions. Already up to 50 percent of employers' labor requests to the US Employment Services could not be met, especially in major industrial centers in New England and the Midwest and on the West Coast.[81] Likewise, agriculturalists warned of food shortages if farmhands were not left to work in the fields, pens, and barns. In response, Congress passed the Tydings Amendment in November 1942 to protect the nation's 1.5 million farmers from the Selective Service.[82] President Roosevelt referred to the nation's manpower needs as a giant "jigsaw puzzle," while *Time* magazine called it "a vast, sticky pudding which the Administration stirred and stirred, hoping that something in the way of solution would come to the top."[83]

This "stirring" led Roosevelt to create the War Manpower Commission in February 1942. The agency was an attempt to coordinate the needs of the Department of Labor, Department of Agriculture, the War Department, Navy Department, the War Production Board, and the Civil Service Commission. Paul V. McNutt, a star in the New Deal machine who had almost attained the vice presidential nomination in 1940, was appointed as its head, but, as became clear very quickly, was given too little real power to initiate change or enforce recommendations. As part of a plan to rectify this situation, Roosevelt issued an executive order in December 1942 that, among other things, ended voluntary enlistments, forced the Departments of War and the Navy to gain the WMC's approval before issuing manpower requests, and gave McNutt the power to issue "policies, rules, regulations, and general or special orders" as he deemed fit. It also specifically put Hershey and his agency under the direct control of McNutt and his.[84]

Shortly thereafter, McNutt tried to exercise his new authority, hinting that he would have the Selective Service begin drafting fathers who did not switch to a job defined by the WMC as essential to the war effort. It was not his first foray into "work or fight" policy, but while his earlier statements had been unpopular, this one hit a particularly sensitive nerve within Congress and among the general public.[85] He encountered immediate pushback. Representative Wadsworth angrily rebutted that the Selective Service "never was intended to be used a club to be wielded or cracked down on the heads of civilians [to make them move] from one place to another place in civilian occupations."[86] Both the House and the Senate started debating bills that would automatically defer all pre–Pearl Harbor fathers.[87]

The subsequent nine-month political battle over whether fathers had an obligation to serve in the military was one of the uglier Washington power struggles of the war, and it resulted in McNutt being stripped of his control over the Selective Service. It is not by accident that it was fought over deferments in general—an issue that encapsulated the question of whether military or civilian manpower needs took precedence—and the role of fathers in particular. Practically speaking, opponents of drafting fathers believed men with children were more entangled in the civilian economy than single men, as "they maintained more elaborate establishments" than their single counterparts.[88] McNutt strongly disagreed with this interpretation. He defended the conscription of fathers, explaining that factory workers supported the war effort in a more tangible way than fathers in nonessential jobs. In the struggle for manpower during a total war, he explained, occupational deferments had to take precedence over those for dependency, especially since the United States was the "only nation engaged in th[e] war that ever required dependency deferment and [was] the most generous one in allotments and allowances for dependents."[89] In other words, American children would not starve if fathers were taken in large numbers, nor would American society disintegrate.

As this chapter has shown, however, a man's status as a father symbolized the cultural importance of breadwinning, family guidance, and morality, and the pull of this argument was powerful. For many, fatherhood, and by extension "the institution of the home," represented the very "backbone" of American "civilization."[90] The Selective Service had no choice but to acknowledge this fact. It could not function without public or political support.

And the debate raged in Congress and other public spaces. Republican senator William Revercomb of West Virginia warned the Senate Military Affairs Committee that the induction of fathers would throw the people into "a turmoil" and result in orphaned children prowling the country in "wolf-packs," causing mischief.[91] Members of local draft boards in Pennsylvania, New Jersey, Massachusetts, Texas, Alabama, North Carolina, and Ohio resigned in protest over the prospect of drafting fathers. Hershey had to dismiss the entire membership of the local board in Haverhill, Massachusetts, for flatly refusing to induct a single father.[92] Enemy propaganda even used the political debate over dependency deferments as fodder. One intercepted broadcast from Tokyo to Latin America tried to make the case that America's resort to the use of fathers as soldiers was evidence of a cover-up of the extent of American casualties.[93] For its part, the American public remained firmly opposed to the conscription of fathers well into 1943. In September of that year, a Gallup Poll found that 68 percent of respondents preferred to draft unmarried men employed in war industries before touching fathers. An even bigger majority reported that it would rather draft single women into noncombat positions in the military before calling men with children.[94]

Bills and counterbills were introduced in both houses of Congress as the war of words heated up in the press. At one point, Democratic senator Burton Wheeler of Montana tried to call the Senate back into session early from its summer recess specifically to pass a bill to forbid the drafting of any father prior to January 1, 1944.[95] Finally, in December 1943, Congress sent the president a compromise measure. Faced with unwavering opposition to blanket exemptions for fathers from military officials and significant pushback from Hershey, who claimed that it would be impossible to fill draft calls without turning to fathers, the various bills' sponsors had no political choice but to back down from their initial position that fathers simply should not be conscripted.[96] The final law, however, confirmed the basic principle that all other available men should be taken before those with families. This was to be accomplished by convening a five-man medical panel to determine if physical standards could be lowered even further, combing the files of men deferred for physical or mental reasons to see if any of them could be considered physically fit, and by altering the way draft quotas were allocated nationwide. Rather than issuing calls at a local level, the law shifted the burden to the states so that all eligible childless men throughout an entire state would have to be called before any men with children could be inducted. This change eliminated the problem of some localities exhausting their supply of childless men before others.[97] The law also removed the Selective Service from the control of the WMC.

With his renewed independence, Hershey went about collapsing the Class III category of deferments. A new subcategory, Class III-D, was created for men whose families would face "*extreme* hardship and privation" if the man in question were conscripted: single fathers, for example.[98] Everyone else who had held a dependency deferment was then shifted into other categories, assuming that the government's allotment would make up for the loss of the soldiers' civilian wages. Those who held essential occupational or agricultural jobs were put in the appropriate Class-II subcategory, but the majority were reclassified as I-A, or available for service, albeit with certain limitations. By law, men with children were given preference for occupational and agricultural deferments, and men without children in the I-A category were to be drafted into the military before I-A fathers.[99] By mid-1945, only one half of one percent of all registrants aged eighteen to thirty-seven held dependency deferments.[100]

Throughout the war years, tens of millions of American men served in the military. Many enlisted, and when that avenue was cut off in late 1942, many more volunteered to be drafted early. The majority, however, waited for their induction notices to arrive. Except for a small number of radical pacifists, American men did not publicly challenge the *existence* of the draft, leading later generations to believe that most male members of the so-called greatest generation served willingly. Filtered through the shadows of memory and time, the narrative of willing service took root.[101] In fact, the plurality of men probably did serve more or less willingly once the Selective Service came calling. In the absence of comprehensive data, it is impossible to determine individual men's motivations. Careful mining of the sources available, however, shows that many men tried to work the system to avoid conscription.

The Selective Service handled slightly more than 4.5 million appeals of individual classifications throughout the course of the war. Two-thirds of these were reviews of occupational deferments, as required by a 1943 amendment to the Selective Service and Training Act. The remaining 1.4 million appeals originated from men who were classified as I-A or from their employers.[102] At one point in 1943, one out of every six inductions went to appeal, as men tried to avoid serving in the military.[103] According to a congressional investigation, government workers, 35 percent of whom were men between the ages of eighteen and thirty-eight, submitted their own "impressive-looking applications" at an alarming rate.[104] They were trying to gain the legal deferments from service that more than 57 percent of registered men already held.[105] While this percentage lessened over the remaining two years of war, the reduction in deferments was not because men stopped trying to obtain them.[106] Individual men continued to look for new ways to avoid induction even as new regulations closed avenue after avenue for deferment, making draft avoidance more and more difficult.

While officials acknowledged the importance of deferments, the existence of loopholes demonstrably frustrated them. Otherwise dry reports on employment in West Coast shipyards questioned the motivations of able-bodied workers. At the Mare Island Naval Shipyard, for example, men under the age of thirty-seven who held occupational deferments turned over at a rate of only 2.7 percent, while 8.8 percent of IV-F men quit in any given month. In other words, according to the authors, young, healthy men remained "even in the low-pay unattractive jobs" in order to shirk military service.[107] Across the country in North Carolina, state officials worried that men specifically took jobs in mica production to avoid the military. They were so concerned about the possibility that men were "digging for deferment," that they asked the War Production Board in Washington, D.C., to initiate an investigation.[108] The Department of Agriculture reported an uptick in men with dependents seeking farm employment as dependency deferments dried up. After congressional action in early 1944 gave extra protections to agricultural workers, men started to leave higher-paying industrial jobs for farming.[109] Hershey became so annoyed by "job jumpers," or men who took defense jobs in order to gain occupational deferments but then immediately quit, that he amended the Selective Service regulations at the end of 1944 to ensure that any man caught leaving his place of employment without the permission of his local board would be reclassified as available for military service and subject to immediate induction. In six months, close to 129,000 men were so reclassified.[110] The term became so common that newspapers stopped defining it.[111] "Farm jumpers" similarly plagued states with large rural populations.

Historical sketches written by clerks of local Selective Service boards in Kansas in 1946 offer another window onto the ambivalence of men from America's heartland. Reports from Sumner and Thomas Counties both opened with statements disavowing scandal and draft dodging in their localities. Yet both then went on to describe men who rushed into marriage, had children to avoid the loss of occupational deferments, sought employment at defense plants in order to "escape the draft," and who "got the jump on the draft board" by moving to farms.[112] The sketches' exuded unrelenting positivity, but the accounts were shot through with exceptions.

"Good War" myth aside, it should come as no surprise that American men's aggregate attitude toward military service hovered somewhere between resignation and ambivalence during World War II. If Americans had been eager to serve, Selective Service would not have been necessary. Similarly, the notion that married men's contribution to the state derived from their roles as breadwinner and father was ingrained in American legal and political culture by the 1940s.[113] The nation's commitment to selective conscription meant that the agency charged with operating the draft would have to grapple with a polity that believed military service interfered with its masculine responsibilities.

Nevertheless, as mobilization deepened, the requirements of total war demanded that domestic concerns be placed on the back burner for the duration. Once manpower needs could no longer support the privileging of domestic masculinity, manpower policy followed suit with the dramatic reduction of dependency deferments. Politicians like Senator Wheeler capitalized on Americans' general distaste for the drafting of fathers as he tried to forbid their induction by statute. Ultimately, however, Americans resigned themselves to the eventuality.[114]

Agricultural and occupational deferments, meanwhile, continued to be justified as necessary elements of the war effort. Planners defined them as critical to national defense—defeating an external enemy—even if this was not how individual men used them. At the same time, it became increasingly difficult for men under the age of twenty-six to obtain these types of deferments. Beginning in the spring of 1944, local boards were instructed to take age into account when classifying registrants, who were broken into three separate brackets. Men between the ages of eighteen and twenty-five from that point forward not only had to prove that they were "regularly engaged" in activities "necessary to" the war effort, but they also had to be approved by their state directors in order to obtain an occupational or agricultural deferment. Men between the ages of twenty-six and twenty-nine similarly had to demonstrate the critical nature of their work but did not need additional permission, and the burden of proof was lifted from men between the ages of thirty and thirty-seven.[115]

Gradual changes to the Selective Service regulations by the end of the war, therefore, accounted for American men's overwhelming participation in the United States military during World War II, not their immense desire to defeat the Axis through the personal use of force. As this chapter has shown, even though the system of manpower procurement established by the Selective Service was hugely successful, it was far from seamless. Uniformed service was contested during World War II, a situation frequently elided in postwar works that focus on the myth of the "greatest generation." Although public debate over conscription rarely strayed into the liberal language of male citizens' right to choose service as it would in later years—African Americans' fight for the right to serve in the military on an equal footing with whites being the notable exception—widespread service in the armed forces was not the result of broadly internalized civic republican understandings of the responsibilities of citizenship.[116]

While certain federal, state, and private sources labored mightily to link masculine citizenship and military service in the minds and hearts of individual Americans, others flat out rejected that message, leaving the Selective Service—and many individual men—caught in between. Hershey charted a middle course for his agency. He acknowledged the economic necessity of deferments as a war measure and bowed to public opinion on the question of dependency early in the war when it was possible to do so. He never wavered from his civic republican idealism, however, and continued to view military service as each man's responsibility in wartime. Individual men continued to do what they had always done during America's wars. Those who actively wanted to serve joined up. Many looked for ways to avoid service by working the system to their advantage, but when they ran out of options they served more or less willingly when the draft came calling.

CHAPTER 2

"To Rub Smooth the Sharp Edges"

Universal Military Training, 1943–1951

During Harry Truman's administration, tens
of thousands of Americans wrote to the president to express their opinions
on matters relating to military service. They wished to weigh in on their
nation's evolving foreign policy and defense strategy as the United States
transitioned from war to peace to Cold War. Unsurprisingly, their suggestions were as varied as the populace itself. Letters juxtaposed the necessity
of military preparedness against that of diplomacy; they contained pleas for
large armed forces and for disarmament.[1] But citizens' missives debated more
than the comparatively simple question of how best to defend the country
against potential foreign aggressors. These letter writers, like policymakers
and lobbyists during the same years, were attempting to define national security in an uncertain age by weighing the very purpose of military service.
Was the primary role of soldiers, sailors, marines, and airmen to defend the
territorial borders of the United States and American interests abroad, or
should military training have deeper aims? One set of deliberations focused
on whether the United States should instate a program of universal military
training (UMT), keep a program of selective service, or return to an all-
volunteer force, as had been the country's tradition in peacetime. For a short
time, UMT gained the most traction in public discourse.

Over the span of its political life, UMT passed through many iterations, as
planners varied the features of their proposals and argued over details, but all

plans for UMT required some period of military training for all able-bodied American men, generally in a civilian capacity. This meant that although the training would be on military subjects, in military camps, and under modified military discipline, the men themselves would not be *in* the military. Instead, upon successful completion of training, they would be part of a large general reserve and subject to call-up in the event of a national emergency. In essence, UMT was supposed to give the mobilization process a jump-start. Men, once mobilized, would need refresher training, but theoretically they would already be familiar with topics like military organization, discipline, and weaponry. Under some plans, men also would receive specialized assignments, in infantry or artillery, for example, ideally lessening the logistical burden of mass mobilization.

On its surface, UMT was a defense measure, but its advocates always acknowledged its potential social benefits. If legislation had passed, UMT would have established a standardized, compulsory, residential training program for virtually all American men under the auspices of the federal government. In that capacity, it would have offered an opportunity not available anywhere else in American society. Proponents argued that instructional programs offered in training camps could eradicate illiteracy, remediate health care deficiencies, provide vocational training, teach moral values, and promote tolerance of difference. In short, they claimed, UMT would strengthen the nation internally as well as protect it from external enemies.

These potential benefits appealed to many of those writing President Truman. Letter writers claimed physical training would "make *men* out of . . . weaklings."[2] They hoped leadership training would help boys develop initiative, conscience, and character.[3] Authors asserted that moral guidance would end juvenile delinquency and venereal disease, while military discipline would teach "loosely jointed . . . slouching yokels" the "little courtesies of everyday life."[4] These benefits appealed to others as well. From roughly 1944 to 1948, Presidents Roosevelt and Truman and officials in the War Department advocated UMT, at times so vociferously that the Department of Justice eventually censured the latter for circulating propaganda. Public opinion polling indicated that the majority of the population favored some sort of military training for all men, so long as the men did not have to go on and actually serve in the military once their training was complete.

Meanwhile, a small but determined opposition developed, composed primarily of religious, pacifist, education, farm, labor, and civil rights organizations. Americans who opposed UMT penned letters to the president complaining that compulsory military training would deny men their religious liberty, invite war, militarize the nation, waste resources, and destroy the "moral and spiritual fiber of American manhood" by, among other things, "turning the brewers loose on them like a bunch of ravenous wolves."[5]

In their deliberations, interested parties used UMT as a cipher. To proponents, it represented the most efficient way to protect the United States from external enemies, the most democratic way to build an educated citizenry, and an excellent way to strengthen America's manhood. Opponents vehemently disagreed. They saw UMT as a threat that put the nation's security, democracy, and youth at risk. They could not accept military training as an essential component of male citizenship or the military as the best place to teach economic or domestic responsibility. The question of whether America needed a militarily trained male populace forced all those invested in the plan's outcome to evaluate not only their visions for postwar national defense but their conceptions of democratic citizenship as well.

UMT's supporters and detractors grounded their positions in different theoretical bases for citizenship. For those who preferred a civic republican definition, universal experience in the armed services seemed the most democratic way to forge male citizens. They believed that a year of common training would create common opportunities for all American men, provide a measure of equality to men from diverse backgrounds, and teach individuals how to function as informed citizens in a democratic republic. Those who defined citizenship in the classically liberal mold viewed UMT as the first step along the path to fascism and totalitarianism. They thought the regimentation of military life would destroy America's independent manhood, undermine the liberty on which American citizenship was based, and arrest the moral development of boys as they grew into men. They also pointed out that universal military training was not, in fact, envisioned as a universal measure, as it would have been a racially segregated, single-sex program.

In the end, UMT failed, dying a slow death between 1948 and 1951. Its failure confirmed the nation's commitment to a system of selective rather than universal service. From 1948 until the end of the draft in 1973, the Department of Defense struggled with a system of conscription that ostensibly subjected all men to military service but did not compel service from every man. As later chapters will show, deciding which men to select for military service and which men to defer or exempt became an increasingly time-consuming and problematic task for the agencies responsible for classifying the nation's manpower.

But UMT was important for more than just its failure. The terms of the debate illustrated the contested nature of American citizenship and masculinity as well as their difficult relationship with military service in the mid-twentieth century. From one perspective, universal military training should have been an obvious measure coming out of World War II. Messages about male responsibility to serve were everywhere. Most men of military age were in uniform, and however they had ended up in the services, most viewed that service as beneficial.[6] The United States had entered the war after a devastating surprise attack and had spent years building up its forces before undertaking major military operations in Europe. In the immediate aftermath of the war, before the Cold War coalesced, the so-called next war remained a nebulous, frightening, potentially atomic possibility that could come from anywhere. Yet UMT was not an obvious measure. It was one that sparked intense debate. This was partially because the political and military events of the early Cold War introduced geopolitical conditions that made such a program seem outmoded, but it was also because Americans could not agree on the potential consequences of using the military as a major socializing agent for all young men. At a moment when the civic republican conception of citizenship might have triumphed, it did not. As had been the case in the past, military training would not be a prerequisite of male citizenship in the United States. Moreover, the political campaign failed to convince Congress, detractors, or the American public that the army was the proper place to instill the virtues of citizenship or masculinity into American men; UMT was a level of militarization they were unwilling to accept. Ultimately—for pragmatic and ideological reasons—the federal government backed away from a universal male requirement to serve.

The political history of universal military training is relatively simple. It ran in two waves, the first of which crested during World War I and the second in 1947. UMT originally emerged from the preparedness movement of the pre–World War I years, members of which believed American involvement in the European conflagration was inevitable. Proponents advocated the development of a large, well-trained military in advance of a congressional declaration of war. And they backed their beliefs with money. With the help of the U.S. Army, members of the Military Training Camps Association (MTCA) established twelve voluntary civilian training camps, the largest of which was at Plattsburg Barracks, New York. By 1916, more than sixteen thousand men, primarily from the East and Midwest, had paid thirty dollars each to complete basic training. The political clout of these members of what became known as the Plattsburg Movement helped the MTCA successfully lobby for federal funding for civilian training camps under the direct supervision of the Department of the Army in the National Defense Act of 1916.[7]

After World War I, the MTCA continued to push for UMT as part of a larger plan of army reorganization, hoping that a militarily trained populace would deter any future war. Congress, however, demurred. Democrats, pledged their support to the concept of a League of Nations and rejected a system of universal military training as antithetical to the principles of global peace and cooperation. In the name of political expediency, those Republicans who supported UMT backed down. The MTCA contented itself to add an amendment to the National Defense Act of 1920 allowing for voluntary training at civilian camps for all citizens who requested it.[8] By 1940, 500,000 men had volunteered for training at these camps, but UMT was off the legislative table.[9]

High-ranking veterans of the Plattsburg Movement, however, brought the idea back during World War II. Long-time advocates, like Army Chief of Staff George Marshall, Secretary of War Henry Stimson, and Brig. Gen. John McAuley Palmer, believed that a lack of centralized postwar planning had severely weakened the American military and the United States' position in global politics, leading to what Marshall termed the army's "Dark Ages."[10] They treated congressional failure to include UMT in the National Defense Act of 1920 as a deficiency of political will and blamed the measure's defeat on the wild swings in public opinion that followed the 1919 armistice. They argued that if Congress had acted with greater expediency in 1918, prior to the Fourteen Points and the introduction of the League of Nations, Americans would have enthusiastically supported a plan of universal military training. In turn, they reasoned, the large, trained reserve that would have resulted from the law would have deterred German and Japanese aggression in the late 1930s. According to Marshall, if the country had only "followed through" in the 1920 Defense Act by training a large civilian reserve, "Germany would not have dared to involve herself in a war that would draw the United States into the conflict."[11] In 1944, when every American felt the consequences of war, members of the MTCA began the second push for universal military training.[12]

Once the War Department, under Stimson's leadership, had made UMT its priority, the idea began to appear in the media with increasing frequency, first as the result of a directed campaign and then as the press began to cover the effects of that campaign. Under the direction of Under Secretary of War John J. McCloy, senior military and civilian leaders, especially from the army, began publicizing their desire for UMT. They placed features in publications with broad appeal like The Saturday Evening Post and The American, and they targeted specific constituencies through journals like The Nation's Schools and the American Association of University Professors Bulletin.[13] Others gave public addresses that were covered by the press as news items or appeared on radio programs.[14] Soon, interested citizens took up the issue themselves, which was precisely McCloy's goal.[15] In the first week of March 1945 alone, one hundred local newspapers ran editorials on the issue of UMT. While not all of them came out in favor of the program, it was clear that the question of whether the nation needed such a program had gained a foothold in the public sphere.[16]

In June 1945, the House Select Committee on Postwar Military Policy, chaired by Clifton A. Woodrum, a Democrat from Virginia, began weighing American options for postwar national defense, including universal training. Though not a legislative committee with the power to propose bills, the Woodrum Committee's July 1945 report endorsed a plan of universal military training as part of a larger program of national security.[17] In November 1945 and February 1946, the House renewed hearings on UMT, this time weighing a specific plan outlined by Rep. Andrew May, a Democrat from Kentucky and the chair of the House Committee on Military Affairs. The primary focus of both sets of hearings was how best to avoid the "next war" through the development of a strong national security program. Between the Woodrum and May hearings, more than three hundred witnesses, including government and military officials, representatives of concerned organizations, and private citizens presented testimony or prepared statements outlining their positions on a program of compulsory military training.

Witnesses representing the military and civilian arms of the federal government, including Marshall, Palmer, Secretary of the Navy James Forrestal, General Dwight Eisenhower, and Admiral Chester Nimitz, overwhelmingly focused on universal military training as a key element to the United States' defense policy. They emphasized their belief that America would not enjoy "a reasonable degree of national security" without it.[18] Several themes ran through their testimony. First, although the shape of the postwar world had not yet been determined, they assumed that another war would occur if the United States appeared weak.[19] Second, any future war would begin with a surprise aerial or missile attack on the United States. In that case, America would not have the luxury of time to marshal its resources and train its men. Instead, the military response would have to be immediate. Although they admitted that some retraining would be necessary, the military men felt that the knowledge citizens would gain during a year of civilian training would invaluably speed up mobilization in the event of a war.[20] Finally, although government witnesses vocalized their support for the United Nations, then in its infancy, they strongly recommended a show of military strength from the United States as the best way for America to back up its commitment to the new international body. The United States would only be able to act as the UN's moral anchor if it had the military strength to support its claim to world leadership. Further, should the UN require its member nations to commit a peacekeeping force in the future, the United States needed to have enough troops to spare.[21]

With the exception of Stimson, a former participant in the Plattsburg Movement and member of the MTCA, government witnesses limited their discussion of UMT's social benefits. Although they acknowledged the education and training men would receive as applicable to civilian life, they purposely kept the defensive goals of UMT as a security program at the fore of their statements. Nimitz wrote a letter to the committee in which he called these educational and vocational "byproducts" "entirely beside the point." Vice Adm. Aubrey Fitch, the deputy chief of naval operations (air), complained that focus on the civilian benefits of military training tended to "confuse the issue."[22]

Witnesses less immediately connected to the government were more likely to extol the nonmilitary virtues of UMT, but they also argued primarily from a national security vantage point, albeit with heightened rhetorical flourish. According to John Thomas Taylor of the American Legion's national legislative committee, UMT's opponents were the "one group to bear the blame" for American involvement in World War II. Anyone who failed to support UMT would be responsible for the next war.[23] Jay Cooke, president of the Citizens Committee for Military Training of Young Men, an ad hoc lobbying organization with strong ties to the War Department, colorfully highlighted the protective benefits of UMT. "Few people rush up to [boxers] Joe Louis or Jack Dempsey and slap them in the face," he asserted.[24] No one would attack the United States if it appeared suitably strong. UMT, in these witnesses' eyes, was required to guard the nation.

As testimony at both sets of hearings illustrated, however, detractors heartily disagreed that UMT made the United States safer. They defined national security quite differently. Rather than emphasize UMT as a possible deterrent *against* external threats, activists from educational, civil rights, pacifist, and religious organizations tended to view it as a threat *to* American values. As early as November 1944, staff representatives from a number of organizations, including the National Education Association, the National Women's Christian Temperance Union, the Friends Committee, the Women's International League for Peace and Freedom (WILPF), the National Council for Prevention of War, and the newly formed National Council Against Conscription, met to coordinate a defense against UMT proposals. As a result of their efforts and organized outreach sessions, the chorus of voices attacking what they viewed as the destructive characteristics of UMT steadily expanded.[25]

Many of the hostile witnesses at both the Woodrum and May committee hearings grounded their objections to UMT in the unstable international political climate of the immediate postwar period. They argued that
it would be impossible to know the United States' military needs until the
war with Japan ended, American soldiers stationed in both Asia and Europe
could rotate home, provisional governments could be set up in the countries
under occupation, and the organization and mission of the United Nations
could be established.[26] The detonation of atomic bombs at Hiroshima and
Nagasaki in August 1945 further bolstered opponents' hostility to UMT. If
any nation possessed the ability to obliterate another with one weapon, they
reasoned, then international cooperation through the United Nations was
the only way to prevent global destruction.

Arguments of this ilk spoke as much to the defense of the United States as
those that called for universal military training. Pacifists like Dorothy Detzer
of WILPF; educators like George F. Zook, president of the American Council
on Education; and civil rights activists like federal judge and former dean of
Howard University Law School William Hastie all advocated international
cooperation, primarily through the United Nations, as a safer, more effective
means of national defense. Zook told the May Committee that the United
States could not "hold, or even merit, the confidence of other nations" if it
paid "lip service" to the ideals of "international peace and cooperation" but
"at the same time repudiate[d] them with [its] actions."[27] Hastie warned,
"There is no tolerable future in an international jungle in which each lion
calls himself the king of the beasts and keeps sharpening his claws to prove
it."[28] These detractors clearly believed that training the nation, even through
a so-called civilian program, was akin to arming it, a state more likely to
heighten rather than limit danger.

By early 1946, public opinion on military manpower policy was split. Dissatisfaction with the Selective Service System ran high. Many men who had
been serving overseas at the end of World War II remained stationed as occu-
pying forces throughout Asia and Europe. With support from their families,
they demanded immediate discharges. The army, however, needed 1.5 million men to fulfill its commitments abroad. It would only be able to maintain
this number and simultaneously rotate veterans home through continued
conscription.[29]

As Soviet intransigence delayed the reunification of Germany, communist
forces continued to gain traction in China, and the "iron curtain" dropped
over Eastern Europe, Truman and others determined that the United States
would not be able to demobilize quickly. Congress passed a series of extensions to the Selective Training and Service Act of 1940, allowing the draft to

continue until March 31, 1947. These extensions were compromise measures, and although they passed Congress fairly easily, their provisions caused controversy. Since the immediate emergency had ended, the new laws exempted eighteen-year-olds and fathers from the available pool, creating a dearth of manpower just as the Cold War was beginning to take shape. Demobilization rates slowed in early 1946 as the Selective Service struggled to meet its commitments. Americans with family members serving overseas and those whose loved ones faced induction criticized the Selective Service in equal measure. Many Americans questioned the existence of a draft during peacetime, denouncing it as un-American.[30]

At the same time, the public appeared to support universal military training. While the strategic details of how millions of American men with limited training would or could be deployed were never ironed out, the majority of Americans seemed willing to accept UMT as a military necessity. In a series of nine Gallup polls conducted between December 1945 and January 1956, support for UMT dropped below 65 percent only once.[31] Approval in other, smaller surveys ranged as high as 83 percent.[32] But such support was "soft."[33] Most Americans may have approved of UMT in theory, but they prioritized other economic, political, and social concerns and were not likely to agitate for its passage into law.[34] They wanted to wait for American soldiers to return home, for the geopolitical shape of the postwar world to become clear, and to give the new United Nations the opportunity to foster international peace before they made any decisions about domestic military training or service. This left only a core group of lobbyists, led by the American Legion with support from civic organizations like the US Chamber of Commerce, Kiwanis International, and the Lions Club, to try to shape public opinion in favor of UMT. These enthusiasts faced a broader range of pacifist, educational, religious, labor, and civil rights organizations, all of which took their dissent to Capitol Hill and to the media.

Opponents of UMT quickly capitalized on public antipathy toward the Selective Service by eliding the differences between military training and military service. In speeches, radio addresses, newspaper articles, and their organization names, they referred to UMT as "universal military conscription," "peacetime conscription," and "universal military service."[35] Even though the Truman administration and Selective Service repeatedly explained that the main point of the program was for men to train *with* the military as civilians rather than *in* the military as soldiers subject to the same hierarchy, rules, and obligations as enlisted men, public confusion remained. People's comprehension was further muddled by contradictory media accounts and congressional debate. Several congressional bills did propose universal service *in* the military instead of just *with* it, although these did not receive backing from the president, War Department, or most civilian advocates of military training.[36]

As a result of this confusion, supporters, especially within the executive branch, struggled to control the terms of the debate. They tried to educate the public on the difference between plans for universal military training and the role of conscription under the supervision of the Selective Service System. Truman, for example, in an October 23, 1945, speech to Congress, was very clear that he did not consider UMT the same as a draft. "Conscription is compulsory service in the Army or Navy in time of peace or war," he argued. "Trainees under this proposed legislation . . . would be civilians in training."[37] But his attempts to delineate the difference led to charges of deception from his political enemies.[38]

In response to criticism of the draft and in the face of continued public uncertainty over UMT, Truman and the War Department began exploring a return to voluntarism as the best way to meet America's military manpower needs.[39] Conscription and universal training could not exist side-by-side, they reasoned; the democratic and egalitarian rationales for UMT would evaporate if the armed forces inducted some men for a period of several years while others merely trained as civilians for one. War Department officials, therefore, wanted to suspend the draft, both to prove that enough men would enlist voluntarily to maintain the vital nucleus of America's military and to allow the political space for a UMT program to pass. In January 1947, the army officially abandoned its policy of advocating another draft extension. The expiration of congressional authorization for the Selective Service System in March would further open the political doors to universal military training, or so military planners hoped.

The winter of 1946–47 also marked a turning point in the way Truman and the War Department chose to market their proposal. Over the previous two years, they had insisted that UMT's main purpose was national defense and labored to keep the program's potential educational, vocational, and health benefits in the background. Maintaining control of their message, however, became increasingly difficult as Congress, lobbyists, and concerned citizens insisted on bringing these other issues to the fore, especially as evidence of military overreach.[40] Truman and Secretary of War Robert Patterson, therefore, began to attack these criticisms head on, defending their proposed program through an unprecedented public relations offensive. What resulted was a shift away from discussion about the efficacy of UMT as a national defense strategy and toward public debate over the purpose of military training, the meaning of masculine citizenship, and how or if the former could be used to build the latter.

Boosters of universal military training had acknowledged the links between compulsory training and democratic citizenship since the days of World War I. MTCA members, by underscoring the principles of duty, responsibility, and patriotism that training would instill, had touted a trained civilian reserve as a deterrent to militarism rather than as a potential threat to American liberty. They also used the perceived nonmilitary benefits of UMT as selling points. Former assistant secretary of war Henry Breckinridge, for example, promised that the extra training illiterate and non-English-speaking trainees would receive would "yank the hyphen out of America."[41] The MTCA's World War I–era plan included provisions for naturalizing immigrant aliens who completed training, teaching illiterate trainees how to read, and providing vocational training to those men who needed it.[42] According to enthusiasts, universal training would bolster the American economy, educate the populace, strengthen American values, and unify a divided nation, thus providing domestic security as well as security against external aggressors.

Thirty years later, the meaning of citizenship in relation to compulsory military training was a question raised continually through the Woodrum and May hearings, despite the War Department's initial attempts to stay clear of it. Witnesses at both sets of hearings used UMT as a symbol for the America they wished to create in the aftermath of World War II. Those who favored universal military training tended to base their opinions on a civic republican understanding of citizenship, framing their support with the obligation of the male citizen to defend his nation. Detractors, on the other hand, rooted their arguments in a more classically liberal interpretation of citizenship. They concentrated on the right of the individual in a free society to make choices for himself. These differing visions of citizenship led witnesses to define universal military training as either a democratic measure or a totalitarian one.

The one thing that united stakeholders on all sides was their insistence on defining citizenship as male. In fact, few activists—either for or against UMT—specifically considered the citizenship rights or obligations of women.[43] None of the plans proposed or considered in Congress required any type of contribution from the nation's women. Women would not be obliged to sacrifice their time or their bodies to earn the rights of citizenship, nor was it the state's responsibility to defend their rights against the infringement of universal training. Even more telling, not one witness in either of the two sets of hearings—or in subsequent hearings—complained that the educational, health, vocational, and moral benefits of military training would accrue only to men. Those in favor of the measure argued that UMT would strengthen the nation by strengthening its men, bodily, economically, and morally. Like the GI Bill, UMT legislation assumed that men, as bread-winners, needed these benefits more than women, who would be supported by their husbands.[44] Proponents used this expectation to argue that the vocational and leadership training men would receive in military camps would help them advance after their terms of service ended. Opponents used the same assumption to claim that ripping men away from college and apprenticeship programs would harm their future vocational status and deprive the nation of qualified scientists and engineers. No one suggested that women could fill the extra admissions slots at colleges or universities as they had during World War II.[45] Public discourse on UMT centered on the rights and responsibilities of men and the role they were expected to play in American society as both soldiers and civilians.

Supporters justified the compulsory nature of the training based on their belief that citizens owed service of some type to the nation that nurtured them. They stressed duty, obligation, and responsibility. "All American citizens and resident aliens enjoy the protection and freedom of our way of life," wrote Admiral Nimitz in his letter to the Woodrum Committee. "They must share the obligation to defend that freedom."[46] Republican representative Frances Bolton of Ohio declared, "Citizenship in a free society holds within it the responsibility, and the duty on the part of the individual to protect it, and the principles for which it stands."[47] This framework emphasized a government of, for, and by the people. It could not survive, especially in an unstable global geopolitical climate, without the active participation—in this case through military training—of its citizens.

Training would be worth the temporary sacrifice of time, individual choice, and life, if mobilization ever proved necessary. It would deter outside aggression and provide security to the nation, allowing the United States—and thus its citizens—to thrive and prosper. But more importantly, it would "provide the trainee with a larger return than [he] would give to his Nation."[48] Proponents cited remedial health care, educational and vocational training, self-reliance, a sense of responsibility, leadership skills, the opportunity "to rub smooth the sharp edges of prejudice, sectionalism, and lack of understanding between groups," and the physical strength brought on by basic training as some of the benefits to be reaped from a system of universal military training.[49]

Taken together, these advantages would help equalize many of the inequalities that existed within American society. Graduates of the training system would begin their adult lives on more equal footing—physically,

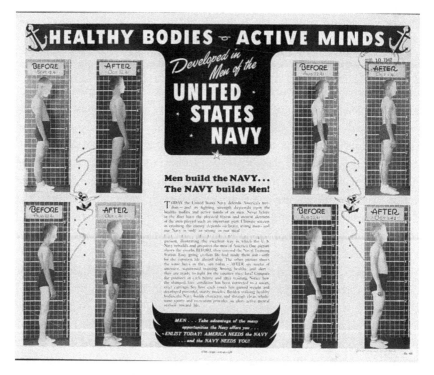

FIGURE 2.1. "Healthy Bodies, Active Minds." Proponents of universal military training often advertised UMT using the same idea present in this 1942 poster: basic training would better America's manhood. Photo courtesy of Northwestern University Library, https://images. northwestern.edu/multiresimages/inu:dil-6cd9f216-134a-4862-9b9d-ed1353f16fea

educationally, and socially—than they would have without training. Such equality of opportunity epitomized the promise of American democracy, enthused boosters.

Detractors, on the other hand, relied on a more liberal interpretation of citizenship. Rather than emphasizing the responsibilities of the citizen to the state, they highlighted the obligation of the state to guarantee the rights of the citizen. They focused on the ideals of individual liberty, free choice, and independence as the essence of American democracy. Therefore, they argued, UMT, because of its compulsory nature, was not democratic. It infringed on the free choice of the men who would be "dragooned" into service, and it encouraged a militarized society in which citizens would be discouraged from thinking for themselves.[50] This would be particularly oner- ous for those with religious objections. Samuel L. Harrison, representing the Michigan Council to Oppose Peacetime Military Conscription, pointed out that "American tradition has always held to the rights of religious liberty and that recognition that . . . men must obey God and conscience rather than men." He worried that for many, "universal conscription would be a complete violation of their own best conscience" and therefore the antithesis of everything America stood for.[51] "We consider it the last vestige of slavery," opined Dorothy Detzer of WILPF in no uncertain terms.[52]

Compulsory military training, which was "largely authoritarian in its methods," would make the United States no better than Nazi Germany or Soviet Russia.[53] "To adopt the essence of the system we are fighting to destroy is to be victimized by victory," stated University of Detroit president William J. Miller, representing the Michigan Council to Oppose Peacetime Military Conscription. "Nothing is more dangerous to democracy than the conditioning, regimentation, and uncritical obedience to arbitrary authority that most compulsory military training induces," he warned. Moreover, he observed, the regimentation and authoritarian nature of UMT would destroy the values of discipline and self-control that supporters proclaimed would be gained through military training. These principles, he noted, "are inwardly induced by voluntary acceptance. . . . They cannot be externally superimposed or cultivated under compulsion."[54] Rather, it was freedom of thought and action that led to the innovations that fueled America's greatness. UMT would infringe on these freedoms and lead to the "death and destruction" that befell all militarized nations, contended Guy E. Snavely, executive director of the Association of American Colleges. "The best brains of country," he declared, would be "occupied continuously with devising weapons of destruction instead of developing plans for the happier, fuller life."[55]

The meaning of a happy, full American life was of great concern to the opponents of UMT. Daniel Marsh, president of Boston University, rejected outright the notion that military training would improve the nation's male citizenry. "We go to war when we have to," he admitted, "but there is no reason why we should lie about it and pretend that it makes for finer manhood."[56] Exposure to the alcohol and sex on which military encampments supposedly thrived would corrupt the nation's youth, assured some witnesses at the Woodrum and May hearings, but more importantly, claimed others, compulsory training would interrupt their proper, rightful civilian pursuits.[57] Educational activists worried that if men did not complete their vocational and higher education immediately after graduating high school, they would not resume training for civilian careers after life in the military.[58] Simply put, claimed opponents, UMT was destructive to the American way of life.

Truman's answer to these criticisms was to create an independent commission to study all facets of universal military training and make recommendations based on its findings. He began assembling what was to become the President's Advisory Commission on Universal Training (PACUT) in November 1946. Over the next seven months, members, led by chair Karl T. Compton, president of the Massachusetts Institute of Technology, met with more than two hundred witnesses and traveled throughout the country to discuss the issue with concerned citizens. Ultimately, their report, *A Program for National Security*, confirmed universal military training as indispensable to the nation's defense. Members grounded their recommendations in national security concerns, but they also used *A Program for National Security* to categorically refute opponents' charges that UMT would destroy America's democratic ideals and superior morality.

The commission's findings served as the Truman administration's contribution to the public discourse on the contested nature of citizenship and democracy in relation to universal military training. PACUT members, in fact, took their lead from the president. Where he had recommended UMT to Congress in October 1945 as a key element of the nation's security program, calling all other benefits provided by the program "byproducts," he had changed his emphasis by December 1946. In his opening statement to PACUT's members, he explained that he had explicitly left the word "military" out of the commission's title, calling the term "incidental." He now claimed a universal training program that taught men to be good citizens would make America stronger. As he saw it, a program of mandatory training would ameliorate some of the ills caused by modern living. It would teach the nation's "young people" about democracy, how to "get . . . along with one another," and help them care for their bodies, the "Temple[s] which God gave [them]." The end result, he concluded, would be to "have sold our Republic to the coming generations as Madison and Hamilton and Jefferson sold it in the first place."[59] This charge set the tone for all future work the committee undertook.

Members spent their first meeting debating the president's stance and their own opinions on universal military training. Compton and Rev. Daniel A. Poling, the editor of the *Christian Herald* and a former army chaplain, had already testified in favor of the idea before Congress.[60] In fact, pacifists fiercely criticized PACUT's composition.[61] Most of its members had close ties to the White House and the military establishment. Anna Rosenberg was an industrial relations consultant who had formerly served as the regional director of the War Manpower Commission and as Franklin Roosevelt's personal observer in the European Theater of World War II. She would be appointed an assistant secretary of defense in 1950. Joseph E. Davies was the former chairman of the War Relief Control Board and had served as an ambassador to the Soviet Union, Luxembourg, and Belgium. Former New York State Supreme Court judge Samuel I. Rosenman had been the special counsel to the White House until mid-1946. Attorney Truman K. Gibson Jr. had served as a civilian aide to the secretary of war during World War II. The vice president of Georgetown University, Rev. Edmund A. Walsh, had served as a consultant to the American chief of counsel at the Nuremberg Trials. Harold W. Dodds, president of Princeton University, and Charles E. Wilson, president of General Electric, rounded out the commission. Gibson, an African American; Poling, a Protestant clergyman; Walsh, a Roman Catholic priest; and Compton and Dodds, both university presidents; had supposedly been appointed to the committee to lend it diversity and authority, but none represented the majority opinion of their broader constituencies on UMT. Although they claimed to be open-minded, most members admitted their predisposition toward passage of a training program at their first meeting.[62]

Members did not, however, ground the basis of their support solely in the military needs of the country. They took Truman's charge to heart, acknowledging the importance of looking beyond the country's immediate external defense requirements to investigate the possible moral, educational, and health benefits of UMT to national security. As Rosenman declared, "Insofar as this program promotes public health, literacy, intelligence, general citizenship and high standards, I think the program promotes national defense."[63] Specifically, Rosenberg expressed the hope that physical training would improve the well-being of American men in light of high rejection rates by Selective Service during World War II.[64] Gibson saw UMT as the "only form of universal education" that the United States had "any chance of putting into effect." While he acknowledged that military education might not be ideal, he felt "it [would be] better than none," especially for young African American men, whose literacy rates were abysmal.[65] Poling admitted that his "primary interest was in moral and religious values."[66]

These biases influenced the committee's final report, *A Program for National Security*, which was submitted to Truman on May 29, 1947, after the committee heard testimony from witnesses with a wide variety of civilian and military backgrounds.[67] In it, they unanimously and wholeheartedly recommended universal military training as a necessary and (relatively) economical element of the country's national security program, but only "under circumstances that w[ould] strengthen the spirit of democracy and prove of lasting value from a physical, mental, and moral standpoint to the youths in training." These "byproducts," they concluded, would be appropriate goals within a military setting only if universal training offered a tangible benefit to national security, but no program of UMT could function without paying special attention to the citizenship training the men would receive.[68] The United States needed to cultivate its strengths—both moral and military—in order to maintain its global "position of leadership" and prevent "the mantle of totalitarianism" from spreading "its darkness over still larger sections of the earth."[69]

According to the report, lack of preparedness on the part of the United States led to World War II. Therefore, it behooved the United States to remain prepared for all future contingencies, including war. The advent of air power and atomic weapons, however, made this option virtually impossible. The commission foresaw sneak attacks against the United States, possibly with atomic weapons, and defensive wars in allied and nonaligned nations, especially in Latin America, as equally viable methods for drawing America into military action. In either case, the United States would have to mobilize quickly—perhaps within as little as sixty days—in order to meet the threat of highly mechanized atomic warfare.[70]

The only effective way to protect the nation was through the combined effort of skilled active-duty professionals equipped with the most modern technology and militarily trained men spread throughout the country, "ready and able to meet disorder, sabotage, and even invasion."[71] This type of balanced approach would require either a force-in-being large enough to meet threats overseas and maintain active-duty personnel in every major American city, or a trained civilian populace. Both for economic reasons and to maintain the character of American democracy, PACUT concluded that a program of universal military training, as part of a larger, integrated national security program, was the best way for the United States to meet its defense obligations to the world and to its own populace. Most importantly, any such program had to be anchored by a "strong, healthy, educated population" that could "stand as a beacon of inspiration to those who believe that freedom and respect for the dignity of the individual are superior to security based on domination by the state." Members assumed that "want, ill health, ignorance, race prejudice, and slothful citizenship" were as dangerous to American existence as Hitler, Mussolini, or Tojo. A healthy and happy populace, assured the report, would provide the "bedrock" of American defense and prevent discontent from allowing American democracy to "degenerate into spineless ineffectuality."[72]

Members of PACUT made several recommendations for domestic reform. They advocated full production and full employment, improved health care, and quality education for all Americans, regardless of background. When these pieces came together, they argued, citizens would gain an "understanding of democracy and an increased sense of personal responsibility."[73]

America would gain a healthy, well-educated male populace with a clear understanding of what it should be fighting for and the knowledge that it should fight. For men, citizenship would rest on their military responsibility. Internal strength was essential for external power, and universal military training was the key to meeting this goal.

The report also made its case for training by directly refuting the arguments against UMT. It stated what universal military training was not. It was not conscription any more than were compulsory taxes or education. It was neither "un-American" nor undemocratic so long as a democratically elected government approved of it and so long as all men had an equal obligation to participate. The report rejected the notions that military preparedness would lead to war or turn the United States into a militaristic society.[74] Camp life would not necessarily be the moral cesspool certain detractors claimed. With carefully selected cadres, strict regulation of sexual behavior and alcohol consumption, good moral and religious training, and community involvement, universal military training could be a wholesome experience that developed the qualities of good citizens in American men even as it provided needed security to the nation.

PACUT received a fair amount of public attention, but it was the army's response to criticism of UMT that gained the lion's share of publicity. On January 13, 1947, the Army Ground Forces (AGF) opened an Experimental Training Unit at Fort Knox, Kentucky, under the command of Brig. Gen. John M. Devine, who had spent the last year of World War II leading the Army's 8th Armored Division across Europe. The AGF designed the unit to test the basic training component of the War Department's plan for universal military training, but it quickly became the centerpiece of a public relations campaign.[75] In order to publicize the virtues of universal military training, the War Department brought reporters to Fort Knox to observe— and presumably to write favorable articles about—the experimental unit. It also provided speakers to interested civic organizations and panel members to radio programs to highlight the various benefits a national UMT program could provide.

These publicity materials focused on how UMT could mold responsible, upright, democratic male citizens. The War Department noted the varied arguments against compulsory training, especially concerns about the religious and moral well-being of trainees, the disruption a year of training would cause to the educational and vocational lives of the men, and the fears over the destruction of democracy that training could signal, and it opted to take them on one by one.[76] How UMT would operate as part of a plan for national defense was all but lost among discussion of UMT's domestic benefits.

In all, 664 trainees took part in the first round of the experiment.[77] The army acknowledged that conditions could not fully mimic a national UMT program, since participants were regular enlisted men rather than conscripts, but it actively worked to approximate the conditions a national UMT law would create. All members of the initial cohort were under age twenty, and the men represented a large geographic swath of the United States. Only fourteen were married, and none had children.[78] Trainees averaged a tenth grade education, and only thirty-one had any schooling beyond high school.[79] In an attempt to match the population at large, another thirty-one men whose aptitude scores would have disqualified them from military service were accepted into a special training unit, known as the Pioneer Platoon, which was designed as a laboratory to test how these men would fare in a regimented environment.[80] All the men in the Experimental Training Unit were literate, and none had any major physical ailments.[81] Race was the major exception. Although the AGF had originally included plans for a segregated African American company in the Fort Knox experiment, the War Department overruled it, deeming the creation of separate facilities for a single company impractical. In fact, the War Department wanted to avoid calling attention to the army's institutionalized segregation, so it whitewashed the unit.[82]

Although the men were regular army recruits, the UMT experiment demanded that they be treated differently than the average GI. The War Department and the AGF were quick to highlight the unit's different training focus, judicial system, and regulations. They published pamphlets, produced informational films, and provided speakers to interested civic, religious, and educational organizations.[83] The unit itself possessed a dedicated public relations office, which produced its own materials and hosted members of the public and the press. According to Devine, almost two thousand visitors toured the facility between January and July 1947. Officers conducted press tours and assisted reporters.[84]

The printed materials produced by these offices clearly revealed a common desire to assuage the public's fears of UMT by portraying the experimental unit at Fort Knox in the most positive, nonthreatening light possible. Devine personally wrote letters to the families of each of the trainees. The Public Relations Office at Fort Knox sent copies of the unit's newspaper, the *UMT Pioneer*, home to parents of current volunteers each week.[85] Publications invited parents to visit their sons to put their minds at ease.[86] The 1947 informational pamphlet *Universal Military Training*, for example, did not mention, picture, or even allude to any form of martial endeavor until page 27.

When publicity did highlight the military elements of the program, it extolled the secondary benefits of training. According to the publicists at

Fort Knox, "the primary mission" of the unit was to turn out "hardy soldiers" who were "strong both in mind and body."[87] Publications pointed out that drill, calisthenics, and aerobic exercise would all lead to stronger, more muscular bodies, while classes in personal hygiene would help remediate some of the problems faced by the country's more disadvantaged youth.[88] Moreover, UMTees would come in contact with people of differing backgrounds, which would help individuals overcome their prejudices and solve some of the country's class and ethnic tensions. The hope was that "All [would] live and work together in the great democratic fraternity typical of America; bunking in the same barracks, eating the same food, wearing the same distinctive uniform, and sharing the same worth-while experiences."[89] The abundance of nutritious food, health care, and increased understanding of others was supposed to lull parents into a sense of well-being for their sons.

Lobbying groups, however, posed a much greater obstacle to the passage of a UMT bill than did individual parents, most of whom theoretically supported the measure, at least if public opinion polls were to be believed. Of these, religious organizations and other associations concerned with UMTees' moral welfare were among the most vocal and were therefore perceived as the greatest threat. The program at Fort Knox dealt with these concerns in a number of ways. The enhanced role of the base chaplains was perhaps the most novel. Within one week of arrival at Fort Knox, each trainee met with a Catholic or Protestant chaplain for an initial interview to ascertain his "willingness to support the unit's religious program."[90] Chaplains provided a series of seventeen mandatory "Citizenship and Morality" lectures, and attendance at worship services was compulsory during the first four weeks of training.[91] Devine and the Public Relations Office described the results of the chaplains' program as "phenomenal."[92] They were happy to report that most men continued to attend worship services after they were no longer required to do so. Moreover, 102 Protestant trainees took steps to be baptized or confirmed, as did 35 of the 135 Catholics in the first group of volunteers.[93]

Given the importance of morality, publicity materials depicted sex—or the promise thereof—carefully. The army's version of masculinity included an expectation of chaste, heterosexual love with an eye toward future marriage and families. Thus the trainees needed access to women, but only under controlled conditions. Unit dances and visits to homes in the local community provided wholesome, chaperoned contact with the opposite sex. *Universal Military Training*, for example, showed one image of trainees gathered around a piano with young women from the local community for a sing-along. Another photograph, of a young couple sitting under a tree, was captioned, "Old buildings are not the least of the local attractions."

These images left the reader to infer that a training post did not have to be an all-male environment and that marriage could be one of the benefits trainees would accrue through UMT.[94] Sex, however, was only for marriage. Two chaplains' lectures on "Sex Morality" stressed abstinence rather than prophylaxis. In fact, according to General Devine, "all references to mechanical preventives, or statements that penicillin is [a] cure-all were avoided. . . . The basis for these lectures was the place of sex in the plan of God and the necessity for keeping one's body and mind pure."[95]

In case moral and religious instruction were not enough to keep trainees out of trouble, unit regulations prohibited pin-ups, gambling, profanity, and alcohol consumption. The Post Exchange contained a soda fountain rather than the usual bar because, according to the Public Relations Office, "the average 18 year old prefers a soda."[96] To prevent carousing on weekend passes, post regulations required trainees to register at the USO and to inform the unit headquarters of their intended whereabouts. Devine measured the success of this endeavor by the low venereal disease rate exhibited by UMTees (10.2 per thousand) compared with that of the regular army soldiers also stationed at Fort Knox (41.2 per thousand).[97] Local statutes forbade bartenders throughout Louisville, the nearest city, from selling alcohol to trainees. In order to keep the UMTees visible, unit regulations required them to wear distinctive badges on their uniforms at all times while off post.

Planners also instituted a plethora of after-hours activities to occupy (or possibly exhaust) the UMTees in a wholesome manner. As one *UMT Pioneer* columnist rhetorically asked, "How is a guy going to particularly good movie, attend glee club practice, see a company basketball game, and go to dance in one night [*sic*]?"[98] Volunteers could also take advantage of GED, correspondence, or vocational classes; a hobby shop; a music room; a sports center; a swimming pool; a radio station; and a theater in their off-duty hours. Publicity surrounding Fort Knox made sure to highlight all these options in order to de-emphasize the military nature of UMT, reassure Americans concerned about the moral lives of the young trainees, and underscore the ways military training would benefit men's futures as civilians.

Military publicity also aimed to quell fears of "Prussianism." Public relations officers stressed the democratic features of UMT rather than weapons training or drill. Pamphlets assured their readers that trainees were not "taught to kill." UMT, such publications claimed, could never foster the violence and terror that characterized militaristic societies because military training avoided "regimentation" even as it taught "discipline and respect."

The men at Fort Knox were never to be considered merely numbers or cogs in a machine. Each man was encouraged to "respond . . . as an individual, develop . . . as an individual, [and] think . . . as an individual."[99] Instructors were to present lectures and standardized curricula "in the democratic American way," complete with "open discussions rather than formal lectures." "Learning is motivated when each man is made to feel that his ideas are important and original," explained one informational pamphlet.[100]

Even the army's system of discipline was modified to avoid the threat of military hierarchy. Unit regulations prohibited drill sergeants and junior officers from haranguing the trainees or using profanity. UMTees were to be disciplined through a demerit system rather than with verbal threats, hazing, or other forms of abuse. Infractions too severe for the demerit system, such as going absent without leave for less than twenty-four hours, disorderly conduct, or drunkenness, were turned over to a Trainee Court. This disciplinary body consisted of a jury of seven trainees who decided cases argued by trainee judge advocates and defense counsels.[101] Devine particularly lauded this system as a means to instill individual responsibility, stating, "Every court case is a lesson in justice and that is a lesson in citizenship."[102] In other words, planners believed that trainees would develop democratic values and learn active citizenship when they were encouraged to raise their voices and participate in discussion and self-government. Militarism simply could not flourish in such an environment.

In the process of producing publicity materials to allay fears about universal military training, the War Department and army constructed an idealized form of virtuous, moral, middle-class male citizenship. The War Department promised boys poise and confidence, education and skills. They would learn discipline but maintain enough individuality to think for themselves. UMT would reinforce the values of church, home, and family. Thanks to the remediation any illiterate trainees would receive, all UMT graduates would meet at least minimum educational standards, and the available vocational training ensured that all would be prepared to be wage earners. Training would also harden soft bodies and correct the health defects of the nation. In return for their time, trainees would gain confidence, new interests, and new knowledge. They would be "more tolerant and understanding," "physically fit," and "mentally alert." Each individual would "look . . . a man" upon completion of the program and be "ready to take on his new job or school work with satisfaction." UMT would strengthen the nation internally by remolding its manhood. Moreover, each trainee would graduate a "responsible citizen." Military training would constitute that citizenship, and a particularly masculine ideal of citizenship at that.[103]

The public responded well to this publicity. Gallup polls conducted in February 1947, as PACUT was meeting and the Fort Knox unit was operating, indicated that 72 percent of the general public favored one year of compulsory military training for all young men.[104] Of the 2,750 letters expressing opinions on UMT that members of PACUT and the president received from Americans between December 20, 1946, and February 6, 1947, 67 percent were favorable.[105] The Fort Knox unit even managed to impress certain critics, including *New York Times* military affairs correspondent Hanson W. Baldwin.[106] In other words, the media blitz spurred by the formation of PACUT and the experimental unit seemed to be working. The press picked up on the relentlessly positive image of UMT furthered by army public information officers. Stories referenced UMT at least 115 times in 95 newspapers across 33 states during the first week of February 1947 alone.[107] But as historian William A. Taylor has argued, the measure of its success in the media generally focused on "the conduct and morale of the young soldiers rather than any actual military efficiency."[108] It seems that many of those Americans who approved of UMT in 1947 supported it as much for the image of wholesome masculine citizenship it offered as for its benefits to national defense.

Similarly, those who argued against UMT connected their belief that universal training would be detrimental to American security interests with their belief that it would harm American values. An analysis of letters sent to members of PACUT showed that of the nine hundred writers opposed to UMT, 90 percent thought such a plan "inconsistent with American ideals" and 85 percent argued that it would "cause rather than prevent war." In other words, there was significant overlap between Americans who believed compulsory military training would infringe on the rights of young men, militarize the nation, and create geopolitical insecurity.[109]

Remarkably, these positions crossed party lines. Public opinion polling conducted in April 1947 showed that 73 percent of Americans believed that the United States was likely to be involved in another global war within the next twenty-five years, making national defense an issue of major concern to both parties, but whether Americans favored or opposed UMT was not based on political party. In July 1946, a Roper survey done for *Fortune* magazine found that 65 percent of Republicans and 69 percent of Democrats favored training while 27 percent of Republicans and 23 percent of Democrats opposed it. This same survey showed that age, sex, level of educational attainment, geographic region, veteran status, and occupation also did not seem to affect a person's likelihood of endorsing the measure.[110] In the end, as the letters to Truman and PACUT showed, it was an individual's vision for America that determined whether or not he or she backed universal military training. Public support seemed to hinge on Americans' personal calculations of how UMT's domestic benefits balanced against its potential for protection from external enemies. When press accounts focused on how compulsory training could build strong, breadwinning men with a strong sense of civic responsibility, UMT enjoyed greater approval.

Despite strong public support, a bill for UMT's instatement introduced by Republican Harry L. Towe of New York, the chair of the House Armed Services Committee, stalled in the summer of 1947. Towe's committee and then a separate subcommittee of that body held hearings throughout June and July, but the issue became a political hot potato. Opposition groups clamored to have their objections heard before the hearings, but the Armed Services Committee shut them down before they could all have their say. In its report, the committee defended itself, declaring that the issue had been "thoroughly debated" and a "singular uniformity of argument" had been presented. Since "no new light would have been shed on the subject had hearings been extended," the hearings ended.[111]

Moreover, Republican senator Robert Taft of Ohio decided to throw his considerable political weight behind the opposition.[112] Taft had always disdained compulsion in manpower policy, believing it an infringement on American liberty. He had voted against the Selective Training and Service Act of 1940 and had advocated an all-volunteer military in the wake of World War II. By late 1947, he had turned his attention to UMT, bringing many Republican members of Congress with him.[113] The House Armed Services Committee ultimately reported out the Towe bill favorably, but only because of the absence of eleven of its Republican members. It moved on to the Rules Committee, where it languished.[114]

At the same time, a special subcommittee of the House Committee on Expenditures in the Executive Departments, chaired by Republican Forest A. Harness of Indiana, convened to investigate whether the military had acted inappropriately in its UMT publicity campaign. The hearings concluded that civilian employees of the War Department and enlisted men from the Fort Knox unit had used federal funds to finance speaking engagements with civic, educational, women's, parent's, and patriotic organizations. Further, the military had chartered planes at taxpayers' expense to fly visitors, especially reporters, to Fort Knox, who subsequently received heavily biased tours.[115] Congress censured the War Department for engaging in propaganda, and in early 1948 the Department of Justice initiated its own investigation. Publicity in favor of UMT from the War Department (later Department of Defense) all but stopped.[116] It could no longer advertise UMT as a measure to strengthen America's manhood or teach citizenship obligations.

The number of articles on UMT featuring its domestic benefits slowed to a trickle, while unraveling events in Europe brought national security back to the fore. When communists staged a successful coup in Czechoslovakia in February 1948, alarm rippled through the defense establishment. Not only had the last remaining democracy in Eastern Europe "fallen" to communism, but the emergency highlighted the woeful manpower predicament faced by American ground forces. The army's available force was 117,000 men below its congressional authorization, while the Marine Corps fell short by approximately 30,000.[117] Moreover, soldiers were mustering out of the army faster than new men could be recruited. Force strength was falling, leaving the army, according to Secretary of State Marshall, "a hollow shell, over-deployed."[118]

On March 17, in a speech addressed to a joint session of Congress and broadcast over most major radio stations, Truman outlined his emergency plan. He requested that Congress approve the European Recovery Program without delay, enact a plan for universal military training, and temporarily reinstate the draft. "We have found," he declared, "that a sound military system is necessary in time of peace if we are to remain at peace."[119] The United States, according to the president, was in a liminal state, neither at war nor at peace. The old objections to a peacetime draft had no place in a Cold War world. New exigencies called for a rethinking of national security policy.

Truman had performed another about-face, combining UMT with conscription. His administration's previous position had been to separate the two measures, and the push for UMT had been part of the rationale for allowing the draft to expire in 1947.[120] But now he tried to reconcile the two, reassuring the nation that Selective Service would be necessary only "until the solid foundation of universal training [could] be established." In the meantime, UMT would support the reserves, and conscription would fill the ranks of the active forces.[121] Gone was any reference to UMT's possible benefits for the nation's moral, educational, or social welfare; discussion of the meaning of democracy; or consideration of the responsibilities of citizenship. From 1948 on, the administration framed universal training solely as a defensive measure in an increasingly hostile world. With this change, the measure steadily lost support.

As Cold War tensions escalated with the Soviet blockade of West Berlin, congressional debate shifted away from whether the United States should arm itself and toward the best way to do it. Although some Republicans, like chairman of the Senate Armed Services Committee Chan Gurney of South

Dakota and chairman of the Senate Foreign Relations Committee Arthur Vandenberg of Michigan, continued to support universal military training, most did not. Many followed Taft and lifted their objections to conscription, finding it "more important to be anti-Soviet than antimilitary."[122] Instead, they chose to support the findings of the President's Air Policy Commission, a fact-finding committee formed by Truman in July 1947 that advocated the expansion of the newly independent Air Force as the most efficient and realistic way to defend the country.

Other opponents, meanwhile, had not substantially changed their line of attack since 1944. They continued to object to UMT based on the assumption that the measure would infringe on the citizenship rights of individual men and destroy the moral fabric of American society. More than one hundred witnesses either testified or submitted statements to this effect at the Senate Armed Services Committee's hearings. Despite the publicity campaign of 1947, not one major organization or constituency that had opposed UMT in 1944–45 supported it in 1948, although several, including the American Federation of Labor, the American Council on Education, and the American Farm Bureau Federation, lifted their opposition to selective conscription on a limited basis.[123] And by this time, Department of Defense officials could not counter these concerns with their own idealized vision of civic republican citizenship, even if they had wanted to.

But it was the issue of race that drove the final nail into the coffin of universal military training. Despite propaganda that painted UMT as an unmitigated good for the nation, the War Department/Department of Defense could not escape the central contradiction of a program that promised a common, leveling, democratic experience to all men but only within a segregated system. While African Americans had protested this inherent discrimination since the War Department's earliest proposals, labor and civil rights activists A. Philip Randolph and Grant Reynolds forced the issue in 1948.

In late 1947, the two men founded the Committee Against Jim Crow in Military Service and Training to lobby for the desegregation of the military. Testifying before the Senate Armed Service Committee under the auspices of that organization, they warned members of the committee that if integration was not made part of whatever training program Congress settled on, they would initiate a broad campaign of civil disobedience against any compulsory service or training. Randolph promised to "personally . . . advise Negroes to refuse to fight as slaves for a democracy they cannot possess and cannot enjoy." He pledged himself to "openly counsel, aid, and abet youth, both white and Negro, to quarantine any Jim Crow conscription system."[124]

Randolph and Reynolds' call for civil disobedience initiated a firestorm of protest. Liberal allies in Congress were furious. Oregon Republican and civil rights supporter Senator Wayne Morse suggested that Randolph be tried for treason.[125] Other civil rights organizations, including the Congress of Racial Equality, the NAACP, and the National Urban League objected to Randolph's tactics, even as they were able to take advantage of the publicity garnered by his demands to push their own antisegregation agendas. It is impossible to know how much influence this agitation had over Truman's decision to order the desegregation of the armed forces in 1948, but it is clear that young black men were thinking about the issue. No polls were conducted in rural southern or urban northern areas where the majority of black youth lived, but a survey conducted by the Youth Division of the NAACP found that 71 percent of black college students favored a boycott of segregated compulsory military training during peacetime, while 50 percent stated that they would not serve even during a war emergency.[126]

In July 1948, Truman assured Reynolds and Randolph that segregation would be banned in the military and the draft.[127] Opponents of UMT, however, took advantage of the political upheaval. The majority of the Congress preferred to let the military decide its own racial policy, believing that the nation's protection, not social experimentation, was the first priority of the Department of Defense.[128] Most southern representatives, including those who supported UMT, would not back any program that mandated integration, and some attempted to have segregation specifically written into defense bills. Senator Richard B. Russell, a Georgia Democrat, introduced an amendment to pending draft legislation that would have required the military to assign any man who filed a petition to a unit composed solely of men from his own race. Mississippi Democrat John Bell Williams offered a similar measure in the House.[129] At the other end of the spectrum, Taft and Senator William Langer, a Republican from North Dakota, actively fought to include integration amendments in UMT bills, most likely as a delaying tactic, since they opposed compulsory training in general. Congressional inability to reach consensus on the meaning of "universal" in universal military training meant that no UMT legislation could get past a full congressional vote, even if most members favored the idea.

In the end, Truman signed the Selective Service Act of 1948 into law on June 24 without a training provision. Inductions were scheduled to start ninety days later, but in that time, international tensions calmed slightly. Although the Berlin Airlift continued, it appeared that Soviet premier Josef Stalin was unwilling to start another war. As a result, and because the threat of conscription spurred sufficient men to enlist on their own, draft calls stayed low and were suspended entirely by February 1949. Although the issue of UMT came up in the debates over the fiscal 1950 budget, there was no impetus for its passage. Selective conscription barely seemed necessary, let alone training for all American men.

Truman, however, continued to lobby. With the opening of hostilities in Korea, he appointed staunch UMT supporter George Marshall as secretary of defense, who in turn suggested Anna Rosenberg, a former member of PACUT, as the assistant secretary of defense for manpower and personnel. They seized on the Korean emergency as an opportunity to renew their fight for UMT as part of a long-range plan to expand the country's reserves. They hoped to eliminate conscription after the war ended by authorizing the president to alter the terms of Selective Service legislation. They fought for a law that would allow Truman to shorten the period of training for inductees to six months and either reduce or eliminate the responsibility for active service. This would effectively create a training rather than service program. House and Senate deliberations, however, added restriction on top of restriction to the proposal.[130]

In 1951, Congress passed the Universal Military Training and Service Act. Although primarily designed to extend the draft, the act allowed for a UMT program, but only after Congress had established provisions for it in a separate law. The separate law never passed. Debates over its details and lack of political will sent the measure back to committee, where it died. Military planners continued to shift their focus to mechanization, air power, and a doctrine of limited engagement. By 1951, training a large reserve of infantrymen seemed obsolete. The Truman administration had failed to convince opponents that UMT was an American, democratic, or necessary measure. The idea of universal military training was, in effect, politically dead, as was the civic republican ideal of masculine citizenship it represented.

By the end of World War II, a national consensus had been reached about the necessity of male military service in a time of emergency. The passage of regulations narrowing deferments and the vigorous enforcement of those regulations by the Selective Service sent the message that young, able-bodied men had a responsibility to serve when there were no other options. Military necessity trumped age; domestic responsibilities, including dependents; and, in almost all cases, occupation. A large, strong, conscripted armed force was plainly required when America faced a clear military threat from external aggressors as it did from Nazi Germany and Imperial Japan. Individuals and their families may have balked at this general consensus, but as chapter 1 showed, it is hard to deny that it existed by the end of 1944.

Supporters of UMT tried to leverage this consensus. Stimson, Marshall, and Palmer launched their campaign for universal military training within the War Department in 1944 in an attempt to build on the sense of emergency engendered by World War II. They hoped that Americans' desire to avoid another war combined with the concurrent swell of patriotism and civic responsibility cresting at that historical moment would propel their plan into successful legislation.

But it was not to be. Americans during World War II had not accepted widespread conscription easily, even during total war. As the sense of emergency ebbed at the end of the war and was replaced by one of geopolitical uncertainty, the consensus that seemed to link military service to a widespread civic republican ideal of masculine citizenship broke apart. Individual needs, desires, and circumstances once again became factors in the debate over the purpose of military service.

And deliberations over the passage of UMT *were* as much about the purpose of military service as they were about national defense. By framing training as either an economical way to strengthen the nation's manhood or as a surefire way to destroy American values, supporters and detractors both treated it as a laboratory for building citizens, who were implicitly defined as white and male. Their idealized vision of citizenship differed, however, and whether one viewed civic republicanism or classical liberalism as the ideal framework for citizenship determined whether he or she saw the purpose of UMT as molding ideal citizens or saw it as evidence of massive government overreach.

By 1948, the service branches had split in their vision for America's national security. Where Secretary of Defense Forrestal advocated a "balanced" force, characterized by an expanded Air Force that would be supported by "a strong Navy, a sizable and well-equipped Army, and the many supporting services," including UMT, the Air Force clearly had other ideas.[131] Secretary W. Stuart Symington publicly admitted that he would rather grow the air force than support UMT.[132] For its part, the army latched on to the potential benefits of conducting basic training in the style pioneered by the Fort Knox Experimental Unit, particularly with regard to the enhanced role of chaplains in shepherding recruits' morality.[133]

UMT enjoyed its greatest popularity during the first half of 1947, when the Truman administration through PACUT, the War Department, and the AGF actively promoted its potential domestic benefits. When members of Congress, the press, and the American public were most able to imagine summer-camp-like training facilities teaching physical fitness, critical thinking, patriotism, religious values, and vocational skills to a whitewashed male populace, legislation gained the most congressional traction.

Reality, however, caught up with fantasy. Americans were not all white, even if War Department officials wanted them to be. African American activists called attention to the contradiction inherent in any plan that would segregate black trainees, especially when part of the rationale for such a program was to "to rub smooth the sharp edges of prejudice." Yet segregationists refused to include African Americans, and integrationists refused to pass a segregated bill. There was no universal reality of full citizenship that included black and white men, which made defining the responsibility of universal military training impossible.

UMT also lost ground because the picture of manhood the military created was simply too good to be true. Flesh-and-blood men did not behave as the staged photographs and carefully worded text in publicity materials indicated. Regular soldiers at Fort Knox who were not associated with the UMT experiment derided the special unit's participants by impugning their masculinity. Names bandied about for UMTees included "beardless wonders," "senior boy scouts," and "male Wacs," after the female soldiers of the Women's Army Corps.[134] Journalist Alexander Stewart found that Fort Knox trainees, resentful of being called "the lace pantie brigade [sic]," frequently removed their distinctive badges while on pass in Louisville in order to find beer and women.[135] Clearly the men themselves, fearful that the prohibitions on alcohol and sex would damage their masculine self-image, did not universally buy in to the image of manhood so carefully cultivated by the army. In fact, some of the independent press coverage took the army's carefully controlled message and pushed it further than the publicity officers intended. A photo essay in *Life* magazine referred to the UMTees as "kid-glove rookies." It derisively noted the trainees' individually tailored uniforms, the unit's "polite" and "solicitous" officers, and the rug on the club room floor.[136] The end result was not so much an image of wholesome manhood, but an impression of soft, pampered teenagers.

By 1948, the United States was negotiating an entirely new context for its national security planning. As later chapters will show, changing strategic needs coupled with the declining likelihood of another global war meant that the armed forces required fewer and fewer men. UMT was obsolete, even if Truman and Marshall were not quite willing to concede the point just yet. At neither war nor peace and with the threat of a Soviet atomic weapon looming some time in the future, the Department of Defense and Congress decided to return to a system of selective conscription. This decision made practical sense from a defense standpoint, but it also validated military service as a selective male citizenship obligation, decisively ending the possibility that military service in the twentieth century would be coupled with the responsibilities of male citizenship during peacetime.

CHAPTER 3

"Really First-Class Men"

The Early Cold War, 1948–1953

When President Harry Truman stood before Congress in March 1948 to ask for a reinstatement of the draft, he fervently hoped selective conscription would be a temporary expedient, in place just long enough to bolster the armed forces until a program of universal military training could be implemented. But it was not to be. UMT never passed, and Selective Service continued to operate until 1973, officially through more years of peace than war. The Selective Service Act of 1948 instituted the United States' first true peacetime draft.[1]

Like America's other twentieth-century draft laws, the Selective Service Act of 1948 and its successor, the Universal Military Training and Service Act of 1951, allowed men who met certain requirements to defer their military service, in some cases for long enough that they aged out of eligibility altogether. Like those offered during earlier periods of conscription, these deferments were designed to protect the nation's economic stability, but unlike during earlier wars, conscription during the Cold War was not framed as an emergency expedient. Rather, after 1948, Selective Service was conceived as a semipermanent institution necessary to support the large manpower requirements of the Cold War. The period of prolonged military preparedness engendered by this conflict forced manpower planners to rethink the purpose of conscription and the system used to sustain it. For the first time, deferments were used to support an indefinitely militarized peace instead of a temporary war effort. Within this context, protecting national values while meeting long-range defense goals was of greater consequence than during earlier periods of conscription. Sustaining a functional, vibrant, and distinctly American civilian society became as much a goal of military manpower policy as producing a strong military.

The onset of the Korean War brought these issues into sharp relief. The surprise with which the North Korean invasion of South Korea caught Pentagon officials underscored the need for preparedness in an uncertain world. As a result, the armed forces did not plan to demobilize after the cessation of combat as they had following every previous American military engagement. Thus the policy debates over deferments that occurred during the Korean War took on new meanings, as their results would last long into the militarized peace that followed.

In order to meet the emergency, the United States military tripled the size of its active forces, just as the nation's population of military-aged young men fell to its lowest number in decades. Fewer babies born during the Depression years meant fewer men available to be soldiers in the 1950s. Meanwhile, the Selective Service Act of 1948 deferred all of the same categories of men as the original 1940 law, including veterans and men younger than nineteen years old. Available manpower was spread thin in both the military and civilian sectors. Yet in 1951, with congressional and presidential approval, the Selective Service added a deferment category for college students. Moreover, just as they had during World War II, Congress and certain segments of the public proved reluctant to draft eighteen-year-olds or revoke the dependency deferment for fathers even at a moment of heightened concern over the depth of the manpower pool.

Despite downward population trends and vastly increased induction calls, pressure from professional organizations, federal agencies, and the American public indicated these groups' desire to look beyond the immediate emergency. They considered certain men more valuable to the nation as civilians than as soldiers. Science, engineering, and educational organizations argued that American technological superiority depended on maintaining an uninterrupted supply of bright, young college graduates. Civic organizations, including many that lobbied in favor of universal military training, hoped to lower the age of induction to eighteen, but the same pacifist and religious groups that fought against UMT also maintained that military service at such a young age would destroy America's youth. Finally, individual citizens and lawmakers alike fretted over what would happen to the institution of the family if fathers were drafted away from their homes on a regular basis. To these groups, national security included training future generations of scientists, engineers, and doctors; nurturing boys into men; and protecting the nuclear family. The decision of who to draft and who to leave at home would have lasting repercussions. Conditions established during the Korean War would not be temporary; they would become the new "normal" for an indeterminate length of time into the future peace. Therefore, it was imperative that new regulations protect national security and American values.

In many ways, the Selective Service, Congress, and the president responded to competing pressure groups as they had during World War II. They weighed all of their options and ultimately chose to induct men from those groups they felt could best be spared from civilian life. Constituencies granted the possibility of deferment were those deemed most essential to the nation's defense, but the advent of the Cold War changed how that essentiality was determined. Whereas by the middle of World War II, a man's contribution to the external war effort—how his civilian job would help the United States defeat the Axis—was the determining factor, the indeterminate nature of the early Cold War subtly shifted the calculus from the man's current contribution to national defense to his potential for future contributions. This was particularly evident with the addition of a student deferment at a moment when the military needed men terribly.

As during World War II, fathers lost their deferments toward the end of the Korean War after heated public debate. Unlike during World War II, however, it was not out of military necessity. It was as a trade-off to protect the new student deferment from charges of elitism. If anything, deliberations were even more intense than they had been in 1943, as advocates of fatherhood argued that ripping fathers away from family on a semipermanent basis would leave American youth more susceptible to delinquency at a moment when unraveling the social fabric made America vulnerable to communism. Such arguments left legislators, lobbyists, and the Selective Service struggling with how they would define service to the nation under Cold War conditions.

In short, the definition of service began to expand in the early 1950s to more clearly encompass civilian pursuits. Through that expansion, deferment policies during the Korean War privileged economic and domestic forms of citizenship over martial citizenship in the civic republican tradition. Their unintended result was to further the process of separating military service from masculine citizenship, especially for the white, middle-class men who were most able to take advantage of the student deferment.

In many ways, the Selective Service Act of 1948 was an equivocal measure. On one hand, the very existence of conscription during peacetime indicated the intensified militarization of postwar American society. Traditionally, the United States had depended on involuntary inductions only during war-time because the American people historically harbored a deep suspicion of peacetime conscription. In the late 1940s, however, fear of a third world war trumped such misgivings. In the emerging Cold War environment, national security was seen by many as a more critical issue than the threat of compul-sion, which was why many former isolationists, including Senator Robert Taft, the Republican of Ohio, dropped their opposition to conscription in 1948. On the other hand, Congress responded to Truman's request with a limited bill.

Members made it clear that the Selective Service Act of 1948 was not uni-versal military training in disguise. The legislation itself stated that all men did not have an equal responsibility for military service. The text acknowl-edged that "the obligations and privileges of serving in the armed forces . . . should be shared generally," but went on to qualify that men should only be drafted "in accordance with a system of selection which is . . . consistent with the maintenance of an effective national economy."[2] In other words, while universal military service theoretically should be an obligation of citizenship, such a program was not a practical reality. The nascent Cold War demanded partial mobilization. Men should expect to serve if called, but the Selective Service would not call all men equally.

Because the United States was at peace in 1948, the law reflected the same peacetime conditions as the 1940 law had. But because conscription was now seen as an indefinite measure, how to maintain postsecondary students in the educational pipeline became one of the first new issues for stakeholders to address.

Student deferments had a short history. Educational groups lobbied for student deferments during World War I, but Secretary of War Newton D. Baker repeatedly denied any blanket exemptions, explaining to President Woodrow Wilson that privileging wealthy students would create "class feel-ing," and ultimately class resentment among those who could not afford a postsecondary education.[3] Since the Selective Draft Act only conscripted men aged twenty-one or over until three months before the war's end, those college students who had not volunteered for the armed services had not been subject to induction.[4]

The Selective Training and Service Act of 1940 allowed students to post-pone their inductions until the end of their academic year or until July 1, 1941, whichever came first, but as with World War I, it was not until Con-gress considered dropping the age of draft liability to eighteen in the fall of 1942 that the issue of student deferments gained much political momentum.

In response to the protests of college administrators, the Selective Service piloted a limited student deferment program in 1943. Students who majored in one of twenty science, engineering, or related fields; whose university would certify that they were in good standing; and who would graduate before July 1, 1945, could receive a deferment.[5] As manpower needs increased, these deferments were limited to a total of ten thousand students nationwide in the fields of chemistry, engineering, geology, geophysics, and physics.[6]

World War II, however, jump-started the militarization of civilian science and highlighted its importance to military strategy and tactics. The advent and military application of technologies such as radar, synthetic rubber, penicillin, and especially the atomic bomb brought scientists firmly into the realm of national defense, frequently under the auspices of the federal government. The War and Navy Departments both undertook limited research agendas and awarded contracts to private laboratories to work on specific problems. Defense-related research was conducted in other major agencies as well, including the Departments of Agriculture, Commerce, and Interior.[7] In 1941, the White House created the Office of Scientific Research and Development (OSRD) to coordinate research and development efforts between federal and military agencies; liaise with foreign governments and civilian institutions, including universities, the National Academy of Science, and the National Research Council; and develop some of its own programs, including the Manhattan Project. It even stationed civilian geologists, physicists, architects, biologists, and civil and electrical engineers in overseas theaters of operation through its Office of Field Service.[8] But Vannevar Bush, OSRD's director, envisioned a much stronger connection between science and national defense as the country moved toward peace.

In *Science: The Endless Frontier*, a 1945 report commissioned by President Franklin Roosevelt, Bush encouraged the federal government to promote scientific education and encourage the development of new talent. He argued that this was the government's responsibility since science "vitally affect[ed the nation's] health . . . jobs, and . . . national security." Science, he claimed in no uncertain terms, had won World War II. While he acknowledged that science alone was "no panacea," he advocated the notion that "scientific progress" was necessary for American liberty. Basic scientific research, or work exploring how the natural world functioned rather than that attempting to solve a particular problem, was key to America's continued safety since no one could predict what applications new knowledge would yield. In order to further such inquiry, he advocated the creation of a permanent Science Advisory Board to help guide the president and Congress as they shaped future scientific policy for the country and a congressionally funded civilian organization to "supplement and strengthen" military research. Government funding would ensure that the work got done, while civilian control would guarantee intellectual freedom.[9]

Adequate numbers of trained personnel were essential to Bush's vision. "The limiting factor is a human one," he wrote. The nation's rate of scientific advancement would depend on "the number of really first-class men" who engaged in the work. And Bush stressed the importance of numbers. He worried that too many scientifically talented and trained men had entered the military during World War II. He estimated that their widespread enlistment and conscription had created a deficit of approximately 150,000 science and technology students who would have received bachelors degrees and another 17,000 men who would have earned advanced degrees in chemistry, engineering, geology, mathematics, physics, psychology, and the biological sciences by 1955. Therefore, he argued, it was incumbent upon the government to compensate for this imbalance by opening wide the doors to scientific education. Federal programs should encourage improvement in science education and offer scholarships and fellowships to talented students looking to pursue advanced degrees. The security of the nation depended on scientifically trained manpower, be it military or civilian.[10]

Bush's report implicitly gendered such trained manpower as male. While he never suggested the deferment or exemption from military service of male college students, most likely because World War II ended while he was compiling his data, neither did he offer viable alternatives in the event of another war. Although Bush argued that "a larger number of men and women of ability" should be "encourage[d] and enable[d] . . . to take up science as a career," *Science: The Endless Frontier* did not discuss any method to attract or encourage women to enroll in STEM programs. Perhaps more tellingly, it made no reference to the large number of women who had gained scientific and engineering training during World War II. Women's enrollments in STEM programs had spiked during the war, largely due to recruitment efforts. While their absolute numbers had remained small, women earned 75 percent more undergraduate engineering degrees during the war than they had in the period immediately before, and they had flooded special training programs like that established by aircraft manufacturer Curtiss-Wright.[11] Nevertheless, for all its urgency, Bush's report did not explicitly suggest that women—as professors, students, or researchers in private industry—could help make up for the deficit of scientific personnel or provide national security into the future. So long as women remained an afterthought in recruitment and training efforts, defense through scientific research would remain a masculine obligation, even in the presence of female scientists.[12]

Despite this oversight, Bush's advocacy helped scientific manpower become a subject of great concern to the federal government as it demobilized after World War II and then reorganized its many agencies during the early Cold War. In October 1946, Truman appointed his assistant and former director of the Office of War Mobilization and Reconversion, John R. Steelman, as the chairman of the President's Scientific Research Board. Truman charged this body with reporting on all of the federal government's scientific undertakings across agencies. Its goals included cataloguing the availability and allocation of resources and determining how scientific personnel were trained.[13] Its membership consisted of the heads of those federal agencies most involved in scientific research, including Robert Patterson, secretary of war; James Forrestal, secretary of the navy; Clinton P. Anderson, secretary of agriculture; Vannevar Bush, as the director of the OSRD; and David Lilienthal, chairman of the Atomic Energy Commission.

These men took for granted the idea that science was vital to national security. Their five-volume report, *Science and Public Policy*, issued between August and October 1947, opened with the claim that "the rapid extension of scientific knowledge" would be a "major factor in national survival." Not everyone in the civilian world agreed. Scientists, like other types of intellectuals, took on a more equivocal role in the popular culture of the early Cold War, where they were portrayed simultaneously as subversives and as saviors, who could unleash supposedly uncontrollable forces of destruction but who could also better humanity by harnessing those same forces.[14] Within government circles, however, federal funding firmly yoked science to national security.[15] The white-coated, laboratory-based scientist became an "indispensable warrior," a masculine savior rather than an effete—or potentially communist—"longhair." Civilian scientists were key to national security, as they performed a vital service to the protection of the nation as "the first line of defense."[16]

The members of the President's Scientific Research Board did not find the shortage of trained scientists quite as dire as Bush had in 1945. Their report found that the war had directly cost the United States approximately 90,000 bachelors degrees and 5,000 doctoral degrees in scientific subjects, but it expected these numbers to rise to 100,000 and 8,400, respectively, "before the effects of war-reduced enrollments [were] overcome." Steelman further estimated that only one-third of science majors entered research or teaching careers, reducing the deficit to a mere 40,000 scientists and engineers on the bachelors level. Ninety percent of PhDs tended to enter similar professions, leading to a loss of approximately 7,600.[17] Nevertheless, the report warned, the nation could not afford to sit idly by and wait for the manpower shortfall to correct itself. To do so would be "dangerous not only to . . . national welfare but to national security." As an example, it pointed out that at the moment of the report's publication, neither the Atomic Energy Commission nor the army could fully staff their research and development programs.[18] Therefore, recommended the board's members, the federal government needed to stimulate the growth of America's scientific manpower pool.[19]

The report concluded that the nation's universities were the key to solving the scientific manpower crisis. They were sites of both training and basic research. Financial support through grants to improve facilities and equipment, fellowships to augment professors' salaries, and scholarships to assist the brightest students would all help ease the deficit.[20] But it would be a long process. Scientists, according to Steelman, could not be "mass-produced."[21] America's colleges and universities would need 15,000 additional science instructors, including 4,500 with PhDs, to reach the prewar student-teacher ratio, a process that would take at least ten years. Yet given the huge postwar increase in demand for scientists, that number, according to the report, was not guaranteed to be sufficient.[22] In short, policies to encourage students to enter scientific fields were vital to national security.

Like Vannevar Bush's *Science: The Endless Frontier*, Steelman's *Science and Public Policy* did not identify the training of women in STEM fields as a remedy for the nation's science deficiency. Unlike Bush, Steelman did not nod toward girls or women as a hypothetical solution. Where Bush advocated that the educational doors be open to both "men and women of ability," no reference to women appeared anywhere in Steelman's five volumes. "Research," volume 4 claimed, was "essentially the product of a highly trained intelligence, requiring not only techniques and knowledge but the imponderables of personality—imagination, persistence, keen analysis, organizational and creative ability." But, it continued, "the essence of training such men" was in connecting male students with trained male scientists.[23] Female scientists, as students or university faculty, did not appear even as an afterthought. When the members of the President's Scientific Research Board recommended a broad-based program of federal grants, scholarships, and fellowships, therefore, they envisioned such aid accruing only to men.[24]

Science and Public Policy also never specifically mentioned Selective Service or conscription as a current or future policy. At the time the report was submitted, the draft had been deactivated, with the hope that it would no longer be necessary. The army was trying to fill its ranks with voluntary enlistments, and Truman was lobbying hard for UMT. Volume 4 of the report, however, viewed the decision to draft science students during World War II with skepticism. It acknowledged that the pressures confronting policymakers at the time had been "complex," but the report also pointed out that in "stripping" the nation's colleges and universities of scientists and students, the United States had followed a policy vastly different than its allies, Great Britain and the Soviet Union, which had expanded their science education programs.[25] "In light of the effect of the policy in contributing to the present shortage," it concluded, "the wisdom of the decision [not to defer science students] seems dubious."[26] The message was clear. In the event of another war, at least some student deferments would be necessary to protect America's scientific development and, by extension, its national security.

By including broad provisions for deferments in the Selective Service Act of 1948, Congress left room for the president to authorize the protection of students from the draft. With presidential approval, therefore, the Selective Service designed subsequent regulations to create as little disruption to a student's academic year as possible. High school students over the age of eighteen who met the physical requirements for induction were classified as I-S and automatically deferred until they graduated from high school or turned twenty, whichever occurred first. College students who received draft notices were granted administrative deferments that allowed them to postpone their inductions through the end of the current academic year.[27] Although this type of classification prevented the loss of a semester's tuition or academic credit and essentially granted deferments to all college freshmen, it left postsecondary students vulnerable to the draft before they earned their degrees.[28] The director of Selective Service, Lt. Gen. Lewis B. Hershey, realized that further regulations needed to be developed.

In November 1948, the Selective Service and the National Security Resources Board jointly convened the first meeting of six Scientific Advisory Committees and asked them to develop a workable plan for classifying and deferring students in the national interest. Members represented professional organizations and public and private universities in six fields— agricultural and biological sciences, engineering sciences, the healing arts, humanities, physical sciences, and the social sciences—but representatives quickly realized that they shared common goals and opted to work as a committee of the whole. They elected M. H. Trytten, the director of the Office of Scientific Personnel of the National Research Council, as their chair.[29] None of the men present at the two-day November meeting or its December successor questioned the need to defer college students or the urgency of protecting scientific fields in the name of national security. That these goals were of paramount importance was considered obvious; how to achieve them was not.[30]

How deferred students should be utilized ultimately became one of the committees' major points of contention. Was the purpose of this program to allow students time to gain special skills for use within the military or to further civilian research? How did committee members, as a group, define service to the nation? Even as members hammered out the details of their proposal, the rationale for such a proposal remained unspoken until late in the second day of the December meeting, when Harvard professor and economist John Kenneth Galbraith proposed an embargo on occupational and dependency deferments after graduation for men who already had received a student deferment. He feared a public relations disaster if the American people believed college students could go on to become an "elite group" singled out "for protection from the Draft."[31] George O. Curme Jr., a vice president of Carbide and Carbon Chemical Corporation, took issue with Galbraith's assumption "that the only way in which a man can serve his country is by being in uniform," a statement that led Hershey's assistant, Col. Louis F. Kosch, to ask, "Where is the man most valuable to the national defense?"[32]

Answers to Kosch's question varied as committee members tried to weigh multiple factors, including public perception. If only certain men could afford college and these men received repeated deferments, the student program would create a privileged class that, by virtue of its wealth, would never have to face down an enemy gun. Charles W. Cole, president of Amherst College, colorfully and perhaps presciently explained, "while it won't be nearly as acute in peacetime as in wartime, I do think we will separate the sheep from the goats in college, and all through life and make a very bad situation publicwise."[33] Other representatives firmly believed that American security depended on the research of talented civilian scientists. Men could contribute just as much to national defense in civilian laboratories, if not more, than they could by serving in the military. As Charles E. Odegaard, executive director of the American Council of Learned Societies, put it, the idea that "the only real way to defend your country is in a uniform . . . is an old idea and is a medievalist one." Unless the men present at a scientific advisory conference could jettison the "old tradition that when there is a war Johnny gets his gun and goes off to defend the country," there was no point in continuing to meet, he opined. If the committee members themselves could not agree that civilian scientists performed a valuable service to the nation, they would never be able to convince the public at large that a student deferment program was necessary. "We have got to face the facts of an altered technological situation in our society," Odegaard expounded. "If we don't believe that it is essential to have this trained personnel, then this whole training program doesn't make sense and there is no point in our sitting here talking about utilization outside the Army. . . . I think we have to work against a popular conception that war is fought only by the man in uniform." In his eyes, service was service, whether military or civilian.[34]

Ultimately, committee members came to agree with him. They proposed a plan that they believed carefully balanced the democratic values of equality and open access to education with the selectivity necessary to a program defined by its need for special skills. Since no one could determine which skills would be important in the future, they called for a liberal system of deferments, for which students from all fields, not just those related to science and engineering, could qualify. To be eligible for the program, students would have to rank in the upper percentile of their college class and score highly on the Army General Classification Test (AGCT), an aptitude exam given by the army to all prospective soldiers at induction and enlistment centers. Committee members wanted to make sure that only the best and brightest would earn the privilege of a deferment. But in order to prevent the perception of elitism, they strongly recommended the creation of a widespread, government-funded scholarship program for qualified men. Moreover, they endorsed the possibility of further deferments for graduating students. Their plan proposed a four-month grace period for graduates so they could start graduate school or find a job that qualified for an occupational deferment. If they failed to do so, then they would be reclassified as I-A and treated as any other draft-eligible male citizen.[35] The plan created, in Odegaard's words, "a genuine selective service system in a much wider sense" that took "into account . . . other kinds of service that [were] essential to the national interest."[36]

The Scientific Advisory Committees submitted their report to Hershey on December 21, 1948, but the Selective Service shelved it and dissolved the committees in early 1949, once inductions were suspended. Without a monthly conscription quota to meet, the issue of student deferments lacked urgency. It was not until Cold War tensions erupted into war on the Korean peninsula in June 1950 that the issue of the draft moved back into the public eye and onto the floor of Congress. The Selective Service resumed inductions as the military mobilized to meet the emergency. Congress quickly extended the Selective Service Act of 1948, which had been due to expire at the end of the month. Lawmakers began working on the legislation that would become the Universal Military Training and Service Act of 1951. In doing so, they were forced to prioritize those values that they believed deserved special protection.

Although there is some historiographical debate about when planners in the State and Defense Departments began to envision the Korean War as more than an isolated emergency of limited duration, it is clear that this viewpoint had crystallized by 1951.[37] As Anna Rosenberg, assistant secretary of defense, testified before Congress in January of that year, legislation authorizing the continuation of the draft should not be "an emergency measure." Rather, her request for conscription was "a proposal for permanent legislation designed to provide the greatest long-term security" available in an unstable world.[38]

Rosenberg and other officials contextualized the draft within an environment of Cold War militarization and based American foreign and military policy on their belief in the existence of a continuing global struggle between American democracy and Soviet communism. As the recently issued, top-secret National Security Council report NSC-68 made clear, the consequence of losing the war in South Korea would be an ideological victory for the Soviet Union. The United States would have to mobilize accordingly to defend its ally, but it would not be able to demobilize after the war.[39] Any peace of the 1950s, therefore, would be a militarized peace. American civilian society as well as the military would have to remain at the ready. To maintain a flexible force ready to meet any contingency, the army, officials believed, would have to rely on conscription to meet its manpower needs. Thus when the Selective Service sprang into action to meet its quotas in June 1950 after having suspended all inductions the year before, the question of which men to safeguard through deferments quickly became a political issue.

The vast majority of American men between the ages of eighteen and twenty-six could not be conscripted because they had not yet reached the legal age of induction, already held deferments, were already in the military or reserves, or were veterans.[40] Moreover, low birth rates during the Depression years had their greatest impact on the draft-age population during the late 1940s and early 1950s, when just over one million men turned eighteen annually.[41] Hershey feared that if the war continued, too few would qualify for induction to replenish active-duty soldiers who rotated out of service.[42] His anxieties escalated when the Truman administration asked for a total military force of 3.5 million men by early 1951, an increase of just over two million. Hershey and the Defense Department worried that the available pool of manpower would not be deep enough to meet the need, especially as mounting casualties in Korea created a need for ever-greater numbers of men.[43] Nevertheless, under pressure from a variety of sources, the director of the Selective Service returned to the Scientific Advisory Committees' plan for deferring college students, primarily in order to protect scientific and engineering fields.

Hershey hastily recalled the members of Trytten's advisory groups in July 1950, asking them to review their recommendations and issue a new report, which they did in December.[44] Their new report confirmed the Scientific Advisory Committees' commitment to a liberal deferment program, citing the mercurial nature of scientific advancement. "It is quite possible," it noted, "that fifteen years ago nuclear physicists would have been dismissed as a scientific luxury—as a group of theoreticians not essential to the national defense."[45] Now, with the advent of the atomic bomb, the report left unsaid, theoretical physicists were indispensible to national security. More importantly, men with specialized training needed "a broad basis of knowledge of men, things and affairs" in order to maximize their adaptability to new circumstances. "And if there is anything a nation cannot now afford to lose," members assured Hershey, "it is ingenuity in planning and research at a higher level."[46]

Trytten went on to claim victory in World War II as "primarily the triumph of a virile technology based on the skills and knowledge of scientists, engineers, and other specialists."[47] Deferments for scientific training, therefore, were not only an acceptable masculine alternative to military service, they were crucial if the United States was to maintain its military and technological superiority. Equally important, he believed, college students contributed to "national preparedness just as certainly as . . . men in training in the armed services."[48] Odegaard confirmed this notion at a conference to present the committees' findings to the public. He explained, "National defense is now more than a military affair. It requires as a correlative a concept of civilian defense that involves far more than putting out fires or directing traffic to bomb shelters."[49] Civilian work was not throwaway work. It was imperative to national security. Men did not need to carry a rifle in order to defend the nation.

Hershey did not entirely agree. While he supported the group's recommendations regarding the importance of student deferments, he adamantly believed that a deferment should be a postponement of military service, not an exemption. Not all national service was created equal, at least in his view. He warned members of the Preparedness Subcommittee of the Senate Armed Services Committee, which was evaluating the new Selective Service bill, that Congress must carefully frame the legislation, "otherwise a deferment becomes simply a means of evading service by staying out until the program ends or the law expires."[50] Lawmakers had to balance Odegaard's and Hershey's competing points of view as they worked to overhaul the 1948 law.

In fact, legislators had to untangle a welter of competing interests, contradictory scenarios, and contingent statistics in order to hammer out a workable bill that would increase the size of America's eligible manpower pool. Length of service, age of eligibility, mental and physical standards, and deferment criteria all faced congressional scrutiny in 1951 as lawmakers wanted a plan flexible enough to meet both the Korean emergency and any future contingencies. Moreover, Congress and the Department of Defense wanted to put the issue of Universal Military Training to rest. "The time has come when we must look beyond the end of our nose," declared Democratic senator Lyndon Johnson as he opened the Preparedness Subcommittee hearings that January.[51]

At issue was the delicate balance among military preparedness, the country's economic welfare, and its social values. That the armed forces needed to pull millions of men out of civilian society was not up for debate, but who to pull certainly was. Representatives from the Pentagon quickly dismissed groups they viewed as unlikely to be able to fill manpower needs. Assistant Secretary of Defense Rosenberg eliminated the possibility of drafting veterans with less than twelve months of service, pointing out that most of those within the eligible age range would be disqualified for reasons of

FIGURE 3.1. Draft protest meeting. As during World War II, Americans during the Korean War worried about the effects of conscription, a situation with which Congress had to contend. For example, on May 8, 1952, a group of seventy farm families from nine Wisconsin counties met with State Selective Service Director Bentley Courtenay in the state assembly chamber to discuss the expansion of agricultural deferments. Photo courtesy of the Wisconsin Historical Society, WHS-75880.

dependency, occupation, or poor physical condition.[52] Moreover, the public outcry had been fierce when reservists, most of whom were veterans of World War II and many of whom had wives and children, had been called up for service during the early months of the Korean War. A renewed draft of veterans was not expected to gain public support.[53] Further, the Department of Defense adamantly rejected lowering its physical and mental standards for induction amidst fears of increased rates of disciplinary problems and high projections for pension expenditures into the future.[54] Gen. Omar N. Bradley, chairman of the Joint Chiefs of Staff, worried that men who could not meet high mental qualifications would be a "liability," while Adm. Forrest Sherman, chief of naval operations, called lowered standards "a pain in the neck all along the line."[55] Neither veterans nor IV-Fs could be expected to resolve the military's dire manpower predicament.

Just as during World War II, the major point of contention, therefore, became whether to draft eighteen-year-olds or married men, either with or without children. Defense officials preferred the younger men. First, they were cheaper. Witnesses estimated that the military could save between $456 million and $513 million annually on dependency allotments by inducting eighteen-year-olds instead of older men with family obligations.[56] Second, they believed, inducting younger men would cause less social damage. As Rosenberg argued, the "older family man" was more likely to be heavily enmeshed in local businesses, education, and the "life of the community generally," which meant that drafting men with dependents would cause "a great loss . . . to the purchasing power of families" and be "more costly in social values."[57] At the hearings before the House Armed Services Committee, she also speculated that men with dependents might be less efficient soldiers than those without. She explained that the government could never lose sight of "the morale factor of calling a man in who has dependents and who therefore is at heart and mind somewhat at home while he is in the military."[58] She cited experts who had assured the Department of Defense that younger men had less difficulty adjusting to military life than slightly older men because many had "not married or developed permanent roots in their careers."[59] Of especial social benefit was the fact that inducting eighteen-year-olds was less likely to break up families and therefore less likely to contribute to divorce rates. Finally, multiple witnesses insisted that eighteen-year-olds made excellent soldiers.[60] Gen. Dwight D. Eisenhower, then supreme commander of the North Atlantic Treaty Organization and staunch UMT supporter, insisted that young men "deserved" the privilege of military training so that they could defend themselves and their country in the event of war.[61] Eighteen-year-olds, from the Defense Department's procurement perspective, were the most reliable and economical source of additional manpower.

Civilians outside the defense establishment, however, were less certain of the wisdom of drafting men just out of high school. They tapped into several of the arguments that had been made by opponents of universal military training. Witnesses from a variety of backgrounds argued that drafting eighteen-year-olds, who could not vote, would further militarize American society and regiment boys' minds. Boys' immaturity, testified John M. Swomley Jr., director of the National Council Against Conscription and an anti-UMT activist, was one of the major reasons for the "higher prevalence of neurosis among younger persons in the Army," a situation that could be avoided by keeping this age group out of the military.[62] Mrs. William L. Slagle of Dayton, Ohio, lamented, "Our country is not in such dire straits that we need to conscript our babies for a global crusade comparable to the Children's Crusade of the Middle Ages."[63] Other opponents agonized about young conscripts' moral well-being. Rev. Ezra Ellis, chairman of the Public Affairs Committee of the Minneapolis Church Federation, fretted that the "boys" would be stranded in "strange places" and exposed to "gambling, prostitution, and drinking sources of unusual temptation."[64] Charles W. Elliott of Chicago, Illinois, worried that contact with military education programs on the prevention of venereal disease would both "corrupt" and "debase" draftees.[65] Finally, some educators warned that conscripting eighteen-year-olds would "liquidate a substantial portion of the higher education" system in the United States.[66] They feared that if men were taken into the military before they completed one or two years of college, veterans would never return to complete their degrees.[67] Others believed the measure would demoralize high school seniors.[68] In all, these arguments capitalized on the notion that eighteen-year-olds were boys who required nurturing rather than men who would thrive under military discipline. Conscription at such a malleable age could irrevocably harm their educational, vocational, and moral futures.

Legislators had no choice but to take these concerns seriously, especially since constituents espoused them just as strongly as witnesses before congressional hearings. Letters from average American citizens flooded the White House, the vast majority of which opposed drafting eighteen-year-olds.[69] In one random sample of three hundred letters taken by White House officials in January 1951, only seventeen writers favored the idea. In an April sample, only one did. Analysis of the selection showed that the authors hailed from across the country, in what the report referred to a "bona fide citizen response." Writers based their opposition on several points, but in the aggregate, they believed eighteen-year-olds were too young and immature for compulsory military service, especially when the men in question were not enfranchised and therefore had no input into the policy; the proposal would militarize the nation, jeopardize liberty, and interrupt men's educational goals. Letters suggested drafting prisoners, aliens, refugees, and older men instead.[70]

Lawmakers, therefore, were left with a conundrum. The nation needed military manpower. One group or another had to be tapped to fill the armed forces' need for 3.5 million men, leaving legislators with questions about who the nation valued and how. Which men were most needed on the home front and which on the battle front? Who had done their duty, and, for that matter, how was duty to the nation to be defined in the fraught environment of the Cold War? How was manhood to be defined? Were eighteen-year-olds sufficiently men to be considered eligible for compulsory military service? Was fatherhood, a man's responsibility to his family, enough justification to exempt a man from military service, his responsibility to his nation? Most of these questions were never explicitly asked, either on the floor of Congress or in citizens' letters, but their themes appeared repeatedly.

While opponents of the eighteen-year-old draft defined teenagers as boys, other Americans, especially women, used their missives to plead with the president to exempt fathers and married men without children from military service.[71] They argued that "married people [were] the nucleus for the future families of America," the foundation on which the country was built.[72] Wives needed their husbands' financial contributions and emotional support. Without these, writers assured Truman, "newly established homes" would "break up," wives would have "to go out and find work or live off [their] parents," and "heartbreak and sorrows" would follow.[73] Mrs. Joseph Pepe of New Britain, Connecticut, complained that she would not be able to maintain payments on her home or furniture if her husband were drafted. "This may not seem important to you," she wrote the president, "but it is to us and to many of my friends who are in the same position." The loss of her husband would mean the disintegration of this young wife's entire world. More importantly, she complained, "a married man would be dragged away from home and work," unable to fulfill his masculine obligations. "How can you raise children and serve your country at once?" she concluded. Mrs. Pepe's implied answer seemed to be that child rearing *was* an important form of service. In a later passage of her letter, she directly asked President Truman how he, as an individual and the head of state, could draft the married men who were "raising *your* families and working in *your* factories."[74] Her casual use of the personal pronoun conflated male domestic and occupational responsibilities with vital service to the state. Meanwhile, she argued, since eighteen-year-olds were the last to be drafted, they sat in a state of limbo, caught between child-hood and adulthood. Employers were "afraid to take a chance" on them, so unruly teens sat "in confection parlors all afternoon, or in pool rooms," unable to take on the responsibilities of men. Younger, single boys could use military service as a vehicle toward manhood, while that same military obli-gation undermined older, married men's masculine responsibilities.

As these letters indicate, the issue of dependency was complicated, as it had been during the century's previous conflicts, but at mid-century, it was loaded with the era's unique cultural baggage. The end of almost two decades of depression and world war led to a new emphasis on the home and family. Renewed economic prosperity, the availability of a broad range of consumer goods, and, perhaps most importantly, the restoration of close to ten million men to civilian life placed a new emphasis on a "return to normalcy." Marriage and birthrates skyrocketed.[75] According to contempo-rary prescriptive literature, social stability depended on the "togetherness" of happy families.[76] In the first three months of 1951 alone, readers of Look magazine learned that married men and women lived longer than those who were single and that couples with children were less likely to divorce than those without.[77] The social message was clear: having children led to better marriages and marriage led to longer lives.

Perhaps more importantly, experts warned that children would neither thrive nor be able to be effective parents themselves unless "Dad" offered them the opportunity to develop "a warm regard for some of the best quali-ties of masculinity—tenderness, protection, strength."[78] Involved fathers were essential to healthy families. Philip Wylie's 1942 screed, *Generation of Vipers*—named one of the major nonfiction books of the first half of the cen-tury by the American Library Association in 1950—blamed "male default" for the rise of overbearing women and incomplete sons.[79] More concretely, in their landmark study on juvenile delinquency, Sheldon and Eleanor Glueck argued that if boys did not form strong emotional attachments to their fathers, they were much more likely to develop "grave insecurity, frustra-tion, and resentment," leading to "psychoneurotic symptoms."[80] Fathers could counterbalance the negative effects of overbearing mothers and pre-vent sons from becoming "sissies." According to advice manuals, the very future of American society depended on the firm hand and tender heart of a loving, engaged dad.[81]

By the start of the Cold War, the idealized image of the nuclear, male-headed household had political symbolism as well. It represented order in a disordered world. The weakening of the nuclear family during World War II was blamed for everything from a rise in homosexuality to juvenile delinquency to creeping communism. Many Americans worried that without a shoring up of the American social and cultural foundations, "pernicious outside influences could . . . breach the walls of community and family institutions."[82] FBI director J. Edgar Hoover, among others, attributed many of America's post-World War II woes to "the failure of parents to provide proper homes."[83] The Gluecks' research supported Hoover's contention, warning that American society would "continue to suffer from excessive delinquency and crime until it focuse[d] much greater attention on childhood and family life."[84]

While there is no direct evidence that members of Congress read parenting manuals while deliberating, Americans' fears over the disintegration of the family did appear in the Congressional Record, primarily through constituents' letters. Donald W. Wyatt of Rhode Island, for example, explained that ripping "a man away from home and family needlessly" was "national suicide," primarily because enforced separation through military service led couples to divorce. According to Wyatt, after World War II, "there were countless children fated to . . . spend . . . part of the year with each parent or hear . . . the taunting of schoolmates." Young people, he warned, shunned the children of divorce, a debilitating and demeaning result of drafting fathers.[85]

Whether for practical or ideological reasons, lawmakers heeded such warnings and largely sided with those who favored the conscription of eighteen-year-olds, believing the alternatives to be worse. Witnesses at congressional hearings offered enough justification to overcome legislative reluctance. High-ranking army and navy officers argued that there was no material difference between an eighteen-year-old and a nineteen-year-old. Anna Rosenberg, assistant secretary of defense; Maurice J. Tobin, secretary of labor; and Edward J. Overby, assistant to the secretary of agriculture; as well as several prominent educators, all testified that taking men immediately after they graduated high school would cause the least amount of disruption to their lives. In a bid to protect men who had already served and to encourage young men to accrue the benefits of military service, veterans' organizations unanimously came out in favor of the measure.[86]

The final version of the bill, which Truman signed into law as the Universal Military Training and Service Act on June 19, 1951, was a compromise that tried to balance all the competing interests. Men would be required to register with the Selective Service at age eighteen and would become liable for the draft at eighteen-and-a-half, but only under certain circumstances. A particular draft board would not be able to conscript any eighteen-year-olds until it had exhausted its entire pool of eligible men aged nineteen and over. To ensure a larger supply of older men, married men without children lost their deferments except in cases of extreme hardship. Moreover, conscripts would be responsible for twenty-four months of active service followed by an eight-year reserve commitment. The Department of Defense reasoned that a longer term of service would offset its need for more men. Finally, minimum physical and mental standards were lowered so that more men would qualify as acceptable for service. Taken together, these elements both qualified more men for the draft and held them in active duty for longer, thus lessening the number the Selective Service needed to induct each month.

The law settled, at least temporarily, many of the outstanding questions about the relationship between military service, American manhood, and citizenship. Congress safeguarded fathers, deeming them more important as civilians than married men without children. Protecting children, therefore, was of paramount importance. Young children, even those who did not live with their fathers, needed their fathers present in their lives. Older children, according to the law, also needed certain protections. The law defined eighteen-year-olds as men rather than as boys, but with limits. They were to be soldiers of last resort. Conscripted eighteen-and-a-half-year-olds could only be deployed overseas after four months of basic training, all but guaranteeing that they would not reach enemy shores before their nineteenth birthdays. Finally, the law itself contained language designed to ensure their moral well-being. It gave the secretary of defense the power to regulate the sale and consumption of alcoholic beverages near all military bases, posts, and camps.[87] Intoxication was deemed dangerous—a gateway to moral corruption—and eighteen-year-olds were to be protected wherever possible.

Tellingly, as badly as the nation's armed services needed manpower, legislators proved unwilling to touch college students throughout the entire debate over the draft. In fact, the implementation of a student deferment—rather than the administrative postponement until the end of the academic year that already existed—proved the least controversial proposal of the new conscription bill. Not one single witness testified against the idea at the Senate Preparedness Subcommittee Hearings.[88] Even the secretary of labor preferred to see occupational deferments completely eliminated before the student deferment.[89] Instead, Congress merely debated the mechanism for administering it.

Hershey, in late 1950, assuming he would receive congressional approval, started designing a new program for student deferments based on the recommendations of Trytten's six Scientific Advisory Committees. He wanted local boards to have access to students' scores on aptitude tests before their initial classifications rather than wait until after their preinduction exams. The Selective Service, therefore, would have to administer its exam before students received their induction notices.[90] Hershey contracted the Educational Testing Service (ETS) of Princeton, New Jersey, to develop a standardized test of verbal and quantitative reasoning for the Selective Service.[91] Additionally, instead of insisting that a man be eligible for the deferment by passing the qualifying test with a minimum score *and* ranking in an upper percentage of his college class, Hershey proposed that an individual should be able to receive the deferment if he achieved one *or* the other. Using "or" rather than "and" provided the program greater flexibility when dealing with the nation's range of students and academic institutions.[92]

Truman approved Hershey's plan, and on March 31, 1951, he issued an executive order to implement it. To prevent the deferment from becoming an exemption, Congress added a clause to the Universal Military Training and Service Act that extended to age thirty-five the draft liability of any man who accepted a deferment before the age of twenty-six. It also added an amendment confirming the autonomy of local draft boards, essentially guaranteeing that they would not be required to defer anyone. In other words, the law affirmed that all recommendations from Selective Service's national headquarters regarding deferments, including those granted to students, were to be considered guidelines for local boards rather than hard-and-fast rules. Local board members would have to take local conditions into consideration when classifying individuals. This provision would lead to much controversy in the future, but it was added to stave off any claims from the public that the law created a protected class. Congress wanted to make it clear that the student deferment was not a statutory exemption. Students needed to qualify for the deferment, and even then it was up to the local board whether or not to grant it.

Meanwhile, the Selective Service plunged ahead with the establishment of new regulations. In the summer of 1951, it added the II-S category for deferred students to its classification system and started offering the ETS-administered Selective Service College Qualification Test (SSCQT). Approximately 80 percent of the estimated 450,000 draft-eligible men on American college campuses took the new standardized exam during its first four administrations in 1951.[93] These numbers were significant enough to catch scholars' attention.

In May 1952, three Cornell University sociologists initiated a study of male college students' attitudes toward military service, the draft, and deferments. Close to three thousand students from eleven college campuses across the nation responded to their questionnaire, and of these, 83 percent expressed negative opinions toward service in the military. College men did not want to be drafted, especially to fight in Korea, a conflict that only 46 percent of respondents supported. Moreover, they embraced their newly won deferments. Only one in ten of the students surveyed believed the law granted special privileges, while a full 96 percent claimed they rarely or never felt guilty about not being in uniform, even with their country at war. Nevertheless, as much as they did not wish to be called up, students, by a margin of four to one, acknowledged that military service was a responsibility of citizenship and viewed their deferments as a temporary reprieve. Ninety-one percent believed they would be inducted within three years of graduation, but they hoped the war, at least, would be over by then.[94] They may have understood military service as their duty, but they did not extend their obligation to fighting in an unpopular war.

The instatement of the student deferment did not immediately soothe the panic the war had caused within the scientific community. Leaders in science and engineering fields agonized over what they saw as an impending shortage of trained personnel, regardless of the government's careful planning and new initiatives. Community members held a series of publicly and privately sponsored policy conferences between 1950 and 1953 to discuss the problem and issue recommendations.[95] An industrial employers' report cited by *Scientific American*, which devoted its entire September 1951 issue to the problem of manpower, stated that an additional sixty thousand engineers alone would be needed in the public and private sectors by 1954.[96]

Otherwise, however, the student deferment program proved a great success. In fiscal 1952, 204,446 men received II-S classifications.[97] Although some labor unions, most notably the United Auto Workers, and a few educators, such as Harvard University president James Conant and Princeton University president Harold Dodds, publicly labeled the program "undemocratic" because it granted special privileges to an elite group, the majority of Americans supported it.[98] In one 1952 Gallup opinion poll, 69 percent of respondents favored inducting students only after they had completed their studies.[99] Hershey reluctantly accepted the program as a necessary element of modern manpower planning, even as he lamented his own agency's liberal deferment policies.[100]

Although the expectation both from within the Selective Service and among the students themselves was that students would serve in the military eventually, the addition of the II-S deferment set an ambivalent precedent. It created a situation in which the military establishment purposely kept a particular category of men out of the armed services in the name of national security, not because of what those men actively contributed to the defense of the nation in the moment but because of their potential to contribute in the future. The Selective Service, with the support of the president, Congress, the Department of Defense, and professional and educational organizations, found students more valuable as civilians than as soldiers. Additionally, because the student deferment program hoped to encourage science education in particular, it helped militarize the scientific fields by tying them to the nation's defense efforts. It privileged civilian forms of masculine citizenship at the same time that it militarized them.

Dependency deferments similarly offered advantages to men who took up domestic responsibilities as husbands and fathers by allowing them to avoid the uncertainty of conscription. In wartime, however, rising manpower needs directly conflicted with the national desire to keep families intact. The loss of the deferment for married men without children in 1951 had been a blow to many families, especially as the number of applications for marriage licenses took a marked upswing in June 1950, just as the war began.[101]

By mid-1951, the Public Health Service of the Federal Security Agency certainly noticed a trend related to new marriages: a significant increase in first births to new parents. A press release in August noted that the birth rate for the first five months of the year was 8.4 percent higher than that for the same time period in 1950, putting 1951 on track to break 1947's record-high birth rate. The rate for May 1951 was a full 14.3 percent higher than May 1950, a phenomenon the Public Health Service directly related to the increase in marriages caused by the start of the Korean War the previous summer. Moreover, the increase in births in 1951 was almost exclusively caused by first births, as opposed to any increases seen in 1948 or 1949, which had been caused by second, third, or fourth children.[102] While we cannot know exactly why these couples decided to procreate, it is not hard to surmise. Most of the men in these families were of the proper age to face conscription, they chose to marry and have children immediately upon the outbreak of war, and Americans continued to resist drafting fathers. A June 1952 Gallup poll found that only 43 percent of Americans favored keeping the armed forces at their current fighting strength through the induction of men with children. By way of contrast, 60 percent supported conscripting men working in vital defense industries. Only the student deferment received more support than that for fatherhood.[103]

Even so, both classifications faced criticism, especially from those who felt unfairly targeted by the Selective Service System. Foreshadowing the Vietnam War, the Korean War acquired a reputation for being a poor man's fight.[104] Those who could afford higher education soon learned to pyramid their deferments, moving seamlessly from II-S (student) to III-A (dependency) or II-A (occupational) deferments. A student who graduated from college and went on to graduate school, had a child, or found a job in the national interest could transform a temporary deferment into a de facto exemption. A few members of Trytten's Scientific Advisory Committees had foreseen this possibility in 1948, but the other members of the committees had largely dismissed their worry with a wink.[105] Hershey also downplayed the phenomenon, claiming that no more than 3 percent of II-S registrants took this path, even as negative publicity embarrassed the Selective Service.[106] Magazines and newspapers worried about privileged young men shirking their patriotic duty as they "babied out" of military service.[107] In mid-1953, local draft boards complained that thirteen thousand men per month were applying to change from student to dependency categories. This was especially egregious as the nation's manpower woes continued to escalate, despite the 1951 reforms. The military badly needed men.

In response, various agencies that handled the nation's manpower policy began studying the issue, including the Selective Service's Scientific Advisory Committee on Specialized Personnel. Hershey had constituted the committee in 1951 based on Trytten's Scientific Advisory Committees to help make policy recommendations on issues relating to students and scientists. The group's primary goal was to protect the student deferment. Since the program deferred no more than 5 percent of any particular cohort, explained one report, it did not "markedly make inroads upon the total manpower pool." Members recognized, however, that the program had a serious public relations problem.[108] If students continued to pyramid deferments, public outrage could call the whole program into question. Revoking the possibility of the dependency deferment from any man who had availed himself of a student deferment would not solve the nation's manpower crisis, but it would make the public feel better about the student deferment program as a whole. The National Manpower Council and the Department of Defense agreed. They both recommended ending dependency deferments for anyone who had used a student deferment.[109]

The Selective Service, as an agency, however, was divided. Something needed to be done, but if students were the only men denied further deferments, it could cause an administrative nightmare and public backlash. The issue went around and around. A first draft of a proposed executive order for President Eisenhower suggested ending III-A deferments for any man who had held a different deferment previously, but ultimately, the agency's Manpower Policy Committee suggested fatherhood should no longer be grounds for deferment for any man.[110] Eisenhower agreed, and in July 1953 he ended the III-A deferment for all men except those for whom military service would cause extreme hardship and privation, just as President Roosevelt had at the end of 1943.[111]

Eisenhower's revocation of the fatherhood deferment was different from Roosevelt's in its context, however, and these differences were significant. First, the new regulation took effect several weeks after the Korean armistice was signed. Even though fighting had ended, defense planners did not foresee American demobilization.[112] Unlike during World War II, this was not an emergency measure necessary to defeat an external aggressor in total war. Instead, it was a nod toward the growing importance of scientific research and development to national security. In that historical moment, the country needed fathers to protect their families by defending their nation as soldiers more than it could afford to revoke the student deferment, or so planners believed. Scientists and engineers, and by extension students, were defined as performing national service. Second, the change in regulation occurred during a flurry of bad publicity. Fatherhood ceased being a protected category only amidst explanations that the change corrected an injustice. As Hershey put it, he had to "trade students for fathers."[113] Under the new regulation, students who did not go into protected occupations after graduation would not be able to shirk their duty as citizens by pyramiding deferments, at least in theory. Rescinding the privilege was a public relations ploy to avoid the appearance of elitism, solve the manpower crisis, and continue training the next generation of defense professionals. But the need for such justification turned out to be short-lived. Fatherhood in 1950s America was simply too important an institution to go without special protections.

As during any modern war, manpower policy during the Korean War was complex. It involved coordinating the preferences and needs of multiple government agencies and civilian special interest groups. The military had to be staffed, war production stepped up, the civilian economy maintained, food produced, and daily life continued, all while allocating a finite number of men and women to military, agricultural, essential, and nonessential occupations in a democratic fashion. Workers, therefore, had to be encouraged rather than coerced to enter particular fields, stay on the job, and increase production, or the United States would risk becoming no better than its communist enemy. But, as during the two world wars, the armed forces could not depend on voluntary enlistment. The federal government and the public deemed the military threat imminent enough to justify conscription. Once again, the United States had to figure out how to balance the ideal of democratic participation with the practice of selective service.

The Korean War was different from earlier wars, however, in that it was not considered the main event. Even though it was a hot war with devastating consequences for the people who lived it, it had limited strategic aims. American policymakers believed it a mere distraction from the real threat posed by the Soviet Union. The Cold War would not end when the shooting in Asia stopped, especially with the threat of atomic war persistently looming. Thus demobilization after the armistice was not an option. Viewed through a longer lens, then, the Korean War signaled the beginning of the heavily militarized peace called for by NSC-68 rather than its own discrete conflagration.

Debates over deferments during the Korean conflict, therefore, took on a special significance. Policymakers were aware that the decisions they made would have consequences that lasted longer than the war itself. Conscription would become the new normal in American society, at least for the immediately foreseeable future. One of the Selective Service's basic premises was that any policy "adopted with a short range perspective" that could impact "the American way of life and its cultural and social values," could "freeze into a pattern" that could "take centuries to eradicate." Consequently, warned the agency, "never before has it been so extraordinarily important to deal sensitively with these intangible values which in the long run form a very large part of the essentials of the way of life we are trying to defend."[114] The choice of who to defer and who to draft mattered. The United States needed the right men in the right places to engage the enemy, maintain the economy, assure the nation's technological supremacy, and preserve its families, but also to ensure that America stayed "America."

In fact, the nature of the discourse over deferments between 1948 and 1953 did not so much indicate a change in the country's social values as a shift in how policymakers understood its defense needs. This is why the addition of the student deferment was so important. The Selective Service had piloted a student deferment program during World War II, but quickly contracted it when manpower pressures grew too great. Although the military desperately needed men during the Korean War as well, Congress, the Selective Service, and the general public were much more willing to protect a plan designed to produce scientists in the name of national defense in the atomic era. By 1951, science was seen as a key component of national security, and the only way to obtain scientists was to train them. The introduction of the II-S classification, therefore, helped broaden the definition of service to the nation. College students, like men with vital war jobs and farmers, were defined as performing service that maintained the national health, safety, or interest. The Selective Service accepted their potential contributions as equally valuable as those of the infantry soldier. This decision would have significant consequences into the future as the student deferment created a class-stratified system.

Similarly, the debates over the importance of men's domestic roles in the 1950s did not illustrate a significant shift in the country's social values. Fathers and husbands, for example, did not receive more consideration during the Korean War than they had during World War II, when Congress had also turned to eighteen-year-olds before revoking dependency deferments and when local draft boards had gone out of their way to protect family men. But the arguments used by those who wanted to protect fathers in the early 1950s are important to understand, for, as the next chapter will show, the context began to change in the late 1950s. While during the early 1950s, military manpower policies protected national security *and* American values, during the second half of the decade, policies began to conflate the two. Men's domesticity, like science and engineering, came to be considered a key element of national defense as the Selective Service began to explicitly encourage marriage and fatherhood through a new policy called manpower channeling. All in all, military service became less important for many American men, even as militarization suffused their lives.

CHAPTER 4

"A Draft-Dodging Business"

Manpower Channeling, 1955–1965

In January 1958, director of Selective Service Lewis B. Hershey was called before the Subcommittee on Independent Offices of the House Appropriations Committee to justify his agency's expenditures. Questioning was friendly, but apparently the general's responses to inquiries about negative press coverage were not sufficient to quell congressional concerns about waste in Hershey's agency. By early February, several members of Congress had written to Hershey asking him to answer charges that Selective Service was "wasteful, expensive," and "inefficient."[1] In reply, Hershey penned a pointed letter to Congress explaining the purposes of his agency.

In his letter, which he published in the March issue of *Selective Service*, the agency's news organ, Hershey acknowledged the current low level of draft calls, then only about thirteen thousand men per month, but he emphasized that the procurement of military manpower constituted only about 12 percent of the Selective Service System's operations and 6 percent of its expenditures. The rest of its time and resources went into the process of classifying the nation's men, screening those members of the reserves who were on standby status, planning for future emergencies, and channeling men into the reserves and civilian occupations the federal government defined as critical to national survival. "Selective Service has gone so far beyond the simple job of inducting 13,000 men a month into the Armed Forces," he wrote, that it was "practically pointless" to argue that it had become obsolete. Induction was no longer the agency's main function but had become merely a "byprod-uct" of its operations.[2] Global and domestic conditions had caused the sys-tem to evolve past its original function.

Hershey's testimony and the follow-up letter marked one of the first times that the director publicly acknowledged the Selective Service's policy of manpower channeling, a form of social engineering designed to coax men into designated fields by offering them deferments from conscription. He used the term, however, as a label for a procedure he viewed as already in practice. He argued that the agricultural, occupational, and student defer-ments the agency had used during World War II and the Korean War had gently channeled men "in the direction that they had to go." During these wars, explained Hershey, the Selective Service worked tirelessly "to make people think they [had] volunteered when they [were] actually being chan-neled through a process."[3] The results of the practice were stark. "The only reason the Nation is not short 40,000 or 50,000 engineers today," he claimed, "is because they were deferred in 1951, 1952, and 1953."[4]

Hershey explained that America's technological rivalry with the Soviet Union and the ever-present threat of nuclear war meant channeling would take on an even greater importance in the future. America needed more scientists, more engineers, more doctors, and more teachers. Offering defer-ments from military service was one of the most efficient means to ensure that men chose to enter those professions. It was a matter of "national sur-vival."[5] And he proved true to his word. By the first half of the 1960s, infor-mational literature produced by the Selective Service System referred to channeling as one of the agency's main functions.[6]

Manpower channeling solved two distinct problems that arose from the inherent contradictions of a system that claimed military service as a respon-sibility of all able-bodied male citizens but did not demand universal military service. The first was pragmatic. As children of the baby-boom generation started to come of age and the population of young men began to grow in the years after 1955, the number of those eligible for the draft far outpaced the number of men needed by the military. Channeling increased the num-ber of deferments offered to otherwise available men. It reduced the size of the burgeoning manpower pool, making it more manageable, and increased the probability that a man classified as I-A would in fact be drafted. This reduction allowed the Selective Service to show that it functioned as a viable system of military manpower procurement.

Second, the policy provided the Selective Service with an ideological jus-tification for its increasingly liberal use of deferments. Through manpower channeling, Hershey and the Selective Service explicitly defined certain civilian occupations and implicitly acknowledged marriage and fatherhood as essential service to the nation.] The program's development, therefore, signaled full acceptance of a definition of national service that included certain civilian activities as well as soldiering. This position stood in contrast to the grudging tolerance the agency had proffered during World War II and expanded the enthusiasm it had offered for the student deferment during the Korean War. According to the Selective Service System's own publications, military service was not strictly necessary from American men so long as they performed some measure of national service sanctioned by a deferment.

Men of draft age were not generally conscious of this redefinition. Even though Hershey made no secret of his agency's rationale for deferments, there appears to have been little popular awareness of it. Media outlets found Hershey's pronouncements about channeling unremarkable and rarely reported on them. Nevertheless, the policy provided a mechanism through which men, especially those of the middle class, could avoid active-duty military service. Channeling materially limited the number of men who were considered eligible for military service and who actively served in the armed forces. As the regulations defined a broader swath of men's civilian activities as vital to national security, the Selective Service conflated national security and domestic values. In the process, a policy based on a modified civic republican conception of citizenship ironically ended up channeling middle-class, frequently white men toward a liberal focus on personal choice.

Channeling became possible within the context of the Eisenhower administration for several reasons. The first was a shift in national security policy. When Eisenhower took office in 1953, his discomfort with an $85 billion defense budget constituting 60 percent of federal expenditures and 13.8 percent of the gross national product led him to reassess military strategy.[7] What became known as his New Look threatened the use of strategic—and eventually tactical—nuclear weapons as the best deterrent to communist expansion. The United States would continue to support its allies in local disputes, especially against communist foes believed to be Soviet proxies, as it had in Korea, but it would do so with economic, air, and naval support rather than with ground forces.[8] Under this policy, the military, as a whole, enhanced its nuclear capabilities, but with the exception of the Air Force, the armed services scaled back. Emphasis on air power and irregular methods of warfare grew while the strategic prominence of the infantry decreased.[9] Between 1953 and 1961, the overall size of America's active forces dropped from more than 3.5 million men to less than 2.4 million. The army contracted the most, losing more than 700,000 soldiers—or close to half of its personnel—during Eisenhower's presidency.[10]

Second, in an effort to boost the military's dismal retention rate, Congress passed the Career Incentive Act in 1955, offering a significant pay increase to men who remained in uniform after their initial term of service. It also offered extra hazard pay for airmen and submariners and provided an allowance for families to move with servicemen to new permanent duty stations.[11] By all measures, the law was a success. The re-enlistment rate across the branches of service rose from 14.9 percent in fiscal 1954 to 44 percent in fiscal 1956.[12]

Perhaps most importantly from a procurement perspective, the demographic trends that had been such a problem during the Korean War reversed themselves. Throughout the second half of the 1950s and the 1960s, more and more men turned eighteen each year, vastly expanding the available pool of manpower. By 1965, the number of eighteen-year-old men had increased by 50 percent over the number from a decade earlier, growth that had a profound effect on the Selective Service.[13] Where there had been 9.1 million men between the ages of eighteen and twenty-six registered with the Selective Service in 1953, there were 10.9 million in 1957 and 13.9 million in 1961.[14]

Together, these circumstances meant that the armed forces needed fewer men even as more men were accessible to them. Because the size of the active forces was lower and more men re-upped, the services were more successful at filling their open slots with voluntary enlistments. Consequently, an increasingly small proportion of the available manpower pool faced conscription each year. Between the end of the Korean War and the beginning of the Vietnam War, the navy and marine corps utilized the Selective Service only occasionally, and the air force did not use the draft at all. Only the army was left to regularly augment its numbers with draftees. Inductions dropped from 33 percent of total military procurement in fiscal 1954 to 22 percent in 1957 to just 9 percent in 1961.[15]

Small draft calls presented problems for the Selective Service System. Hershey had always insisted that deferments were merely postponements of military service, not exemptions from it. But by the mid-1950s, the numbers worked against him. Where close to 472,000 men had been inducted in 1953, the Selective Service drafted fewer than 153,000 in 1955.[16] Only two years after the manpower crisis of the Korean War had prompted the end of deferments for fathers and three years after the draft age had been lowered to eighteen-and-a-half, state directors of Selective Service started writing Hershey wondering what was to be done with their excess men. R. T. Finks of Missouri reported in August 1955 that his state yielded approximately 2,000 new registrants each month but received induction calls for only 230 men.[17] Illinois and Massachusetts described a similar dilemma.[18]

Members of the defense establishment, including Hershey, continued to insist that conscription was necessary to the security of the nation.[19] When the Universal Military Training and Service Act of 1951 came up for renewal in 1955, Carter L. Burgess, assistant secretary of defense, told the Senate Armed Services Committee that the military would only be able to meet about half of its manpower requirements through voluntarism. Moreover, he firmly believed that the existence of the draft spurred individual men to enlist.[20] Hershey agreed.[21] These defense planners were convinced that when faced with the threat of conscription, many men volunteered in order to choose their branch of service and the terms of their enlistment.[22] Further, the director insisted that only 5 to 10 percent of qualified men, who he defined as those in the I-A category, managed to escape military service. "When we deal with masses," he assured members of the Senate Committee on Armed Services, "we are going to have a loss," just as sawmills, no matter how efficient, always produced "a lot of sawdust."[23] The problem was inescapable, regardless of demographic conditions or the size of induction calls.

Despite Hershey's confidence, the press soon noticed the effects of the decreasing number of calls. Newspaper and magazine articles reported that a young man's chances of seeing military service ranged anywhere from between one in four to one in fifteen.[24] A late-1955 *Washington Post* piece that placed the odds at one in twelve revealed that "many youngsters talk about '12 to 1' being 'pretty good odds'. . . . With no war on, few apparently think much of their obligation to serve, and talk of 'waiting it out.' "[25] In an early 1956 Gallup poll, 26 percent of male teenage respondents believed that they would never serve in the military, a significant change from the 9 percent of male college men who felt they would not serve in 1952.[26] Of the 74 percent of teens in the Gallup survey who thought they would eventually serve, one-third planned to wait for the draft. With no guarantee that the Selective Service would come calling, these men felt no responsibility to pre-emptively join up. Most likely, they hoped to avoid military service altogether.[27]

The seeming capriciousness of the system, which had been exacerbated by decreased calls, added to negative public opinion. By early 1955, the news magazine *U.S. News and World Report* began reporting on the fickle nature of the draft. Because the Selective Service conscripted the oldest eligible men first, the magazine reported, "many a young man apparently is to find that the draft will pass him by in his early years, only to catch him and force him into service after he has a job, a wife, perhaps children." Moreover, logistical strains on the system meant that more and more men were never even called for their preinduction exam. They remained unclassified for years. The shrinking proportion of classified men, combined with the fact that one in three men who was examined failed the preinduction physical or mental exams, meant that a large number of young men were left in their home communities. Most of them, according to the magazine, possessed "no obvious defects" and therefore did nothing but "heighten the public's impression that the draft [was] full of loopholes." Articles also pointed out that "at least several hundred thousand men, now in the draft age bracket, apparently will not be needed" for military service and that "the number of men who escape service could be larger, if voluntary enlistments exceed expectations."[28] The overall message was that men who chose to gamble with their futures could lose big, but the odds ran in their favor.

Reports such as these worried members of the Selective Service System and Congress, who were concerned about public apathy toward military service. One particular article, also from *U.S. News and World Report,* sparked controversy.[29] When, in January 1956, the periodical reported on the "remote" prospect of conscription, placing the odds of being drafted at just one in fifteen, John H. Greenaway, the New Hampshire state director, complained that such reports were "detrimental to the orderly working of the Selective Service." He specifically linked his state's drop in registrations to "such news items," complaining that negative news coverage led to "callous disrespect" among those who were required to register.[30] The article also caught the attention of the House Armed Services Committee, members of which grilled Hershey and Hugh M. Milton, assistant secretary of the army, about whether the one in fifteen statistic was true.

Hershey demurred, claiming that statistics could be used to prove almost anything, but he used his column in the February issue of *Selective Service* to fire back.[31] "A Nation intensely interested in [cars] with innerspring and foam-rubber seats," he wrote, "will not only be looking for the shortest and easiest method of performing service, but will be impressed by those who continually play up the hope that there is a . . . great chance of avoiding any service." But, he warned, such an attitude "risks service at a time when there are far more [familial and occupational] complications." While news coverage indicated the odds of avoiding military service were high, Hershey cautioned that the stakes were even higher. Service to the nation was vital and needed to be inevitable. If too many men decided to wait out the draft, then that "gamble" would compel Congress to take action.[32]

By the mid-1950s, therefore, the military's manpower procurement system was under significant pressure. Although the law that authorized the draft was renewed easily in 1955, the growing draft-age cohort combined with diminishing needs for manpower exacerbated the contradictions built in to a system of selective service that justified itself based on a civic republican model of citizenship. Hershey realized that the Selective Service needed to reassess how the system could reconcile the principle of "universality" with the reality of "high selectivity."[33] Since virtually no one in power was willing to end the draft, the most obvious solution to the oversupply of eligible men was to reduce the number of men considered eligible for induction.

Reducing the size of the available manpower pool would accomplish several things. First, lowering the number of men considered eligible for conscription would increase the odds that the men who remained I-A would be conscripted. Second, the threat of coercion would spur enlistments. Finally, the change would lower the national age of induction or the average age at which men were called by the Selective Service. During the Korean War, when manpower was at a premium, many local boards had exhausted all of the men available to them between the ages of twenty and twenty-six. When these boards started conscripting younger men, the national age of induction fell to nineteen and a half. But as manpower needs had eased, the age of induction had crept back up. By 1955, it had reached twenty-three, with most men receiving induction notices between the ages of twenty-three and twenty-five. This situation created difficulties both for men living under the uncertainty of the draft and for the armed forces. The military preferred younger men. Men without deferments lived under the threat of the draft until age twenty-six and men with deferments until age thirty-five. By then, they tended to be married, to have children, and to be deeply enmeshed in their careers, making a two-year term of service a true psychological—and frequently material—hardship.[34]

Hershey began discussing options for shrinking the pool of eligible men in 1955, devoting at least one national conference of officers in the Selective Service System to the subject. A poll from national headquarters solicited state directors' opinions on the best way to "reduce and control" the growing number of available men.[35] Of the options provided, which included postponing the inductions of fathers under the age of twenty-six and men in scientific and related fields, the state directors preferred delaying the initial classification of registrants until at least the age of twenty and postponing the induction of all men over the age of twenty-five. These choices would eliminate the oldest and youngest men from the eligible supply, allowing the Selective Service to focus specifically on men between the ages of twenty and twenty-five. Further, the system could continue to avoid blanket administrative deferments, granting dependency and occupational deferments only on an individual basis to men who requested them. Unanimously, however, the state directors voted to delay any action until after the Universal Military Training and Service Act had been successfully renewed.[36]

Hershey followed the state directors' advice on this last point but moved beyond their recommendations when he took "unwritten" action to liberalize induction policies in July 1955, only weeks after Congress reauthorized the law.[37] He chose to postpone induction in all cases brought to his attention where the men were over the age of twenty-six, were fathers, or were employed in the scientific fields. He urged state directors to issue similar directives to all local boards.[38] Classification procedures, including preinduction exams to determine if a registrant should be categorized as provisionally capable of military service, were also delayed until well past the age of eighteen. Missouri, for example, suspended classification until men reached age twenty-one.[39]

Although these were radical—and frequently unilateral—administrative changes, Hershey knew they were unlikely to be controversial. As argued in chapter 3, Americans were generally willing to protect fathers and scientists from military service, based on the belief that these civilian roles were more important than any job such men could perform in uniform. Similarly, few Americans were likely to question measures to limit eighteen-year-old men's contact with the Selective Service System. But Hershey realized that these were temporary measures. He would have to find a more permanent policy solution to the problem of oversupply. Manpower channeling became this solution.

It is unclear exactly who named the policy of manpower channeling, but it clearly grew out of practices already performed by the Selective Service System. It was also a policy that dovetailed with Hershey's civic republican definition of citizenship. By the time of his 1958 congressional testimony, Lewis B. Hershey and the Selective Service had become virtually synonymous. Hershey had been helping to shape the agency since he had been assigned to the Joint Army-Navy Selective Service Committee in 1936, and he had been the system's director for eighteen years. He was its public face. He wrote extensively, testified before Congress frequently, and appeared in newspaper articles almost daily. Perhaps more importantly, Hershey's views about the proper role of the Selective Service heavily influenced the agency's policies and practices, especially since the presidents under whom Hershey served usually deferred to his expertise.

Moreover, Hershey's agency was relatively small, especially considering the number of lives it affected. The staff at the Selective Service System's national headquarters in Washington, D.C., had shrunk significantly since

SELECTIVE SERVICE   June 1959
Portrait of Director Displayed at National Headquarters

FIGURE. 4.1. Hershey portrait from *Selective Service*. Portrait of then Lt. Gen. Lewis B. Hershey that went on display in Selective Service's national headquarters in 1959. The power of Hershey's personality steered the agency for almost three decades. *Selective Service*, June 1959, 4.

World War II. In fiscal 1958, it consisted of only 61 commissioned officers and 150 civilians. Together, these roughly 200 people studied manpower problems, analyzed demographic trends, conducted research, liaised with state offices and other federal agencies, and devised new policies.[40] Each state and territory possessed its own state director and related staff, but in

1958, state offices ranged in size from 5 to 30 people, for a total of 1,019 paid employees.[41] The responsibility for classification, sending out induction calls, and handling most appeals went to the system's 4,079 local and appeal boards, which were scattered in communities across the country. Close to 42,000 people worked on these boards, but the vast majority were unpaid volunteers, appointed by the states' governors and approved by the president.[42] In 1958, the total budget for the entire system was a mere $27 million, leading Hershey to complain that he needed to cut off phone service in many of the local board offices due to lack of funds.[43] In comparison, the National Science Foundation, another independent agency linked to national defense, operated on $40 million dollars in fiscal 1958 and, as a result of the Soviet launch of its *Sputnik* satellite in late 1957, received close to $100 million more in fiscal 1959.[44] So, although more than 43,000 people worked with the Selective Service, the system was highly decentralized. Policies, regulations, and guidelines were developed by a small group of people working in Washington and carried out by a large number of volunteers throughout the nation who, with additional guidance from state directors, were free to interpret them as they wished.

Hershey sat on top of the organizational pyramid. Scholars James W. Davis Jr. and Kenneth M. Dolbeare, working in the late 1960s, suggested that the force of Hershey's personality held the entire diffuse system together. Because the Selective Service did not pay most of its members, it could not coerce them into conformity. Rather, it had to "rely on normative appeals and the manipulation of symbols to obtain the behavior it require[d]." Hershey, who cultivated a "homey-folksy air," was that symbol. Davis and Dolbeare pointed out that in twenty-four issues of *Selective Service* between January 1965 and December 1966, twenty-two articles, in addition to Hershey's regular monthly signed column, focused on the director, as did close to half of the photographs.[45] He appeared just as prominently in earlier issues as well.

During the early phases of his career, Hershey used his position to disseminate his civic republican views on the proper relationships among military service, masculinity, and citizenship. To him, men who did not serve the country when it needed them were indeed shirking their responsibility as American citizens. Easy living made men soft, irresolute, and selfish. It made them unmanly. Even as a young National Guard officer in the days before America's entry into World War I, he had been frustrated by his peers' lack of loyalty to their country. "When the spirit of responsibility dodging is abroad to so large an extent," he wrote in his diary, "it certainly seems that only a war with all its horrors can awake us to our obligations."[46] Men, he believed, had a duty to perform military service, especially in times of emergency. Without a spirit of commitment, the spirit of the nation itself would begin to decay.⁆

Hershey's civic republican ideas about citizenship did not change substantially throughout his time in the Selective Service. He designed the agency as a tool to be used to inculcate and "preserve . . . traditional values," including "patriotism, individual responsibility, [and] decentralization of government," in addition to being a manpower procurement agency.[47] In the years following the Korean War, however, his public declarations about what constituted service to the nation evolved, partially out of necessity. When the population of draft-eligible men began to climb, it became clear that not all of them would be needed to serve in uniform. Yet Hershey saw America as imperiled. The threat of nuclear war with the Soviet Union, conventional war with Soviet proxies, and creeping communism at home threatened the United States domestically and its interests abroad. The populace could not afford to become complacent, he believed, even if induction calls were low. While military service may have been the most efficient means of providing service to the nation, Hershey stopped proclaiming it to be the only one. By 1958, he and his officers had combined the practical and the ideological to produce the new policy of manpower channeling.

Hershey's definition of service began to evolve. Between 1956 and 1959, the system began to accept certain civilian activities as the equivalent of military service, a significant shift from the rationale it offered for deferments during World War II and the Korean War. Hershey instructed his staff to study the best ways to select men "for the task where they might give the greatest service to the Nation."[48] Concurrently, he amended his own public attitude toward the agency's role. For example, he altered the basis on which he defended the regulations that extended the age of draft liability from twenty-six to thirty-five for men who received deferments. Where he had argued during the Korean War that the extended age limit would ensure men's military service, he now claimed that the threat of loss of deferment would retain men in essential occupations until an age when other family pressures would probably keep them there.[49]

Crucially, the extension of draft liability pressured men to stay in occupations of national importance rather than ensuring their military service. Where once Hershey had prophesied disaster if Congress allowed too many deferments, writing in 1949, "If we make [a man] too secure [in his job], it will take about three Selective Service Systems to bomb him loose when we finally want him to go out and use [a] weapon," he now started to advocate the expansion of deferments so that men could be released to "make contributions to civil life."[50] The Selective Service's congressional mandate was to secure *military* personnel, but by the late 1950s Hershey had expanded its purpose to guide the choices of *civilian* men, eliding military and civilian procurement in the name of national security.

Such a redefinition of service grew out of the agency's commitment to civil defense. Hershey and his staff believed that if a nuclear attack were to occur, the Selective Service would be invaluable to the country's rebuilding and civil defense efforts. In the wake of a nuclear strike, some form of community organizing would be required to stave off panic and chaos, and all hands would be necessary to rebuild. Since the Selective Service maintained records on all men, not just those found acceptable for military service, in Hershey's view, it was the logical choice to step into the breach that a nuclear catastrophe would create. Its decentralized structure would allow it to continue to procure soldiers even if national or state headquarters were destroyed. Local boards, with their "cellular structure," would be able to function independently to identify, locate, and utilize all manpower if survival ever became "the first and primary necessity."[51] The Selective Service had "become . . . the storekeeper" of America's manpower supply.[52] Its mission, therefore, needed to evolve.

In the July 1956 issue of *Selective Service*, Hershey outlined the place of Selective Service in the past and his vision for the future. Warfare had evolved since World War II. As illustrated by the addition of student deferments during the Korean War, men outside of uniform could be just as important as those in the armed forces. "From the deferment of men to do, came the transition to defer to train to do," he explained. But student deferments were not enough. Hershey derided the methods currently used to inventory manpower. He worried that the system was not sufficiently far-reaching. He particularly decried a system in which a man who had been rejected for military service, especially for reasons of disability or dependency, was given a basis for believing that he had escaped his obligation to serve the nation. "We must . . . cease to encourage large numbers of our young men to believe that they are useless for the primary duty of citizenship," he exhorted readers.[53] Participation in the nation's defense efforts could occur in a civilian capacity as well as a military one.

While masculine citizenship should continue to be based on a man's contribution to the country's security, Hershey explained, eligibility for military service could not and should not be the only measure of that contribution. Rather than conscript all men into military service, Hershey now advocated modifying the meaning of deferments. Instead of signaling that a man had little role to play in the defense of the country, deferments should signify the vital security nature of civilian work.[54]

According to Hershey, encouraging men to pursue particular occupations was the job of the Selective Service, even if the law governing the draft did not specifically grant the agency such powers. The Universal Military and Training Act stated that national security required "the fullest possible utilization of the Nation's technological, scientific, and other critical manpower resources," but as Hershey understood it, Congress also had repeatedly vested the Selective Service System with the responsibility of protecting the populace. Therefore, he reasoned, it had sanctioned the redefinition of service. "The law enumerates the principle of universality of service, which is sound," wrote the director, but "great latitude was given in the application of this principle." Thus the Selective Service was now "in a position where it [could] exercise leadership in the establishment of the ever-changing concepts of what constitutes essential service for survival."[55] Men had the responsibility to serve the nation, but in the militarized peace engendered by the Cold War, when the push of a button could take the world from peace to war and plunge the United States into darkness, the form of that service had to be flexible. Where in 1950 Hershey had disagreed vehemently that a male citizen's obligation to defend his nation could be fulfilled in any way other than through the military, by the end of the decade he had changed his stance, stating that the concept of "duty" should "be interpreted . . . more broadly."[56] By 1958, this shift in reasoning had coalesced into the policy of manpower channeling, and by 1959 the Selective Service had defined channeling as one of its major functions, on par with military manpower procurement.[57]

The agency shared its newly self-defined mission with other members of the defense establishment and civilian agencies. In 1959, the Selective Service received permission from the assistant secretary of defense to pilot an orientation course in Washington, D.C., for any government employee who had a professional interest in the workings of the Selective Service.[58] The course, which was attended by approximately 150 military officers and civilian workers from the Departments of the Army, Air Force, Treasury, Commerce, and Labor and the Office of Civil and Defense Mobilization, was designed around the supposition that channeling was an indispensible function of the agency.[59] Along with information sessions on the process of registration and the Selective Service's classification system, the proposed curriculum for the course included classes on "The Channeling of Registrants into Essential Civilian Activities" and "The Channeling of Registrants into the Reserve Forces."[60]

As part of the planning process for the orientation course, Col. Joel D. Griffing, the Selective Service's chief planning officer, sent a memo to Hershey's assistant, Col. Charles H. Grahl, explaining that the Selective Service

System possessed "the capability to select" as well as the "power to compel."
It could "place men" in supporting civilian roles, since the process of classification actually "indicate[d]" the civilian or military capacity in which an
individual would "serve."[61] Grahl, whom Hershey had charged with planning the session on "The Emergency Role of Selective Service," responded
with an outline for his presentation.[62] In it, he confirmed that the agency
considered the placement of individuals, both civilians and soldiers, "to be
the overriding aim and purpose of its actions." In fact, he claimed that it took
"no great amount of insight into the philosophy and principles of manpower
utilization to realize that attention to the proper placement of men in the
civilian area is quite *as* important as the proper placement of men in the
Armed Forces."[63] What is striking about these words is that they were shared,
not only with the 150 attendees of the pilot orientation course, but with
participants in all of the following iterations of the course, which continued
through and possibly beyond 1965.

George Q. Flynn, Hershey's biographer, suggests that the general developed the practice of manpower channeling as a rationalization to keep his
agency alive during a period of reduced need, but this is an incomplete—and
a cynical—explanation. Selective Service was not in any real political danger,
despite the pointed questions Hershey received from the House Appropriations Committee in 1958. Virtually no one in Congress, the Department of
Defense, or the Joint Chiefs of Staff seriously considered eliminating the
draft during the Eisenhower or Kennedy years.[64] Defense planners believed
that the threat of conscription motivated men to volunteer, and they pointed
to the low enlistment rates of 1947, when the draft had been suspended,
as their proof. Moreover, since the public appeared comfortable with the
Selective Service, there was no impetus to overhaul or terminate the system
through the 1950s and early 1960s.

Instead, as previously argued, channeling grew out of pragmatic concerns over the size of the manpower pool. The Selective Service expanded its
existing deferment structure to accommodate the growing draft-age population and the nation's declining military manpower needs. By defining civilian activities as service to the nation and therefore as essential to national
security, the Selective Service solved the problem created by the growing
population of draft-eligible young men. Offering deferments to more men
checked the expansion of the I-A manpower pool, which in turn allowed the
agency to apply more pressure to those who remained susceptible to the
draft. The increased risk of induction among those men left as I-A spurred
draft-motivated enlistments and ensured that a higher proportion of men
designated as available would be conscripted. Second, the policy stemmed

from Hershey's genuine ideological commitment to a civic republican definition of citizenship. The director of Selective Service was unwavering in
his belief that all men had a "fundamental obligation" to serve their nation,
especially in times of emergency.[65] Since Congress had deemed universal
military training unnecessary in 1951, Hershey was free to expand the definition of national service. The effect of that expansion, however, was not to
strengthen men's commitment to national service in the name of defense, as
Hershey might have hoped.

The first target of channeling was the reserves and National Guard. In mid-
1955, just as Hershey and the states halted the inductions of fathers, men
older than twenty-six, and scientists, Congress was deliberating the best
way to procure manpower for the nation's military reserve programs. New
statutes ultimately increased the responsibilities of the Selective Service and
expanded men's ability to choose the terms of their military service. In particular, they offered men ways to limit their responsibility for active duty.

Mobilization of the reserves and National Guard for the Korean War
exposed deficiencies in the structure and organization of the programs as
they were then constituted. When North Korean soldiers invaded South
Korea in June 1950, President Truman called up the National Guard and
reserves to augment the regular forces stationed in Japan and elsewhere
around the world. Because individuals could be activated faster than organized units, however, the reservists who deployed first were frequently World
War II veterans who had chosen not to fulfill their reserve obligations in
organized training programs. They did not train regularly; did not draw drill
pay from the military; and frequently were married, had children, worked
in essential occupations, or were past the age of eligibility for conscription,
conditions that would have earned them deferments had the terms of their
World War II service not left them vulnerable to call-up. Second, the army
found that many of its personnel records had not been updated since 1945
and were therefore woefully unreliable. Men had moved, become physically
disabled, died, and found new jobs since the end of World War II. Many
reservists requested exemptions from service for hardship, dependency, or
occupational reasons, but because of poor record keeping the reserves and
Guard could not grant the exemptions until the men reported for duty. Other
men simply could not be found.

Mobilization, therefore, created a logistical nightmare. By the end of
August 1950, 96,400 reservists and guardsmen had been recalled successfully,
but their units were understrength by 50 to 75 percent. One signal battal-
ion reported with only 23 of its 1,035 authorized personnel.[66] Finally, once

reservists and members of the National Guard arrived in Korea, their service record was mixed. National Guard members, who were not required to participate in any form of basic training, proved especially inexperienced. The inefficiencies and inequities of this system led to public outcry.[67]

In 1952, Congress and the Pentagon sought to correct these myriad problems through a complete overhaul of the reserve and National Guard system. The resulting Armed Forces Reserve Act of 1952 broke all seven components of the reserve and National Guard into three separate categories of service: the Ready Reserve, the Standby Reserve, and the Retired Reserve. Members of the Ready Reserve could be recalled to active duty immediately in a time of war. They could either be organized into units that trained regularly on weekends and in the summer and that would be deployed as a whole, or they could serve as individuals who did not train regularly and who could be assigned where needed. Members of the Standby Reserve were usually, though not always, inactive. They constituted a backup pool of manpower that did not train but that could be mobilized in an extreme emergency. Men with rare, specialized skills could also be placed in this reserve pool. Finally, all career military men who drew retirement pay were placed in the Retired Reserve.

Second, the law established provisions outlining service obligations for those men who completed their active-duty responsibilities. In short, it created an eight-year term of service for all servicemen, regardless of the method by which they entered the military. Those who enlisted for four years—the only option available in the navy and air force—would accrue an additional four years of duty in the reserves. Those who enlisted in the army or marine corps for three- or four-year terms of service could complete their eight years in the reserves or National Guard, and two-year draftees would have a six-year reserve obligation. Men would begin their reserve commitment in the Ready Reserve, but could transfer to the Standby Reserve after a combined total of five years of military service. In almost all cases, should mobilization be necessary, Ready Reservists were to be called before Standby or Retired Reservists. To avoid the negative experiences of the Korean War, however, the law included provisions to protect veterans of previous wars.[68]

Such restructuring was designed to allow for a more orderly mobilization and deployment in the event of war, but it left open a number of questions. The 1952 law required the armed forces to keep their records up to date and physically examine every reservist and guardsman every four years to ensure that every man could be mobilized if necessary, but it did not prescribe a mechanism for classifying the men.[69] Second, part of the purpose of the act was to increase the flexibility of the military in an emergency by providing trained units as reinforcements, but the law did not contain enough incentives for men to join the organized components of the reserves. Therefore, most reservists did not drill regularly or receive extra training. Further, the vast majority were veterans, who were older and, as a result of the legislation, protected from mobilization if they already had served during wartime. By 1955, therefore, it had become clear to defense planners that further legislation was needed to fix these problems and to find a way to entice or compel younger men, who were more likely to be deployable for a longer period of time, to join the reserves.[70]

[The Reserve Forces Act of 1955, which Eisenhower signed into law on August 9, addressed many of these issues and granted the Selective Service System new responsibilities] Its provisions assigned the job of classifying Standby Reservists to the Selective Service. As the agency responsible for sorting and classifying those civilians eligible for the draft, it seemed natural that it could also catalogue the nation's reservists.[71] Annual vetting and reclassification of reservists undeniably served a military function by helping the Defense Department keep its rosters current. A situation like that which had occurred in 1950, when the reserve had existed largely on paper alone, would not happen again. But the measure fulfilled other functions as well. It protected the families of reservists in the same way that dependency deferments protected the families of nonreservists. Congress wanted to avoid creating "extreme personal or community hardship" by deploying individual men who could not afford to leave their families. Reservists who acquired significant debt to start new businesses or whose family arrangements changed as the result of illness or additional children could be moved from the Ready Reserve to the Standby Reserve and kept there at the discretion of local Selective Service boards. Standby Reservists, moreover, could not be recalled to service without being declared available by the Selective Service. Finally, the law also recognized the need to maintain a "proper balance of military skills" and "critical civilian skills" both in and out of the reserves.[72] If reservists acquired skills deemed as in the national interest, especially in the fields of science or engineering, the law allowed these men to be transferred to the Standby Reserve.

The Reserve Forces Act also authorized the creation of several new programs.[73] The first allowed men to enlist directly into the reserves. The second program offered men between the ages of seventeen and eighteen and a half the ability to enlist for three to six months of active duty and then serve an additional seven and a half years in the Ready Reserve of any reserve component other than the National Guard.[74] If volunteers satisfactorily fulfilled the terms of their contract, their draft liability would be lifted at the completion of those eight years. If not, they would be removed from the program and would face the possibility of conscription until age twenty-eight. The National Guard, which had always allowed men to enlist at age seventeen, was authorized to grant similar deferment benefits if recruits younger than eighteen and a half volunteered for three to six months of basic training. Finally, the law sanctioned the creation of a Critical Skills Reserve, designed to harness the expertise of scientists and engineers.[75] Any man whose job qualified as a critical occupation or essential activity based on lists published by the Departments of Labor and Commerce in 1951 and revised in 1955 could apply for six months of basic training followed by eight years in the Standby Reserve with no further drilling requirement. All these options were designed to benefit the reserves by lowering the average age of members, which, in theory, would increase force readiness. But the enticements these programs offered to potential recruits took the form of draft deferments and reduced expectations for active duty. Such lures sent the message that service in the armed forces was an important obligation of Cold War citizenship, but it was one that should be as painless and short as possible.

The six-month program aimed at seventeen- and eighteen-year-olds started slowly. The services encountered difficulties filling their quotas. In late 1955, the army had enrolled only 4,500 recruits for its 8,000 slots. All the services fell well short of their goals, a combined total of 100,000 men per year, despite "the largest peacetime public relations undertaking of the U.S. Army."[76] The media blitz included close to 66,000 radio spots, 5,500 special radio programs, more than 20,000 television advertisements, 800 special television shows, and more than 7,000 recruitment talks to more than 709,000 people from the army alone. Print ads and articles ran in *Boy's Life, Scholastic Roto, Parade, Life, U.S. News and World Report*, and the Boy Scout's *Explorer Quarterly*.[77] The campaign was so carefully planned that it won a Silver Anvil award from the Public Relations Society of America in the Government Category in 1956.[78]

Ironically, recruiters blamed the poor showing on a lagging information campaign. Graduating high school students simply were not yet aware of the new program, officials assured the public. In Washington, D.C., for example, some high schools had refused to allow recruiters access to students, and in others, principals granted army, navy, marine corps, and air force personnel a mere fifteen minutes to make a combined pitch for all of their programs. Many teenagers, however, when asked, recognized that the age of induction hovered around age twenty-two and still preferred to take their chances with the draft.[79] Still others joined the National Guard, which did not require any active-duty training time.

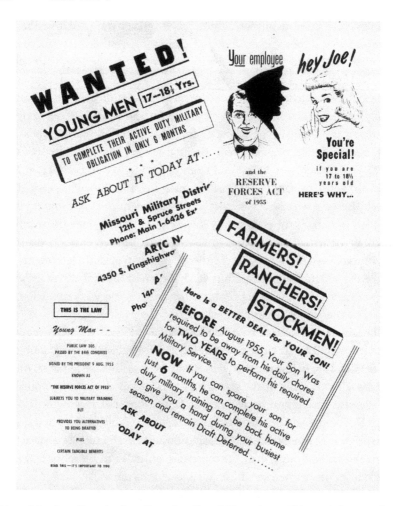

FIGURE 4.2.   Recruiting ad collage. Examples of broadsides and pamphlets created as part of the advertising blitz to enroll young men in a new program for seventeen- and eighteen-year-olds. Ads highlighted the benefits of limited active-duty time and draft deferments for men who entered the program. The Army Reserve created this collage as part of its application for the Public Relations Society of America's Silver Anvil Award in 1956. Photo courtesy of the Wisconsin Historical Society, WHS-140349.

Hershey complained bitterly about the reserve program's detractors, including the teens who ignored their obligations. He hoped the situation could be turned around once men realized the import of their decisions.[80] He claimed that if more men chose to fulfill their responsibility to the military, the overall time requirement for each man eventually would be lowered. Results from a Gallup opinion poll commissioned by the Pentagon seemed to bear out Hershey's admonition. It found that three-quarters of men between the ages of sixteen and twenty thought that military service, whether active duty or with the reserves, was "something to do if [they] must and get it over with." Forty percent claimed that if they had to serve, they were "going to get it over as quickly as possible and get out."[81] Recruitment efforts that emphasized a kinder, friendlier military fell flat in an environment where it was possible to escape military service altogether.[82]

By 1957, the Department of Defense and Selective Service were looking for different ways to entice men to join the Reserves and fulfill their military obligation. Hershey proposed changes to the six-month program meant to attract men otherwise ill-disposed to military service. He suggested reducing the period of active-duty training from six months to the congressionally mandated minimum of three months and "drastically" reducing the seven-and-a-half-year reserve commitment.[83] Opinion polls showed that of those men who did enlist in the six-month program, close to one-quarter did so in order to "curtail their active duty military obligations."[84] Further limits might lead to more volunteers.

The Pentagon agreed with Hershey. In March, the Department of the Army announced modifications to its reserve plan. The army opened the six-month program to any man under the age of twenty-six who had not yet been called for induction and reduced the number of years of service the program required. Men under the age of eighteen and a half would remain in the Ready Reserve for four and a half years, which was later reduced to three years, after which they would be transferred to the Standby Reserve. Men older than eighteen and a half would spend six years drilling with the Ready Reserve.

Additionally, the Army National Guard would henceforth be required to provide six months of active-duty training to all of its members.[85] This issue had become particularly salient as certain guard units defied orders and continued to advertise their lack of active-duty training as an enticement to potential recruits. Battery "A" of the 128th Field Artillery in St. Louis, Missouri, for example, handed out leaflets titled, "Are You 'Draft' Bait?" The handout, which garnered the attention of Hershey and of Assistant Secretary of Defense Burgess, screamed in capital letters that men could be "DEFERRED FROM INDUCTION" without meeting a "stiff selective service college deferment test." In fact, enlistment would mean that a man could "forget Selective Service entirely," an important perk since, as the leaflet warned men, "Your draft board has until age 25 years, 11 months, and 29 days to draft you. Do you think you will escape it?"[86] Recruitment literature such as this, combined with the National Guard's reluctance to encourage men to take advantage of the provision of the 1955 Reserve Forces Act that allowed for voluntary basic training, prompted Secretary of Defense Charles E. Wilson to call the guard "a draft-dodging business."[87] The notion that military service could be minimized was a potent idea that attracted young men and, in the Pentagon's estimation, interfered with recruitment for the six-month program, which, ironically, had also been designed to minimize active-duty service.

The army compelled the National Guard to bring its training standards in line with the other reserve components and to stop publicly deriding the draft. But the promise of a deferment from induction into the regular army combined with military service that did not disrupt men's civilian lives proved ample temptation. Results of the new regulations were overwhelming. By August, the army had to suspend enlistments into the Army Reserve after men flooded recruiting stations. The other branches of service soon did the same, prompting Democratic representative Overton Brooks of Louisiana to exclaim, "We are in harvest season and can't pick the melons."[88] So many men either enlisted directly in the reserves or transferred into the Ready Reserve after completing their regular enlistments that the army could not handle them all. Rather than requiring weekly drills, as the law demanded, many Army Reservists trained only for thirty days during the summer. Within a year, the numbers had increased so rapidly that many men were only called for training every other year. In 1959, the Ready Reserves consisted of 2.5 million men, but fewer than one million drilled regularly with their units.[89]

By channeling men into special programs, then, the Pentagon more than met its Ready Reserve manpower requirements while the Selective Service significantly shrank the pool of men who were available for induction. Where there were 300,000 men deferred from induction into the active-duty forces as reservists and ROTC trainees in mid-1955, the number had expanded to 518,000 by mid-1958 and to 849,000 by mid-1961. It was over one million by 1965. By one estimate, the reserve programs pulled almost 550,000 men out of the I-A category by the late 1950s, and this number continued to grow.[90] The army, as Assistant Secretary Milton testified in 1959, was thrilled. "There is no doubt in my mind," he enthused, "that the Reserve components of the Army have attained the highest degree of mobilization readiness, deployment availability and combat potential in history."[91]

These programs brought men into military service, but it was a limited form of service. Evidence indicates that men joined the reserves to avoid active-duty service, and they were comfortable with this. When President Kennedy mobilized 148,000 reservists in 1961 in response to the Berlin Crisis, negative reaction from those who were called up was widespread and public.[92] Drafts boards were swamped with reservists wanting to report that they had married, become parents, or acquired more dependents.[93]

Without question, Lyndon Johnson's decision to withhold mobilization of the reserves during the Vietnam escalation encouraged would-be draft evaders to enlist in the reserves and National Guard, but the Pentagon reorganized the reserves in 1955 partially in order to channel men away from active duty and conscription. The various reserve components marketed enlistment as means for men to fulfill an obligation for military service while avoiding disrupting their civilian lives, preventing the discomforts of active-duty service, and ultimately avoiding combat. As *Selective Service* reported in 1956, a man's service in the reserves, "free of worries from his draft board," was "about as easy as required military service" could be.[94] Men who enlisted in the reserves during the Vietnam War, therefore, had a decade's worth of tradition on which to fall back as they sought methods to avoid placing themselves in harm's way.

The Selective Service also identified men's occupational choices as a prime area for channeling. As argued in chapter 3, the defense establishment had identified science and engineering as fields of great importance to national security after World War II and instituted the student deferment during the Korean War to encourage men to enter those fields. In the decade after the Korean armistice, the availability of student and occupational deferments expanded significantly, partially as a way to shrink the pool of I-A men and partially to encourage men to enter fields believed to be in the national interest. Both of these rationales helped support the national security state.

Throughout the 1950s, the perception that the United States lacked scientists and engineers and was therefore in danger of falling behind the Soviets continued as a topic of national discussion.[95] According to politicians and intellectuals alike, American superiority rested on outpacing Soviet technological development, both in the domestic realm—as Vice President Richard Nixon and Soviet Premier Nikita Khrushchev's 1959 Kitchen Debate illustrates—and in the military sector. Moreover, the army's strategic plans for countering atomic attack depended on the invention of new weapons, including airplanes that could take off vertically and hand-held atomic rocket launchers.[96] The United States needed a steady supply of men in STEM fields to develop the state-of-the-art appliances and futuristic weapons systems that it so desperately wanted.

In 1955, an interdepartmental committee, chaired by Arthur Flemming, the director of the Office of Defense Mobilization, recommended the creation of a President's Committee on Scientists and Engineers based on the understanding that "the struggle for military supremacy" was "being waged" in the fields of science and technology.[97] Eisenhower constituted such a committee in April 1956 in order to find ways to encourage men to enter scientific, engineering, and technological fields.[98] The committee, composed entirely of men from private industry, was to make recommendations on how public awareness of science could be heightened and how schools' science curricula could be improved.[99] Members, under the leadership of Howard Bevis, the former president of Ohio State University, undertook the objective of raising "public action through public awareness."[100] It also recommended the creation of a President's Science Advisory Committee to stimulate the growth of the scientific manpower pool by developing policy, coordinating federal programs related to science, and liaising with private industry.[101] Eisenhower listened, and in the wake of *Sputnik*'s launch in October 1957, he upgraded a pre-existing Science Advisory Committee in the Office of Defense Mobilization to the level of an executive office.[102]

The Soviet launch of two *Sputnik* satellites in late 1957 gave new life to Americans' fears of being overtaken by their communist rival. Prominent policymakers likened the Soviet achievement to Pearl Harbor, blasting the United States out of its "intellectual complacency." Physicist Edward Teller, the "father of the hydrogen bomb," claimed that the United States had just lost a major battle.[103] *Life* magazine ran several articles on why America had lost the space race and warning of the Soviets' "timetable to disaster" if the United States did not change its priorities.[104] Worries over America's educational system and its potential for scientific advancement abounded. A 1955 book by Rudolph Flesch called *Why Johnny Can't Read—And What You Can Do About It* became a belated bestseller, and a rash of other titles soon appeared.[105] Adm. Hyman Rickover, who oversaw nuclear research and development for the navy, exhorted the nation to use the shock of *Sputnik* to marshal itself to "perform educational miracles," just as it had used Japan's attack in 1941 to mobilize military and industrial miracles.[106] A poll of American citizens by the Opinion Research Corporation found that the public believed the country's prime concerns to be "catching the Russians in the defense race" and "training more and better scientists." Prior to the launch of the two satellites, top worries had been inflation, staying out of war, and racial segregation.[107] The Eisenhower administration responded to the immediate threat by redoubling efforts to advance America's space program, but he deemed long-term solutions to the nation's perceived "education gap" as more important.

By the time of the first *Sputnik* launch, the apparent deficiencies of the American educational system already had a firm place on the national agenda. They had been the subject of congressional hearings in 1956 and were a major topic of discussion for the President's Committee on Science and Engineering.[108] In the spring of 1957, the president had assured the National Education Association that "our schools are strongpoints in our National Defense . . . more important than Nike batteries, more necessary than our radar warning nets, and more powerful even than the energy of the atom."[109] Proponents of school reform, including President Truman, had long advocated federal aid to schools, but for the most part they had been thwarted, caught on the issues of states rights, segregation in southern schools, and the separation of church and state, as Catholic parochial schools demanded support as well.

As a result of political disagreement, federal educational aid had been limited to grants to individuals. The GI Bill, for example, provided educational benefits to veterans. The National Science Foundation awarded scholarships and fellowships to exceptional undergraduates and graduate students studying scientific subjects. But these efforts were severely limited. The launch of the *Sputnik* satellites gave educational reformers and Eisenhower, who had grave misgivings about general federal aid to schools, the opportunity to tie national security to a limited bill designed specifically to aid science education. The result was the National Defense Education Act of 1958 (NDEA), which awarded loans and National Defense Fellowships to undergraduates and graduate students studying scientific subjects. It also appropriated funds to states to update equipment for secondary science and language labs and to encourage math and science education.[110] By 1964, six hundred thousand college and university students majoring in mathematics, science, engineering, and modern foreign languages had received loans totaling more than $404 million from the federal government under the NDEA's provisions.[111]

The Selective Service took an active interest in the discourse analyzing the relationship between science and national defense, especially since the feeling of heightened need for scientists and science teachers coincided with the agency's development of manpower channeling. That the agency would be responsible for deferring the surge of resultant college students was only the tip of the iceberg. In 1955, Hershey convened the National Selective Service Scientific Advisory Group only two years after dissolving its predecessor, the Scientific Advisory Committee on Specialized Personnel. State directors created similar boards of scientific advisers on the state level. They charged these groups with offering advice to local and appeal boards on scientific matters, especially as the boards evaluated applications for occupational deferments. Members of the national and state scientific advisory committees were expected to help laymen in local communities translate technical jargon to determine if a man's job really was essential.

Deferments for scientists and potential scientists took on greater importance in such a climate. In 1955, the Departments of Commerce and Labor revised their lists of essential activities and critical occupations, which the Selective Service used to establish criteria for occupational deferments. Local boards generally would not grant an occupational deferment if a man or his employer could not demonstrate that the man was engaged in a job defined as critical or essential. The new lists were shorter than those compiled in 1951, and they privileged those in white-collar professions, as many production jobs were eliminated.[112] A sense of panic ensued among those seeking deferments.[113] Hershey, however, admitted that although certain occupations were no longer classified as vital, deferments nonetheless would "have to be more liberal" because the military did not need as many men. "Whether they're in the deferred classifications or in I-A will probably be a matter of method rather than results," he wrote to Michigan's state director.[114] In other words, men would continue to gain occupational deferments as a result of local boards' leniency, even if their jobs could not be found on the lists of the Departments of Labor or Commerce. Moreover, after much discussion, secondary school teachers of math and physical and biological sciences were added to the list of critical occupations and "educational services" to the list of essential activities.[115]

These changes, rather than limiting the number of occupational deferments, opened the door to their expansion. The number of men deferred for jobs in science and engineering grew significantly as more sought degrees in these fields. According to the National Science Foundation (NSF), where 89,452 undergraduates earned bachelors degrees in these fields in 1951, 103,653 did in 1962.[116] The numbers of master's and doctoral degrees similarly grew.[117] While the NSF admitted that earning a degree was no guarantee that a person would work in that particular field, it pointed out that a man's educational background and training strongly correlated to the type of job in which he would be hired. It attributed most of the gains to population growth and the rapid expansion of science programs on college campuses.[118] But population growth alone does not account for the rapid rise in occupational deferments across the same time period. Class II-A deferments increased almost 650 percent between 1955 and 1963.[119] Selective Service's national headquarters instructed local boards to severely limit the induction of men who held any job that could possibly be defined as essential such that the induction of men in STEM fields would be "the exception rather than the rule." Local boards, therefore, became more lenient. Between October 31,

1956, and December 31, 1957, the number of men deferred in Class II-A jumped from 27,317 to 34,284, a percentage increase that far exceeded either the growth rate of the draft-age cohort or that of college-educated men during the same time period.[120]

The case of teachers further illustrates this point. Men and women together earned 71,518 bachelor's degrees in education in 1951 and 106,359 in 1962.[121] Part of this increase is, no doubt, because of population growth and the growth of college campuses. These were also years of teacher shortages, which meant publicity and the incentive of a growing job market most likely attracted others into the field. But the growing number of occupational deferments granted to teachers cannot be explained by the simple existence of more teachers. According to a June 1955 Operations Bulletin from the Selective Service, secondary teachers of math and science were eligible for deferments based on the Department of Labor's list of critical occupations. Therefore, national headquarters recommended that local boards give male teachers of these subjects "special consideration" when determining deferments. By 1958, the agency had "broadened informally" its policy of deferring only educators in these subjects and began to include others as well. Hershey publicized the national teacher shortage regularly and encouraged local boards to be lenient in their consideration of all teachers. Moreover, according to Bernard T. Franck III, chief of the Selective Service System's Office of Legislation, Liaison, and Public Information, it was the practice of national headquarters to recommend either postponement of induction or deferment for educators "in practically all teaching fields."[122] In 1960, the agency officially rescinded the 1955 bulletin, noting that teachers in all fields were in demand, even if their specialties did not qualify them as critical according to the Department of Labor. Local boards were told that they should disregard "any implication that teachers in specified fields should receive special consideration."[123] Although local boards were free to defer or induct teachers at will, by 1960 national headquarters had signaled that all teachers should be deferred, a factor that very well may have contributed to the massive growth in the conferral of education degrees.

By the early 1960s, local board members were invited to be as liberal as they wished in the granting of occupational and student deferments. In 1962, the Departments of Labor and Commerce again revised their lists of critical occupations and essential activities, adding categories for those working in "Missile and Space Systems" and language education. National headquarters disseminated the lists to the state directors in a memo reminding them, "Deferments shall not be limited to registrants engaged in the listed activities or occupations."[124] Understandably, this vague policy perplexed local boards, which for the most part tried to apply the standard of "in the national health, safety, or interest" to their deliberations over occupational deferments. But ultimately, as noted above, they deferred more men. One chairman of a local board explained to a new member that the process of deferring was "sort of like an accordion. Sometimes you stretch it out and get generous with defer-ments and then other times you squeeze it up tight."[125] During the first half of the 1960s, the accordion was stretched all the way out.

[Criteria for student deferments, first implemented in 1951, were similarly relaxed. As the age of induction had risen during the latter half of the 1950s, fewer and fewer college men applied for these deferments. Most male stu-dents preferred to take their chances with the draft rather than push their age of liability to thirty-five by applying for special consideration] This reduc-tion prompted Hershey to limit the administration of the Selective Service College Qualification Test (SSCQT) in 1958 to just one sitting per year. In 1962, President Kennedy signed an executive order altering regulations gov-erning the II-S category. Local boards were invited to consider registrants' classification status without holding students to a particular class standing or score on the SSCQT. Selective Service personnel were welcome to con-sider these factors in determining a registrant's classification, but as long as students could demonstrate that they were "satisfactorily pursuing a course of instruction," top grades or a passing SSCQT score were no longer neces-sary.[126] The SSCQT was eliminated entirely during the 1963–64 academic year due to lack of interest. With the relaxed standards, more students chose to take advantage of the student deferment, despite the high average age of induction. The number of students receiving II-S classifications was nine times larger in 1965 than it had been in 1961.[127]

Finally, the Selective Service lent rhetorical support to the Peace Corps, defining it as a program that served the national interest. Although Her-shey was not willing to go so far as to accept service in the Peace Corps as the equivalent of military service and therefore worthy of exemption from the draft, his agency helped Peace Corps members obtain deferments on occupational grounds.[128] When, for example, one man's local board turned down his request for a deferment so that he could volunteer in Ghana, offi-cials at the Selective Service System's national headquarters recommended a complete rewrite of the man's application letter. Rather than simply ask for the deferment, the Selective Service suggested that all requests highlight the Peace Corps as a "civilian activit[y] . . . necessary to the maintenance of the national health, safety, or interest."[129] Men were free to pyramid Peace Corps deferments with marriage, fatherhood, and other student or occupational deferments if they wished. The Selective Service wanted Kennedy to know that the system would "offer . . . its full cooperation in the launching and operation" of the new initiative.[130]

[It is impossible to know exactly how many men entered privileged fields in education, science, or engineering or how many joined the Peace Corps because of Selective Service policies.] Certainly the agency believed it played a major role. *Selective Service* crowed, "Selective Service law, regulation and policy . . . contribute heavily to the Nation's need for teachers and adequately trained citizens."[131] Franck explained, "By its liberal deferment policies of teachers, the Selective Service undoubtedly has influenced men to remain in teaching positions rather than to transfer to some more lucrative calling thereby losing opportunities for deferment."[132] In his 1961 *Annual Report* to Congress, Hershey noted, "Many younger engineers, scientists, technicians and other skilled workers would not remain in their jobs in the defense effort if they did not have occupational deferments."[133] Anecdotal evidence confirms that the offer of a deferment did influence at least some men's choices. For example, twelve of nineteen scientists and engineers profiled in a small study of men working in the weapons industry in 1967 were young enough to have been affected by the Selective Service's policy. Of these, two openly admitted to choosing their jobs, which they had held since before the war in Vietnam escalated, in order to receive a deferment. The reasons the other ten chose their professions were not discussed, leaving open the possibility that more were channeled into their jobs as well.[134]

Regardless of the number of men who actively chose their professions in order to avoid military service, the increased availability of occupational deferments is significant. First, it illustrates the spread of militarization in American society during the Cold War. Legislation like the NDEA defined education at all levels as an arm of national defense, but it was deferments in the name of national security that militarized the teaching profession. Deferments for teachers—like those for scientists and engineers—were rationalized as a weapon against Soviet dominance and defined as a civic contribution equivalent to military service.[135] Second, occupational deferments allowed an increasing number of men to avoid participation in the armed forces. Whether they internalized their jobs as contributing to the safety of the nation or not, they neither donned uniforms nor drilled with weapons. Their lives remained comfortably civilian. However they chose to define their obligations as citizens or their responsibilities as men, military service was not part of the process. And third, these deferments were primarily available to men of the middle class. Production jobs were largely removed from the lists of essential activities and critical occupations compiled by the Departments of Commerce and Labor and used by the Selective Service to determine occupational deferments, while agricultural deferments declined precipitously during these same years.[136] Only those who could qualify for college and postgraduate education had the ability to earn NSF or NDEA scholarships and fellowships. In other words, decisions over who to channel into civilian service and who to continue to draft set the stage for the class and race imbalances that would plague the Selective Service in the coming decade.

While the Selective Service overtly admitted it channeled men into particular occupational fields, its policies implicitly affected men's domestic arrangements. ⌈Whether explicitly stated or not, as during the Korean War, deferments encouraged early marriage and fatherhood.⌉ Men continued to have a moral obligation to protect their women and children, but messages produced by popular and government sources implied that they could more effectively accomplish this goal as civilians rather than as soldiers.[137] The practice of channeling men into marriage and fatherhood further privileged civilian pursuits and unintentionally helped define men's domestic arrangements as service to the state.

As discussed in chapter 3, Eisenhower signed an executive order rescinding deferments for fathers in 1953, just as the Korean War was ending. Married men without children had lost similar protections from the draft as part of the 1951 revisions to the Selective Service Act of 1948. Marriage and fatherhood, however, remained social roles of extreme importance. Fathers had only lost their privileged status because of the combination of high manpower needs, low numbers of available men, and criticism of privileged youth pyramiding their deferments into exemptions. But as manpower requirements eased and demographic factors changed, it once again worked to the military's and Selective Service's advantage to exclude fathers from the draft.

⌈In 1956, Eisenhower issued an executive order changing the sequence of induction so that all eligible nonfathers between the ages of nineteen and twenty-six would be called before any otherwise eligible fathers⌉ Technically, fathers were not deferred. They remained in the I-A pool and were therefore considered eligible to be drafted. With that pool growing ever larger, however, this move all but guaranteed that fathers would not face conscription except in the event of all-out war. In essence, therefore, the president created a de facto exemption for all men with children. From a military standpoint, the new regulation provided the army with younger inductees, since suspending fathers from the draft pool tended to push the average age of available men downward. This shift had the benefit of freeing the military from paying as many family allotments, but Hershey also claimed that the order was "designed to strengthen the Nation's civilian economy."[138] Whether he believed fathers were more likely to remain in stable jobs than nonfathers, enhance the purchasing power of their family units, or strengthen the economy in some other way, he did not elaborate.

The measure garnered little press attention.[139] Wartime fears over the pyramiding of deferments had abated, allowing the federal government once again to define the maintenance of the nuclear family as more important to the containment of communism than widespread military service. In its literature, the Selective Service quietly added the category of "family life" to those of "industry" and "agriculture" as sectors to which the agency owed "essential support."[140] It is impossible to draw a clear causal relationship between Eisenhower's order and the American birth rate, but according to the 1957 *Annual Report of the Director of Selective Service*, the number of fathers in the I-A category more than doubled between fiscal 1956 and 1957, increasing at an average rate of 18,200 per month. No doubt these men chose to procreate for a variety of reasons, but it is more than likely that deferments were at least a factor in the timing of their choice to become fathers. Fiscal 1957 ended seventeen months after Eisenhower's executive order, giving men's wives plenty of time to conceive and bear children.[141]

By the latter portion of John F. Kennedy's presidency, the Selective Service had so many qualified men that it actively sought methods to justify their removal from the pool of eligibles.[142] On March 15, 1963, Kennedy signed an executive order returning fathers to the III-A category, where they had been until Eisenhower's 1953 revision. This action restored official deferments to men with children and eliminated at least 336,446 men from the I-A manpower pool.[143] Ostensibly, Kennedy acted in order to produce a more realistic picture of the available manpower pool since the I-A category was artificially inflated by the inclusion of fathers who, if examined further, would ultimately be excluded from induction for reasons of hardship.[144] But the ruling made no distinction between those families that faced genuine privation and those that did not. In actuality, therefore, moving all fathers to the dependency category projected a cultural assumption that all families were economically and emotionally dependent on a male head of household and sent the message that married men should not be required to perform military service. They were already performing valuable service to their country as fathers and heads of household.

Hershey and Kennedy continued to look for ways to reduce the number of men subject to the draft. In response to an August 1963 inquiry from Kennedy, Hershey reported that the number of men available for induction could be reduced by one-fifth if the president modified the order of call so that all eligible single men would be drafted before any married men without children.[145] The Selective Service's general counsel had already ruled that limiting the liability of married men would violate the Universal Military Training and Service Act of 1951, since the law specifically removed the president's authority to defer married men without children. Gilbert Winter, associate general counsel, wrote, "the placing of these married nonfathers in a separate lower sequence of selection would have the same effect" as a deferment, except that "it would be more permanent" since "under present conditions they would never be reached for selection." In essence, the action would therefore "actually afford them a prohibited deferment."[146] Nevertheless, Kennedy complied with Hershey's request, issuing an executive order putting married men behind single ones.

Once more, the stated rationale for Kennedy's new executive order was to lower the average age of induction, since married men tended to be older than single men, but its subtext was that married men were more important to the nation as civilians than as soldiers; single men could more easily be pulled out of civilian life without disrupting society.[147] Young men got the message. A 1966 Department of Defense study found that marriage rates jumped considerably among young men in the age brackets most vulnerable to the draft in the months following the change in regulation. Marriage rates were 7.5 and 10.9 percent higher for twenty- and twenty-one-year-olds, respectively, between October 1963 and June 1964 than they had been during the previous two years. Marriage rates for all other age groups remained static.[148] Again, the Selective Service's own policies undoubtedly channeled at least some of these men into early marriages, thus privileging domestic masculinity in the name of national defense.

The Selective Service made no secret of its social and civil defense goals through the late 1950s and 1960s. Hershey spoke and wrote openly of the social engineering function of manpower channeling in meetings, articles, letters, and testimony before Congress for close to a decade before the heightened draft calls of the Vietnam War made the practice controversial on a broad scale. Media outlets were aware of the practice. The *Indianapolis Star* complained in 1958, "Selective Service is not a method of channeling all, or even half of our young men into the service of their country. It is merely a device for making a random selection of the relatively small number of men to be conscripted."[149] That same year, the *Washington Post* covered a speech Hershey delivered at an event honoring the District of Columbia's local board members in which he openly discussed channeling.[150] Certainly all those who attended the Selective Service's orientation program between

1960 and 1965 were aware of it. In 1963, an antimilitary flyer circulating in New York City also used the term.[151]

Some academics and politicians had begun remarking on the inequities of the system during the first part of the decade, a message that also trickled down to individual citizens who saw those inequalities in their own communities. Also in 1963, the members of Local Board 56 in Findlay, Ohio, wrote a letter of protest to Hershey, complaining that the Selective Service System's liberal and "undemocratic" policies forced them to perpetuate "rank injustice" and "class injustice" as they granted "blanket deferments for students, teachers, etc." As a result, they saw themselves as "automatons," unable to make independent decisions.[152] They enclosed an editorial from the *Toledo Blade* that espoused similar opinions.[153] Most presciently, Eli Ginzberg, manpower specialist and director of the Human Resources Project at Columbia University, referred to Selective Service policies as "an invitation to national disaster." A 1963 *New York Times* opinion piece by John C. Esty Jr., quoted Ginzberg as saying, "Most young Americans grow up without the understanding of military obligation, with the consequence that if and when they are called to duty they view it as an imposition, an annoyance, or a stroke of bad luck." Esty built on Ginzberg's assertion, writing, "I am afraid that a young man today, instead of feeling guilty about not serving, feels somewhat inept if he can't work out a way to avoid the draft."[154] To those paying attention, channeling undermined the civic republican tradition of the citizen soldier; it made the man who did get drafted a patsy rather than a patriot.

Yet these examples were exceptions. Despite Hershey's outspokenness, most journalists did not find the policy important enough to report on it. Channeling, as a practice, did not register with most Americans until the Vietnam War brought the inequities of the system more visibly to the fore.

In the meantime, the policy of manpower channeling served as a curious ideological bridge. When universal military training failed to pass in 1947 and was then eclipsed by selective peacetime conscription in 1948, those who wished to predicate male citizenship on military service suffered a decisive defeat. The civic republican tradition in the United States was not strong enough to drive legislation extending the obligation for compulsory military training into peacetime. Instead, Congress extended the system of Selective Service that had operated more or less successfully during wartime into the militarized peace of the Cold War. This system, by its very nature, walked a fine line between a philosophical commitment to the participation of all able-bodied men and the pragmatic reality that the military did not need or want all able-bodied men.

While Selective Service functioned effectively as a means of procuring military manpower between 1955 and 1965, it did not function particularly efficiently. The growing pool of available men combined with low draft calls made it appear that too many men could work the system to avoid service. So the Selective Service used its policy of channeling to rewrite the script. By redefining service as civilian as well as military, it tried to use deferments to give the appearance that, in fact, it was the system working the registrants to the nation's advantage. By explicitly conflating national security with men's domestic responsibilities, the Selective Service chose to see men with deferments *as* fulfilling their civic republican responsibility to the state.

Ironically, however, this policy vastly expanded the number of men that could escape conscription while granting them official sanction to do so. For middle-class men, especially, who were most able to become the kinds of professionals granted occupational deferments, military service was viewed more and more as a choice, even in a country with an active draft. Channeling unintentionally strengthened a liberal focus on choice, even as its architects tried to expand the civic republican ideal of responsibility.

CHAPTER 5

"The Most Important Human Salvage Operation in the History of Our Country"

The War on Poverty, 1961–1969

In the spring of 1967, American secretary of labor W. Willard Wirtz shared his expertise with the Senate Subcommittee on Employment, Manpower, and Poverty. The senators were exploring potential solutions to problems created by the Vietnam draft. By the time of Wirtz's testimony, inequities in Selective Service had become national news, prompting a congressional response. Democratic senators Edward Kennedy of Massachusetts and Joseph Clark of Pennsylvania had introduced a Senate resolution two months earlier calling for a complete overhaul of the law governing conscription.[1] The senators designed the April hearings to evaluate the efficacy of their plan, turning a particular eye toward the relationship between military service and poverty.

Wirtz, in his testimony, framed his remarks around the question of fairness. Unlike many antiwar protesters, however, the secretary of labor did not focus on how student deferments allowed men who could afford college to escape conscription. Rather, he claimed that the draft was not fair to the nation's poor, since current regulations did not offer them the *opportunity* to serve. "It has to be recognized," he claimed, "that any military service system which sends a man who has developed himself to battlefield [*sic*] and then send [*sic*] another boy who has wasted his life back to gang warfare in slums or ghettoes is wrong." In his opinion, a draft that rejected approximately one-third of men as ineligible for military service as a result of poor schooling or lack of medical care wasted a chance to lift up America's manhood. Instead, Congress and the Selective Service needed to ask why so many men were rejected and then do something to solve the problem.

[Wirtz spoke as a veteran of the War on Poverty. He, like other committed warriors, had spent the previous several years focused on the problem of poverty amidst American affluence. Along with social scientists, policymakers had been trying to untangle the threads of unemployment, poor education, lack of health care, powerlessness, racism, and hopelessness that seemed to trap nearly one-fifth of all Americans in a seemingly permanent underclass.[2] The Kennedy administration had addressed these issues tentatively as part of its New Frontier. Lyndon Johnson had continued the fight when he launched a full-scale War on Poverty as part of his Great Society initiative. Supporters of the resultant federal programs believed America's great democratic promise included the moral responsibility to guarantee all of its citizens equal economic opportunity and social justice.

Like other liberals in the early part of the decade, Wirtz defined full economic citizenship as both a right and an obligation. All Americans had a right to access the American Dream, which meant access to equal opportunity. In Johnson's words, all citizens deserved "a fair chance to develop their own capacities."[3] At the same time, however, citizens did not have the right to remain in poverty if an alternative was available to them. Democratic senator Wayne Morse of Oregon reflected this position in the 1967 subcommittee hearings. In response to Wirtz's testimony, he soliloquized, "We must try to make clear from the beginning of kindergarten on through that none of us has the right to be illiterate, none of us has the right to follow a course of action that does not assume our citizenship responsibility." Therefore, all men, by "the implied contract that every individual . . . undertakes as a citizen . . . must be willing to submit himself to those conditioning factors that will help make him a responsible citizen. . . . No one," he concluded, "has a right or license to become a burden upon society."[4] The poor not only needed rehabilitation, but they had an obligation to submit to it. This belief undergirded the whole structure of the Economic Opportunity Act of 1964, the keystone of the War on Poverty. Johnson and his supporters eschewed direct welfare payments in favor of programs designed to enhance educational opportunities and job skills training, programs that would allow the "deserving poor" to lift themselves out of poverty.[5]

Between 1961 and 1969, millions of government dollars flowed to private researchers and social scientists searching for a solution.[6] Agencies and departments throughout the federal structure, both on the national and the state level, also conducted studies and piloted programs designed to alleviate the suffering of individuals, train and retrain the un- and underemployed for a modern job market, create new jobs, diminish discrimination, provide health care to those without it, and empower the powerless. The creation of the Office of Economic Opportunity to spearhead many of these initiatives marked the effort's apogee. But the Departments of Health, Education, and Welfare (HEW); Labor; Agriculture; Commerce; and—perhaps surprisingly—Defense all had their roles to play as well.

During the early 1960s, Director of Selective Service Lewis B. Hershey, Secretary of Defense Robert McNamara, and members of Congress used military manpower policy as a weapon in the War on Poverty, which is defined here to include its origins in the Kennedy administration. Programs, both voluntary and compulsory, conducted through the Selective Service and the Department of Defense, were designed to identify and rehabilitate young men who could not pass their mental or physical preinduction and induction exams. Since these men overwhelmingly hailed from the lowest echelons of society, planners hoped that remedial education, health care, and job skills training would allow them to break the cycle of poverty that kept them—and their families—from contributing as American citizens in ways the policy community defined as meaningful. Rehabilitation programs run with the help of the Selective Service and Armed Forces Examining Stations (AFES) aimed to fit men for future civilian or military service, while Project 100,000, a measure instituted by McNamara, attempted to provide low-aptitude soldiers, sailors, airmen, and marines with skills they could use after their enlistments ended.

These initiatives resembled the universal military training proposals of the previous generation in that they were designed to enhance the overall health and productivity of American men. Unlike the push for UMT, however, the programs of the 1960s did not call for universal service across social classes. Instead, they explicitly targeted victims of poverty, especially minority men. Moreover, their goal was to provide poor men with the health care and skills they would need to get and hold good jobs in their civilian lives and thus support their families, a phenomenon the historian Robert O. Self called "breadwinner liberalism."[7] Earlier proposals for UMT had touted vocational training as one benefit of military service but had not isolated such training as the main purpose of the program. New initiatives also served as the inverse of manpower channeling. Where the policy of channeling deferred certain men from military service because they had been identified as more valuable to the nation as civilians, rehabilitation programs sought to add value to underprivileged men through military channels. The rehabilitation programs of the 1960s, therefore, exclusively focused on helping marginalized men conform to a civilian breadwinner ideal in a way that earlier proposals had not.

Rehabilitation programs contributed to the restructuring of the relationship between military service and ideals of masculine citizenship in three ways. First, those run through the Selective Service and AFES as well as Project 100,000 emphasized economic productivity as male citizens' main responsibility to the nation. National security, according to breadwinner liberals, required universal male productivity and a minimum standard of living more than it required universal military service. Only the barest lip service was paid to the civic republican obligation of service in the armed forces. The rhetoric of universal obligation to serve was all but dropped as these programs zeroed in on poor and minority men. Middle-class men were free to pursue other paths toward economic citizenship in the name of national service without remedial help provided through the induction system and by the military.

Second, poor and minority men rejected the programs' linkage of military service, masculinity, and economic citizenship. Voluntary rehabilitation programs failed to attract clients, partially due to the men's fear that remediation would make them eligible for the draft. Targeted men did not want to serve during wartime, despite the job skills such programs promised. In the process, they rejected politicians' justification for the programs, spurning the notion that "every young American" needed to be "develop[ed] . . . to carry his share of the burden of freedom."[8] They rejected military service as their particular obligation.

Finally, the strong connection these programs made between poverty and military service provided another justification for middle-class men to avoid the uniform. The policy of granting deferments for college education and occupations that required postsecondary degrees combined with publicity linking the armed forces with poor and minority men added one more layer of removal between military service and citizenship obligations for middle-class men.

Military manpower policy has been linked to Americans' physical and economic well-being since at least the end of the nineteenth century. The "closing" of the frontier, the simplification of the tasks performed by working-class men as a result of mechanization, and the sedentary, office-based lifestyles of middle- and upper-class men caused intellectuals great worry by the 1890s.[9] Politicians and other public figures, most notably Theodore Roosevelt, advocated "the strenuous life" as a remedy to the neuroasthenia and softness that seemed to plague American men. Intellectuals of the era often linked the concept of civilization with "ideologies of manliness."[10] If America was to evolve as a world power, they reasoned, then its male population needed to perfect itself. Such concerns were one of the major causes of American involvement in the Spanish-American War, as military service was seen by many as a way to reinvigorate the country's manhood.[11]

World War I appeared to confirm fears that the United States was becoming a nation of weaklings. Thirty-four percent of men were rejected from military service for physical incapacity alone.[12] It also marked the beginning of the military establishment's concern with the quality of American manpower, as the draft forced the armed forces to integrate large numbers of poor farmers, urban workers, and immigrants into their operations. The discovery that 7 percent of conscripts could not speak English and 25 percent were illiterate in all languages vindicated UMT proponents' arguments for universal training and fueled new calls for programs to "Americanize" immigrants and for legislation to restrict immigration.[13]

During World War II, federal concern over military rejection rates—and the state of male bodies—climbed. The military rejected just over one-third of all volunteers and draftees examined between November 1940 and August 1945.[14] The Selective Service struggled to settle on standards stringent enough to meet the military's need for capable men but sufficiently lenient to fill the armed forces' manpower quotas. By the end of the war, mental standards had been lowered so far as to admit men who were functionally illiterate.[15]

Officials in the Selective Service, especially Col. Leonard Rowntree, the agency's medical director, viewed many of the maladies keeping men from fulfilling their obligation to serve in the military as remediable. Men with certain dental problems, vision defects, hernias, sexually transmitted diseases, and who were either over- or underweight could benefit from basic medical help, he argued. During the first part of World War II, the agency considered several ideas for voluntary and compulsory rehabilitation programs, including partnerships with the Civilian Conservation Corps and the National Youth Administration.[16] Most of these proposals never came to much, especially because they relied on the voluntary participation of young men who may or may not have had access to local medical care. The Selective Service abandoned its own pilot programs for a large-scale, national rehabilitation program in 1942, deeming the job too large.[17]

The Selective Service did, however, continue to pursue relationships with other federal and local agencies in its quest to create voluntary rehabilitation programs.[18] When Congress established the Office of Vocational Rehabilitation within the Federal Security Agency in 1943, the Selective Service sought out a partnership with the new unit. Along with state vocational rehabilitation (VR) agencies, the Office of Vocational Rehabilitation helped men find state and federally funded medical care in their local communities. The agreement reached between the Selective Service and the Office of Vocational Rehabilitation led to procedures whereby the Selective Service furnished the names of rejectees to state rehabilitation agencies so that eligible men could be "prepared for employment in critical industries."[19] Hershey instructed state directors to liaise with state VR agencies.[20] While the program was beset by troubles, including massive backlogs of names and rejectees' failure to follow up on services, the relationship between the two agencies lasted in some form until 1961.[21]

Moreover, as argued in chapter 2, proposals for universal military training were, at least in part, a response to perceptions that American men had grown soft. Common training, according to some of the plan's proponents, would enhance national security by physically strengthening the nation's male populace. Physical activity combined with military training would ensure men's ability to mobilize quickly and effectively should the need arise. UMT's secondary benefits, including remedial health care and vocational training, would also guarantee that all men had the means to contribute to America's growing postwar economy. Trained individuals, equipped with healthy bodies and the occupational skills necessary for a modern, mechanized economy, would strengthen the civic foundation of the United States.

The military establishment, therefore, was firmly connected to programs, both proposed and realized, designed to enhance the welfare of individuals and the nation through the first half of the twentieth century. Potential soldiers, in theory, required good physical health, educational ability, and an understanding of national values in order to succeed in modern warfare. Ideally, the thinking went, these qualities should be nurtured from childhood, but this was not always possible in the diverse, growing population of the twentieth-century United States. The federal government, including the military, needed to step in to build strong, dedicated, reliable men, who could take the lessons they learned in the military back into their communities after discharge. So when federal initiatives turned toward strengthening the nation's populace and alleviating poverty in the 1960s, it seemed natural that the defense establishment would have a part to play.

The end of the Korean War sharpened anxieties over national strength and manhood. Even though, by most measures, the United States was doing remarkably well—unemployment was relatively low, the economy had grown overwhelmingly since the end of World War II, standards of living for most Americans continued to rise, and the United States was an undisputed world power—fear remained.[22] For the first time, the United States had failed to win a decisive victory in war. Up to one-third of men registered with the Selective Service had not qualified for military service.[23] A handful of American prisoners of war refused repatriation after the armistice, causing many to worry that Americans were mentally weak.[24] The Soviet Union appeared on the brink of technologically eclipsing the United States. The mass media, through movies and publications, capitalized on and spread fear that the nation's citizens somehow were not strong enough for the next war, that America's strength and manhood were on the decline, and that the United States could be easily infiltrated by communists. America in the late 1950s, therefore, was a nation simultaneously at the peak of its strength and wracked by self-doubt.[25]

As a result, the movement to improve national strength that developed in the 1950s and 1960s uniquely responded to the threat of the Cold War. A strong, fully employed, well-educated population came to be understood as a weapon against communism. A particularly masculine cult of toughness and strength arose within political and foreign policy circles during the 1950s.[26] Exhibiting weakness in this environment was unacceptable. Strength of body and mind were essential, as was a refusal to be "soft" on communism.

John F. Kennedy capitalized on these fears as he campaigned for the presidency.[27] Through stump speeches and publications, he painted a picture of a country and a people "in trouble," of a "tired" America, trapped in a period of "decline."[28] He worried that if the nation did not take immediate measures to halt the slow slippage of American prestige, the people would one day take stock and realize that their nation had been overtaken by its communist foe, "like the slow rotting of a great tree . . . which ultimately blows over from the first small wind that passes." Newly independent nations of the world would cease looking toward the United States for leadership if they felt "that the sun of the West [was] setting and that the sun of the East [was] rising," and that the United States was "unable to solve [its] problems."[29]

Strength, according to Kennedy and the men he surrounded himself with, was the key to American greatness—strength of character, strength of body, strength of conviction—and the nation's full potential could not be reached without a well-equipped military and without economic growth.[30] National vigor, therefore, had to be restored through better national defense, renewed economic growth, and a firm pledge to use American strength to uplift the poor, all of which Kennedy vowed to accomplish as president.

One of the areas that the new administration zeroed in on was the military rejection rate. The Interdepartmental Committee for Children and Youth, a task force charged with following up on the recommendations of the 1960 White House Conference on Children and Youth, began to examine the issue in 1961. Committee members worried that men who were turned away when they tried to enlist because they could not meet the military's minimum qualifications would be damaged emotionally, economically, and socially.[31] The Social Security Administration, meanwhile, with the cooperation of the Selective Service, also began investigating how forty thousand men rejected from military service for illiteracy had fared over past decade. Data from Baltimore's old-age, disability, and insurance records confirmed the agencies' hypothesis that those who had been turned away from the military would be poorer than those who managed to enlist.[32] The vast majority of men turned away from military service because they had failed their aptitude tests lived below the poverty line.[33]

But it was a memo sent by Secretary of Labor Wirtz to Kennedy that made the plight of military rejectees a national issue. Wirtz sent Kennedy the memo in early September 1963, following a report by the President's Committee on Youth Employment, explaining that close to one-quarter of all men flunked their induction exams for "mental reasons," meaning they scored too low on the Armed Forces Qualification Test (AFQT).[34] To Wirtz, such a high rate of failure on the test, which measured basic literacy, mathematics, spatial relations, and mechanical skills rather than IQ, indicated a much larger social problem. He estimated that little more than 10 percent of those rejected were "in fact mentally retarded." Instead, these results indicated that inadequate schools betrayed poor American students, especially African Americans, who failed at a rate more than three times that of white men. Wirtz called the failure rate a "national disgrace" and pointed out that men rejected from military service frequently became "a long-run burden to their communities." Their poor educations and low skill levels, which according to the test were not even at a seventh-grade level, often kept them from holding a job and earning a living. Moreover, he pointed to the Selective Service as an "incomparable asset" in locating the "25% or more" of the population that would "unquestionably cause 75% or more" of the nation's "social and economic problems."[35]

As a result of Wirtz' proposal, Kennedy established the President's Task Force on Manpower Conservation on September 30, 1963. The president charged the study group, chaired by Wirtz and composed of Hershey, McNamara, and HEW secretary Anthony J. Celebrezze, with examining why close to 50 percent of all draftees failed their preinduction exams either for physical or mental reasons and with proposing solutions. In his statement, Kennedy repeated Wirtz' warnings that such high failure rates portended a social and economic crisis. "A young man who does not have what it takes to perform military service," he fretted, "is not likely to have what it takes to make a living. Today's military rejects include tomorrow's hard core unemployed."[36] The media agreed that something had to change. The *Boston Globe* called the rejection rate "dismal" and a "crisis."[37] The *Hartford Courant* termed it "ominous."[38]

[During the Kennedy era, therefore, fitness, the economy, and national security became inextricably linked. In Kennedy's words, "Softness on the part of individual citizens . . . strip[ped] and destroy[ed] the vitality of a nation." Unfitness posed "a menace to . . . security" by keeping men from physically fighting the enemy with the necessary vigor and threatening "the activities of peace" as well as "those of war."[39] Men who could not serve in the military could not advance America's economic position, creating a double burden for the nation as it struggled to stay ahead of the Soviet Union.]

In January 1964, the President's Task Force on Manpower Conservation issued its report, *One-Third of a Nation: A Report on Young Men Found Unqualified for Military Service*. Through a study of statistics provided by the Department of Defense and Selective Service, the task force confirmed the earlier finding that almost 50 percent of draftees failed their preinduction exams and approximately one-third of all young men turning eighteen could not qualify for military service.[40]

Members found that of the men who failed for physical reasons, 75 percent could benefit from medical treatment. They acknowledged that some of the conditions considered defects by the armed forces, including not meeting height requirements, would not be considered problematic in the civilian sector, but they argued that most of the men who failed could live fuller lives if they received help. Ten percent of the rejectees had conditions, including syphilis and hernias, that could be cured completely, while another 20 percent could achieve significant relief from conditions like asthma and heart disease with treatment.[41] These findings indicated a deficiency in the nation's health system. Men who should have known of their infirmities frequently did not, and many of those who knew could not afford services.

More disturbingly, the data on men who failed their aptitude tests, combined with the results of a nationwide survey of 2,500 recent rejectees, indicated alarming geographic variability and that mental rejectees were overwhelmingly from backgrounds of poverty. While fewer than 5 percent of men from states like Minnesota, Utah, Montana, and Vermont failed mental aptitude tests, the rate was higher than 30 percent in all of the southeastern states, topping out at over 50 percent in Mississippi and South Carolina.[42] Four out of five of the men surveyed had dropped out of school and only

75 percent had finished elementary school, compared to 95 percent of all American men between the ages of twenty and twenty-four.[43] The report estimated that the unemployment rate for these men was four times the national average and their poverty rate was at least twice that of the rest of the country.[44] One-fifth of their families had received public assistance in the previous five years, when on average only 4.2 percent of children in the United States received benefits from the Aid to Families with Dependent Children program.[45] *One-Third of a Nation* was a striking indictment of many American institutions: the health care system, the schools, and the economic safety net.

The results also indicated the particularly difficult time faced by African American men. Black rejectees had completed more years of schooling than their white counterparts, and yet they were more likely to fail the mental aptitude tests. On average, they were more likely to be unemployed, and those who did work earned over $1,000 less per year than the national average and over $600 less than the white rejectees.[46] The conditions of their lives illustrated both their dire economic straits and the poor quality of their often segregated schools.[47]

The report pointed out that many of the rejectees, both black and white, had already been in the labor force for many years. They had dropped out of school at a young age and worked in dead-end jobs. According to the report, it was "difficult to envisage these jobs making it possible for them to save for contingencies, and to raise families in a manner that would permit their sons and daughters to do better."[48] Thus rejectees had been born into poverty and were likely to pass that poverty on to their children. They were trapped in a vicious poverty cycle. As Wirtz wrote in his letter to the president, "Far too many of these young men have missed out on the American miracle. This level of failure stands as a symbol of the unfinished business of the Nation."[49]

Yet, explained the report, America's business could be completed. Eighty percent of the mental rejectees surveyed claimed that they would participate in programs offering job training and/or basic educational skills. African Americans were even more eager for remediation, with more than 90 percent asking for such services.[50] And members of the task force felt that it was high time that the United States offered help to these men. "The profile of the medical and mental rejectee that has emerged from the studies," they wrote, "leaves no question as to where the national interest lies in this situation." Both "national defense" and "national welfare . . . clearly require[d] that a conservation program be undertaken by the Federal Government, with the fullest possible cooperation of State and local bodies."[51]

The task force recommended taking several steps to maximize rehabilitation opportunities. First, members suggested that all men be fully examined and appropriately classified at age eighteen, when they first registered with the Selective Service, so that defects could be identified and services rendered earlier. Second, they wanted AFES personnel to apprise all rejectees of why they had failed their preinduction exam rather than simply tell them that they were not fit for military service. Third, they recommended that units within the Departments of Labor and HEW coordinate with each other to create referral programs whereby rejectees could be sent, on a voluntary basis, for appropriate help within their home communities. Together, these offices could create "a systematic program of experimental and demonstration projects . . . to develop new techniques for diagnostic testing, basic education, vocational and psychological counseling and methods for motivating rejectees." Fourth, they advocated the creation of Manpower Development and Training Advisory Committees consisting of representatives from local Selective Service boards and members of local educational and welfare organizations that could spearhead a community response to the problem.[52]

According to the task force members, these recommendations could all be carried out through programs that already existed or that were pending before Congress.[53] No new legislation would be required, and additional expenditures would be relatively low. Yet, they explained, the results of such rehabilitation programs would provide the United States with additional tax revenue and save significant welfare costs.[54] In other words, a minor financial outlay now would be paid back many times over in the future, as it would enable this huge group of men—estimated to approach 600,000 per year by 1965—to "become effective citizens and self-supporting individuals."[55]

President Lyndon Johnson used the release of *One-Third of a Nation* to fire one of the opening salvos in his War on Poverty, and its findings added evidence to the argument that such a war was necessary.[56] But the report was also noteworthy because it proposed using the military system to identify and remedy social problems. Any new rehabilitation programs that stemmed from the report would use an infrastructure designed to procure military manpower to prepare men for full economic citizenship as civilians rather than to be soldiers. The resources of the Selective Service and the Department of the Army, which administered the AFQT and ran the AFES, would be diverted toward the new War on Poverty.

Equally important, much like other Great Society programs, the report established the problem of poverty as distinctly male. It identified the AFQT as the most efficient available means to identify those Americans who could most benefit from rehabilitation because the test was the only "major post-school examination" administered in the United States.[57] Only men took the exam, meaning any programs stemming from the test's failure would be open only to men. No equivalent test would be used to locate women with physical and educational deficiencies. The report's authors, like other breadwinner liberals, assumed that offering remediation to men would uplift women and children too, illustrating how ingrained was the notion that breadwinning was a masculine responsibility.[58] Full participation in the workforce remained a male prerogative.[59]

On January 5, 1964, less than two months after taking office, Johnson ordered the Selective Service and the Department of the Army to make plans to examine young men as close to their eighteenth birthdays as practicable. He also asked the agencies of the federal government to study the problem and develop programs designed to rehabilitate those men who failed.[60] The explicit purpose of such rehabilitation was to outfit men with the skills they would need in order to get and hold jobs in the civilian sector. While it was never specifically stated, men whose health improved as a result of treatment would be reclassified as eligible for service. Although several agencies had been studying the issue since 1961, discussion within the Selective Service, HEW, and the Department of Labor stepped up after Johnson's announcement. Officials of these agencies founded an Interdepartmental Task Force on Selective Service Rejectees to coordinate proposals and programs.[61] According to Wirtz, the United States was undertaking "the most important human salvage program in [its] history."[62]

In February 1964, the Department of Labor, with the cooperation of HEW, the Selective Service, and state and local agencies, launched the first phase of a national rehabilitation project for men who failed the AFQT. Officials aimed it at the estimated 63,000 unemployed and underemployed men the department expected to be rejected from the military because of educational deficiencies between February 1 and June 30, 1964. At some point in the future, they hoped to work through the backlog of 3.5 million men between the ages of eighteen and twenty-six who had been rejected prior to February 1964. Local draft boards were asked to "encourage all educationally deficient rejectees," whether employed or not, to report to public employment service offices, where they would be further evaluated to determine which services would be most beneficial. Men in the program were to "receive intensive counseling, testing, job development, and referrals," with a special emphasis on employment counseling.[63] By early March, the Department of Labor had the cooperation of the related state agencies in all states except Louisiana, which came on board that summer.[64]

At the same time, HEW and the Department of Labor began to look for more efficient methods to refer men to available services. In mid-February, they experimented with a joint program in Salt Lake City, Utah. Rather than rely on local boards to notify men via letter, the Public Health Service, Vocational Rehabilitation Administration, and Bureau of Employment Services all stationed counselors directly at the Salt Lake induction center. Counseling personnel could contact rejectees immediately and in person and then conduct follow-up interviews at a later date. The pilot program proved such a success, with 100 percent of rejected men volunteering to participate in follow-up services, that the model was extended to Detroit; Pittsburgh; Philadelphia; New Haven; Newark, New Jersey; and Columbia, South Carolina.[65]

Regardless of how men were singled out, the process of finding them, notifying them, and referring them to appropriate services was an immense undertaking. It involved the coordination of multiple national- and state-level offices. Clients for the new programs were to be identified through the Selective Service, which was responsible for issuing preinduction notices and forwarding men along to AFES for examination. The Department of the Army conducted physical examinations and administered the AFQT. In general, HEW was to handle programs for men who were rejected for physical reasons through its Vocational Rehabilitation Administration and the Public Health Service. The Department of Labor was to handle men who were rejected for mental reasons, primarily through its Bureau of Employment Services. There was considerable overlap in goals, however, so care had to be taken to avoid redundancies. Moreover, local programs were funded through grants from the national offices, but administered on the state and local levels. So, for example, in 1965, Rhode Island's AFES hosted four "overlapping programs" at the same time: a Public Health Service health referral program, a national study of mental rejectees conducted by the Vocational Rehabilitation Administration, a Rhode Island Department of Educational Services training and placement program, and a state-administered Department of Vocational Research demonstration project, which, in turn, was funded by a grant from HEW's Rehabilitation Services Administration.[66] In other states, nongovernmental institutions, including universities, evaluated the programs, adding another layer of bureaucracy.[67]

Funding for the programs came primarily from appropriations for the 1962 Manpower Development and Training Act (MDTA) and its subsequent amendments. The measure, a Kennedy initiative, was meant as a partial solution to the loss of manufacturing jobs to automation. It rested on the assumption that rising unemployment, especially among breadwinners, strained the economy and prevented the United States from living up to its full potential as a world power.[68] The law required participants to be unemployed male heads of household with prior work experience.[69] In 1963, in a bid to catch more clients, Congress amended the law to allow anyone from families where the primary male breadwinner was unemployed to participate, and it lowered the minimum age of participants from nineteen to seventeen. With these changes, Selective Service rejectees, who generally did not yet have dependents, could take part.[70] Men who failed the military entrance exams were seen as a particularly rich source of candidates because, as *One-Third of a Nation* indicated, they were likely to be poor and they were all men. The Selective Service and AFES examinations, therefore, became one of the major sources of participants for MDTA programs by 1964.[71]

The results of the referral programs were mixed. Without question, they offered services and opportunities otherwise unavailable to many men rejected from the military. Job training, literacy classes, and referrals for medical treatment no doubt altered the course of some men's lives. The National Committee for Children and Youth (NCCY), an organization that provided rehabilitation services to men who had tried to volunteer for military service but who had been rejected, for example, crowed about its successes in Washington, D.C., and Baltimore. It declared its final report in 1967 "a valedictory." The report used case studies to illustrate the life-changing effects of the program. Clorester W., Sandy Z., Stephen J., Michael E., Larry W., Larry T., and Larry P.—all from poor or working-class families and all either high school dropouts or experiencing significant academic delay—managed to pass the armed forces entrance exams after receiving intensive literacy and numeracy tutoring through the NCCY. As a result of these successes, Clorester became "a very happy young man," Michael "achieved his ultimate goal," Larry W. was "very proud," and Larry T. would be able to "work as a motor mechanic" after discharge. The NCCY had seen such success in its three years of operation that it had expanded its program to Chicago, St. Louis, San Antonio, Los Angeles, and Rochester, New York, and it was poised to make the entire program permanent through the Bureau of Employment Services in the Department of Labor.[72] The NCCY's report did not dwell on participants' heightened motivation, however. All of the program's clients had failed their exams after attempting to enlist. None had been drafted.

Other demonstration projects proved less attractive to the men they were intended to help. The Department of Labor had originally estimated that it would be able to help approximately one-half of all rejectees, but the results of pilot programs in several states fell well short of the halfway mark.[73] The vocational rehabilitation program at the Rhode Island AFES found that only

12.7 percent of the men rejected for military service were eligible for VR services, and of those, only about two-thirds accepted the proffered help. In total, only 417 of the 8,824 men rejected at the Rhode Island AFES between January 1965 and May 1967 accepted services.[74] The results of a pilot study in South Carolina were no better. This project, which centered on the five counties around the AFES at Fort Jackson, offered physical rehabilitation in addition to VR services, yet in the three years of its existence, only 7.7 percent of the total number rejected, or 165 men, were accepted for services. Of these, only 112 sought the proffered help.[75] These numbers were particularly dismal given that the program offered hospital care, including surgery when needed. Moreover, South Carolina, which rejected close to 66 percent of its potential draftees as compared to Rhode Island's 35 percent, was seen as one of the major prospective beneficiaries of the national initiative.[76]

The two studies listed several reasons for men's failure to participate, including poor communication between counselors and potential clients and staffing deficiencies, but the overarching problem identified by both was that the programs were tied to military service. Correcting men's defects would have made them eligible to be drafted. Both programs spanned the years of major escalation of the Vietnam War. Men who were found acceptable for military service, especially through the draft rather than enlistment, were highly likely to find themselves assigned to infantry units stationed in Southeast Asia. VR personnel in South Carolina termed this threat an "intangible" that "pervade[d] the entire study."[77] Rhode Island researchers similarly believed the "loss of about one in three between screening and actual service would not be expected to be as large if the examining program was a routine one without relationship to military induction." The report emphasized, "Many [men] preferred to retain their disability rather than risk later military induction by undergoing corrective treatment."[78]

A third project, a health referral program in Tennessee with similarly poor participation rates, denied that the draft had anything to do with men's failure to accept services. Yet one of its counselors concluded, "The program would be much more effective if the counselors could be located somewhere completely independent of the examining station. The majority of the boys . . . are either . . . elated to have been rejected, or terribly frightened."[79] He did not elaborate on why rejection pleased the men, but it is fair to assume that it was partly because they could no longer be compelled to serve in Vietnam.

The war affected these programs in other ways as well. As it escalated, AFES stopped examining men as they turned eighteen, focusing instead on evaluating the men who faced immediate induction. Between July 1964, when the army first started examining eighteen-year-olds, and January 1965,

AFES evaluated an average of thirty thousand younger men per month in addition to the usual load of men about to enlist, be conscripted, or be classified by the Selective Service. In September 1965, after all the service branches began to use Selective Service to fill their ranks, AFES examined approximately twelve thousand eighteen-year-olds.[80] By January 1966, the number had dropped so low that *Selective Service*, which since mid-1964 had published a monthly article featuring the number of eighteen-year-olds examined, ceased running the column. Examination stations were too busy inducting soldiers, sailors, airmen, and marines to be able to devote extra resources to the War on Poverty. Older men who failed the AFQT continued to be referred to pilot programs for another two years, but it appears that funding for this particular Great Society initiative petered out after 1968.[81]

Nevertheless, these referral programs are important. First, the failure of men to participate in them, especially during wartime, indicates that many of the targeted men were not all that eager to serve in the military, even with the promise of job skills or free medical care. They did not want to qualify for military service. Whatever they felt their obligations were as citizens or as men—supporting their families, defending their nation, or something else—survival took precedence. These men, who were overwhelmingly from poor and minority backgrounds, joined the college-educated of their age cohort in looking for ways to avoid military service.[82]

Second, these programs illustrate the military establishment's willingness to participate in social welfare programs at a moment when domestic issues were of paramount importance to the rest of the policy community. The Department of Defense and Selective Service System, as members of that community, reflected contemporary values. In that regard, they came to focus on helping poor men achieve full economic citizenship. They committed resources to help other federal agencies train the nation's least privileged men to become breadwinners. Developing domestic strength through a strong economy and full employment became a goal of national defense alongside the projection of military might, at least until the Vietnam War eclipsed the Great Society as the primary priority of the Johnson administration.

As might be imagined, Hershey involved himself in the discourse on physical fitness, national security, and service to the state from the beginning. He sincerely believed that disqualifying a man from military service did both the man and the nation a disservice. By declaring a registrant IV-F, he wrote, "the Government gives him some evidence from which he can infer that he is relieved from further obligation to serve his Government in the Armed Forces," a patent fallacy according to Hershey's civic republican philosophy of citizenship.[83] Eliminating a man from the manpower pool as a result of remediable defects robbed him of the "self confidence and vigor" that would follow from full participation in the military and robbed the government of that man's possible defense contributions.[84] The problem of unfitness, both physical and mental, therefore, was of the utmost concern to the Selective Service.

When Kennedy and then Johnson asked him to take part in the War on Poverty, Hershey threw the full weight of his agency behind the initiative. He sat on the President's Task Force on Manpower Conservation and fully endorsed the committee's findings. He lent the resources of the Selective Service to the referral program for eighteen-year-olds, appearing before Congress in the fall of 1964 to ask for supplemental appropriations to complete the task.[85] He highlighted the Selective Service's role in the War on Poverty at the 1965 annual meeting of state directors and biannual regional conferences for reserve officers attached to the agency, going so far as to require personnel to attend lectures by officials from the Office of Economic Opportunity, HEW, and the Department of Labor.[86] When Johnson asked Hershey to sit on the President's Committee on Manpower and the Economic Opportunity Council, he readily agreed.[87] As a member of the latter group, he solicited suggestions from the entire Selective Service System on how to best meet the problem of poverty, writing an article in *Selective Service*, mailing a letter directly to the reserve officers assigned to the agency, and issuing a state director advice memo. Within two months, he had heard from 70 of the 134 Reserve and National Guard units attached to the Selective Service and from local boards and state offices across the country.[88]

Hershey also proudly described the agency's other contributions. By March 1965, the Selective Service had established a library of reference material on poverty at national headquarters; had "classified, sent for physical examination, and referred as appropriate to the Department of Labor for counseling" approximately 80,000 eighteen-year-olds; had sent letters referring another 250,000 older registrants to rehabilitation services; had participated in at least twenty pilot programs through AFES; had put fliers from the newly created Job Corps in more than four thousand local boards; had employed disadvantaged youth through the Youth Opportunity Program; and had discussed deferment options with representatives of the Volunteers in Service to America (VISTA) program. Moreover, many state directors joined advisory committees on the state level.[89] Hershey wanted his agency to be front and center in the War on Poverty.

Hershey's biographer, George Q. Flynn, argued that as a "conservative Republican," Hershey "was uncomfortable serving as an agent of social reform" and implied that Hershey participated in Great Society programs in order to keep his agency politically relevant.[90] Such an interpretation, however, overlooks the implications of Hershey's civic republican mindset. Hershey strongly believed that service to the state was every male citizen's responsibility, but as shown in chapter 4, his definition of "service" evolved through the late 1950s and early 1960s. Military service was best, but in a technological age when nuclear war threatened the nation's survival, men could serve the state through their occupational choices. Scientists and engineers were vital, as was a successful educational system to train them. The United States also needed a strong economic base and a functioning civil defense structure. These needs could only be met with a healthy, educated civilian populace. As Hershey told the readers of *Selective Service*, ensuring national success was a task "far too big for anything less than a combined coordinated drive by . . . government at all levels and nongovernment at all levels, and citizens everywhere" to help the nation's "youth so they [could] help themselves." The Cold War could not be won unless all young men came "to accept the full responsibilities of American citizenship," including "the will to work" and "confidence that the Nation [was] worth the best they [could] give." "It must be realized by us all," he exhorted his readership, "that our very survival is at stake. The responsibilities [of citizenship] must be shared by all. The burden is too heavy for the few."[91] Training men for national defense, whatever form that defense took, was an obligation of the federal government, even if that meant a war on poverty. By defining social welfare as a security issue, the Republican Hershey was able to support a Democratic president's initiatives. Indeed, growth of the federal government in the name of defense was a hallmark of the Cold War–era Republican Party.[92]

As part of his crusade to make civilians understand their responsibility to the nation, Hershey campaigned for a new system of classification that would shift those men whose physical or mental condition could allow them to participate in civil defense, if not the armed forces, into a separate category of call. He believed this new rating would "tell a young man what he [could] do" rather than allowing him to "escape his obligations because of his unacceptability."[93] Hershey introduced the idea as early as 1956 and finally succeeded in January 1962, when the I-Y category was added to the Selective Service classification system. It encompassed all men with minor physical defects and those who did not meet the heightened mental standards of peacetime but who would have qualified for military service under wartime standards. Approximately 40 percent of the men who had previously failed their preinduction exams were moved from the IV-F category into the new I-Y classification.[94] By early 1964, approximately one hundred thousand new I-Y men were being added to the manpower pool each year.[95]

That same year, in keeping with his desire to use the armed forces to improve American men, Hershey proposed inducting I-Y men into the military for two-year terms, during which time they could be offered basic literacy courses, receive corrective medical care, and be trained in "teamwork and responsible citizenship," all "without overemphasis on military training." After the initial term of enlistment ended, he proposed that they be transferred into the reserves, a move that would have the added benefit of bolstering reserve programs with extra men each year.[96] Secretary of Labor Wirtz and Dr. Stafford Warren, Kennedy's assistant to the president for mental retardation, had proposed a similar "para-military" program a few months earlier as they discussed rehabilitation options for military rejectees. The commissioner of the Vocational Rehabilitation Administration, Mary Switzer, thought that this policy decision "should be considered most carefully," as the military had the camps, personnel, and "vast training experience" necessary for such an endeavor.[97] By the second half of 1964, Secretary of Defense McNamara had picked up on the proposal.

Aside from propagating the Vietnam War, McNamara, a former Ford executive, was probably best known within the Department of Defense for bringing to the Pentagon modern management techniques, including computerized data collection and top-down leadership.[98] But he was also dedicated to using the resources of the Defense Department to achieve social aims. Within three years of his appointment, he had "actively committed the huge defense complex to the struggle against domestic social problems," based on the conviction that the nation's security lay "not solely or even primarily in military force, but equally in developing stable patterns of economic and political growth both at home and in the developing nations throughout the world." In the end, he argued, "poverty and social injustice . . . endanger[ed] . . . national security as much as any military threat."[99]

Based on this belief, McNamara initiated a new battle in the War on Poverty in August 1964. Borrowing from Wirtz' and Hershey's ideas, he proposed a new Special Training and Enlistment Program (STEP) to be run through the army at Fort Leonard Wood in Missouri. It would allow up to ten thousand I-Y volunteers per year to enlist. Their period of basic training would be stretched from the usual eight weeks to fourteen as a condition for acceptance into the armed forces. The extended training interval would include basic instruction in English, math, social studies, and science. Soldiers who, after that time, still could not achieve a passing score on the AFQT would also receive special classes during their advanced individual training.

Those with medical defects would receive specialized medical attention. If, after the men's training, army officials deemed individual STEP men acceptable for service, they would finish their enlistments as privates. If not, they would be discharged as veterans without penalty.[100]

Johnson supported the plan wholeheartedly as another way to solve the problem of youth unemployment, telling his secretary of defense that McNamara could "do it better than the social scientists." McNamara, however, faced opposition from the army, which regarded STEP as a plan to turn its training posts into "moron camps."[101] The plan also faced opposition from Congress. Senator Richard B. Russell, a Georgia Democrat and the chair of the Appropriations Subcommittee of the Senate Armed Services Committee, was particularly opposed, as he feared the induction of large numbers of southern African Americans.[102] Russell worried about the harm to the southern economy that would ensue if too many black agricultural workers were removed from farms through induction. He also believed that arming black men was dangerous. Although requests for supplemental appropriations for the program passed the House, they failed in the Senate, amidst worries that STEP would duplicate the purpose of the Selective Service referral program and skepticism that the military was the proper venue for social engineering.[103] Ultimately, Congress banned the Department of Defense from using any of its fiscal 1966 or 1967 budgets to finance the program.[104]

McNamara, however, continued to look for a way around congressional strictures. He firmly believed that military service could benefit the nation's disadvantaged. He argued that a stint in the armed forces could offer "the hapless and hopeless victims of poverty . . . a sense of personal achievement, a sense of succeeding at a task, a sense of their own intrinsic potential." Military service could free them from the "squalid ghettos of their external environment" and the "internal and more destructive ghetto of personal disillusionment and despair." Such liberation would return men to civilian life "equipped with new skills and attitudes" that would help them "break out of the self-perpetuating poverty cycle."[105] A program to rehabilitate men who had been rejected from military service could bolster national security by eliminating a source of social unrest and benefit American combat readiness by boosting the number of men in uniform.

First, McNamara used the escalation of the conflict in Vietnam and its attendant rise in draft calls to lower induction standards for both volunteers and inductees.[106] Pentagon officials justified this action by claiming that allowing more men to enlist would reduce the military's dependency on conscription. This move had particularly political ramifications once Johnson revoked the protected status of childless married men in August 1965. If more previously ineligible men were able to volunteer, fewer married men would have to be conscripted.[107]

Second, in a speech before the Veterans of Foreign Wars 1966 convention, McNamara announced the Defense Department's intention to bring up to one hundred thousand previously ineligible men into the military each year in order to "salvage" them, "first to productive military careers and later for productive roles in society." Project 100,000, as it came to be known, would "rescue" poor and especially minority men from the "poverty-encrusted environments" in which they had been raised.[108] This new program would focus on Category IV men—those who scored between a 10 and a 30 on the AFQT—and lower the standards for admittance to the military even further. "New Standards" men, as participants were named, were considered eligible for service if they had graduated from high school and had AFQT scores over 10, roughly the equivalent of a fifth-grade education. Men who had not graduated from high school were also given an avenue to acceptance.[109] New Standards men were to be admitted into all branches of military service, both through enlistment and the draft, using a quota system. Overall, under McNamara's new regulations, an average of 22.3 percent of all new accessions into the military—up to 26 percent in the army—had to be Category IV men.[110]

Project 100,000 differed from the STEP proposal in a number of ways. First, New Standards men were not concentrated at one particular training center. Instead, they were distributed throughout the military training infrastructure, receiving their basic training at eighteen different posts around the country. They were assigned to advanced training based on their performance during basic training and personal interviews. Second, they were not told they were part of a special program. The Defense Department kept copious records on their performance and evaluated both the men and program regularly, but the men themselves were officially unaware of their difference from the rest of their colleagues.[111] Third, they did not receive dedicated literacy or numeracy training as STEP men would have. In fact, Defense Department officials specifically emphasized that "Project One Hundred Thousand [was] *not* a literacy project." These differences allowed the Department of Defense to circumvent the congressional stipulations that forbade the use of defense dollars for special education programs. The branches of service had to integrate enhanced training into already existent programs. Literacy training, therefore, would be folded into skills training that all trainees received, and New Standards men would be evaluated using a "job-related curriculum, practical exercises, modern instructional media, and performance tests."[112] Anyone who failed to perform adequately by the end of their period of basic training would be "recycled" back to the beginning to try again or sent to motivational platoons for men with disciplinary infractions. The Army Directorate of Personnel Studies and Research was made responsible for studying the "capabilities, training needs, and uses of soldiers with low aptitudes."[113]

In total, all branches of service added a combined total of 354,000 New Standards men to their active-duty rosters between 1966 and 1971, when the program ended. Ninety-three percent were defined as low-aptitude. The rest had physical ailments that the program planned to remediate.[114] Approximately half volunteered and half were drafted.[115] Their demographic profile was striking. Seventy percent came from backgrounds of poverty and 60 percent from single-parent families. Less than 20 percent had graduated high school, and 40 percent read at a sixth-grade level or less.[116] More than half came from the southern states, and of these, 65 percent were African American. Overall, more than 40 percent of New Standards men were black, at a time when only about 10 percent of all new soldiers, sailors, marines, and airmen each year were African American.[117]

According to researchers Lawrence M. Baskir and William A. Strauss, military recruiters specifically targeted poor, black neighborhoods to find volunteers. For example, of the 125 men enlisted by black recruiters in Oakland, California, in one year, 120 hailed from poor neighborhoods, and of those, 90 percent had AFQT scores that classified them as Category IV.[118] A high proportion of poor and black men were both expected and desired. One early memo referenced the hope that Project 100,000 would be close to 60 percent black.[119]

Supporters of Project 100,000, most notably former Assistant Secretary of Labor Daniel Patrick Moynihan, saw the program as a savior for black men. In his infamous 1965 report, *The Negro Family: The Case for National Action*, Moynihan had identified "the utterly masculine world" of the armed forces as a vital corrective to the "disorganized and matrifocal" family environment in which most young black men were raised. "A world away from women . . . run by strong men of unquestioned authority, where discipline" was "harsh . . . but orderly and predictable" and where rewards were "granted on the basis of performance," could help offset the "tangle of pathology" that imposed a "crushing burden on the Negro male."[120] That 67.5 percent of black men were denied the opportunity to serve in the military because they could not pass entrance exams was heinous, according to Moynihan. High entrance standards denied these men access to the GI Bill, federally backed mortgages, life insurance, civil service preference, veterans' hospitals and pensions. Moreover, these men lost out on valuable skills training and employment. In a 1966 article in the *New Republic*, Moynihan argued that if African Americans served in the military in proportion to their numbers in the population, and if the unemployment rate for young black men was correspondingly reduced, then "the unemployment rate for non-white males in the relevant age group [in 1964] would have been *lower* than that for whites." In light of this, he claimed, the use of the military as "a socializing experience for the poor" was America's "best hope" for "turning out equal citizens."[121]

On the opposite end of the ideological spectrum, southern congressmen lifted their opposition to using the armed forces for social engineering projects. Senator Russell, who had prevented STEP from proceeding in 1964, now advocated the lowering of standards so that "damn dumb bunnies" couldn't escape the draft.[122] To these politicians, it was safer to send a black man to Vietnam than to leave him to the civil rights movement, especially as cities across the nation erupted in violence in 1967. Local boards throughout the South were able to use the policy changes instituted by McNamara to draft African Americans well out of proportion to their representation in the population as a whole, just as more men were being sent into harm's way.[123]

McNamara appears to have split the difference. He continued to advocate the program as a way to offer young men educational skills and economic reward. "If so massive a number of our young men were educationally unqualified for even the least complicated tasks of military service," he asked the crowd at the National Association of Educational Broadcasters 1967 convention, "how could they reasonably be expected to lead productive and rewarding lives in an increasingly technological and highly-skilled society?" Project 100,000, he claimed, offered undereducated men "the Defense Department's experience in educational innovation and on-the-job training" in an "atmosphere of high motivation and morale." But he also alleged that these men would become a danger to society if a solution to poverty were not found. Without a "strong sense of their own worth and potential, they, their wives, and their children would almost inevitably be the unproductive recipients of some form of the dole 10 years from now." More importantly, he warned that "if unchecked and unreversed," the "inner ghetto of the poverty-scarred personality" would "fester into explosive frustrations of bitterness and violence," a meaningful reference after the wave of urban rebellion that had taken place that summer.[124]

The Department of Defense touted the program's successes. Approximately 96 percent of New Standards men successfully completed their basic training requirements, compared to a 98 percent completion rate for those men who had entered the military under the earlier, higher aptitude standards. Eighty-eight percent of these men completed their basic course without remediation, and of those who did not, most only needed two additional weeks of training. Additionally, in the army, 87 percent of New Standards men who were sent for special skills training qualified for their specialties, compared to 92 percent of the training population as a whole. Finally, after twelve to fifteen months of military service, more than 90 percent received a rating of "excellent" in their conduct and efficiency evaluations.[125]

But interpreted differently, these numbers also indicated that New Standards Men failed basic training at twice the rate of all soldiers and were three times more likely to need extra help. In some cases, the men's performance was so dismal that military service seemed to border on abuse. Veteran Hamilton Gregory wrote that the New Standards man he was asked to babysit during basic training did not know his address, could not distinguish between his right and his left, could not tell the difference between an officer and a sergeant, and proved incapable of memorizing his service number, all of which led to excessive punishment. Nevertheless, after a bit of chicanery on the part of a captain, the man passed basic training and was sent to Vietnam.[126] The failure rate was also "deceptively low," since the army, which demanded less of its recruits than the other services, received the plurality of New Standards men. Closer to 10 percent of the first group of Project 100,000 airmen couldn't pass air force basic training.[127] New Standards men also failed advanced training in more complex subjects such as electrical repair, communications, and clerical specialist at significantly higher rates than higher aptitude men. The washout rate for some subjects ranged as high as 44.6 percent.[128]

The Department of Defense expected this type of result. One report explained, "as anticipated, New Standards men perform significantly better in combat-type training courses and the simpler technical courses." They excelled in specialties that stressed "practical work" and that did not require skill in mathematics or reading. Men who were dropped from particular specialties were not immediately discharged. Rather, they were reassigned to jobs "more suited to their aptitudes."[129] In other words, New Standards men were more likely than the military population as a whole to be assigned to combat roles.[130]

Records on the number of Project 100,000 men who were killed or wounded in action do not appear to have been kept.[131] But casualty rates for African Americans, who disproportionately constituted the enrollment of Project 100,000, were. Between 1965 and 1966, the proportion of black active-duty military rose from 9.1 percent to 9.9 percent. By 1967, African Americans were 12.1 percent of all armed forces accessions and constituted 20 percent of the army.[132] Much of this increase can be attributed to the lowering of induction standards.[133] African American military personnel were more likely to have been drafted than to have enlisted and more likely to have been assigned to the infantry, both because volunteers were more likely to be able to choose their specialty and because low educational levels tended to limit black draftees' options.[134] Thirteen percent of army personnel stationed in Vietnam were black, but 21 percent of soldiers killed in action that year were African American.[135] Democratic congressman Adam Clayton Powell of New York characterized Project 100,000 as "genocide," exclaiming that the "brutal" program was "nothing more than killing off human beings that [were] not elite."[136] Powell's New York colleague, Shirley Chisholm, agreed. She scathingly told the House Armed Services Committee that the program's only benefit was to ease "the draft among the middle class whites."[137]

On the whole, the military failed to meet McNamara's stated goal of social betterment through military service.[138] Most New Standards men left the armed forces without receiving the promised training, as the skills needed for combat did not transfer to civilian life. Instructors, funding, and facilities could not be located to implement basic education classes, and only seventeen thousand of the men were able to take advantage of those that were available.[139] By 1968, the Continental Army Command had banned Project 100,000 personnel from 137 of 237 advanced training courses because, it claimed, the men learned too slowly to meet prerequisites. Only five of the remaining available courses were restructured to better meet their learning styles.[140] Additionally, New Standards men were court-martialed more than twice as often as their counterparts and were twice as likely to be discharged early, frequently on less-than-honorable grounds.[141]

Men who entered the services through Project 100,000 frequently did not know they were part of the program, making their reminiscences hard to find. But John L. Ward, who enlisted in the US Marine Corps as part of the corps' Project 100,000 quota did write about his experiences. He successfully became a squad leader in Vietnam and qualified for a promotion to sergeant upon return to the States, yet he had trouble finding a decent job after discharge. In addition to not receiving any special training, he returned from Vietnam with physical and emotional wounds. Posttraumatic stress disorder, the effects of Agent Orange, and his attempts to self-medicate after discharge, all of which he blamed on his time in the marines, held him back. He characterized Project 100,000 as "morally shameful."[142]

The Pentagon under McNamara's successor, Clark Clifford, continued to defend the program, but Melvin Laird phased it out after he was appointed secretary of defense in 1969. Laird cited the general American drawdown from Vietnam and the Pentagon's imminent shift to an all-volunteer force as reasons.[143] Dissent from officials within the military also played a role in the program's demise.[144]

McNamara and his supporters in the Pentagon conceived of Project 100,000 as a way to use the military as a venue to teach American men how to participate fully in American civilian society. Similarly, Hershey, Wirtz, and other warriors against poverty wanted to use the tools provided by the military procurement system to rehabilitate poor men's defects so that they could become breadwinners and full participants in the American polity. For the most part, these programs did not achieve their goals. In addition to sending many participants into combat in Vietnam rather than training them for useful work in the civilian world, they loosened the connections between military service and male citizenship obligations for many middle-class men.

Publicity surrounding Project 100,000 and the rehabilitation programs explicitly linked the military with poverty and minority status. Publications from the *New Republic* to the *New York Times* to the *Muscatine* [Iowa] *Journal* referred to participants as "rejects" in need of "salvation" and likened the military to a social service organization.[145] The *Chicago Tribune* reported on Clifford's continuing support of Project 100,000 by discussing the new defense secretary's "plan . . . to improve American life" through judicious use of his department's budget. "By applying its conscience," the paper reported, "the Pentagon can provide ghetto employment . . . and education for thousands of young men ill-equipped for work."[146] Such coverage juxtaposed the military with the civilian options open to more well-to-do men. The Baltimore *Evening Sun*, for instance, opened an article on the NCCY's rehabilitation program in Baltimore by highlighting a recent CBS news story about "a private classroom in which young men were being taught how to evade the draft by cunning and devious means." Meanwhile, in an echo of Michael Harrington's famous work on poverty among affluence, men from "the other America," who suffered in conditions of "unemployment, poor health, semi-literacy, and bleak subsistence," struggled to volunteer.[147] Those who utilized the NCCY services, however, "felt new self-respect" and became taxpayers able to "share the load," as "new [men] in uniform."[148] Private counselors taught middle-class boys how to stay out of the military, while federally funded programs helped the poor learn how to enlist. The military might have been sold as a way to achieve "a stable job, status, and independence," but what about the men who already had these things?[149] Such publicity did not mention what the army might offer to them other than an opportunity to work and live with members of American society with whom they were thought to have little in common.

More concretely, Project 100,000 and lowered entrance standards had an incontrovertible effect on those who faced conscription during the years of the Vietnam War. As more men qualified to volunteer for military service, the various branches of service required fewer conscripts to meet their monthly accession quotas. Of the men who were drafted, approximately fifty thousand per year were earmarked for Project 100,000, meaning they had to be from Category IV. As these generally poor and minority men filled open slots, the Selective Service needed fewer white, middle-class men. Men with economic resources had far less to fear from conscription and, after Johnson asked all eighteen-year-olds to be examined as soon as practicable, rarely even had to submit to an early preinduction exam. Because it was assumed that all college students would receive a II-S deferment, young men who claimed they would soon start university training, even in the absence of written confirmation, were not subject to the early exams and therefore not referred to remediation programs even if they could have benefited from rehabilitation.[150] This dichotomy exacerbated the inequities based on social class that already existed within the Selective Service System.

Where publicity surrounding UMT a generation earlier had emphasized the democratic nature of military training and the common citizenship classes all men would take, the programs of the Great Society era focused specifically on the rehabilitation of poor men. The rhetoric of universal citizenship, patriotism, and duty almost completely vanished from the discourse. A few internal memos and *Selective Service* discussed rehabilitation as a way to spread the burden of military service into the poorer classes in a more equitable manner, but planning was accompanied by no such discussion about the wealthier classes.[151] As Wirtz' congressional testimony illustrated, civilian planners felt it more important to emphasize poor men's obligation to contribute economically to American growth. Instead of using military service to teach a common form of masculinity based on duty, honor, and strength, the programs of the 1960s focused on building economic and military strength by creating breadwinners and soldiers among those ill-equipped to fill those obligations of citizenship on their own.

The development of these programs indicated the extent to which national security had, by the early 1960s, come to be defined as a function of economic and domestic strength as well as the ability to use force abroad. That the Selective Service and Department of Defense would, through various rehabilitation programs and Project 100,000, participate in the War on Poverty demonstrated just how intertwined economic and military security had become and how far the Selective Service had gone toward defining civilian pursuits as service to the nation. But as the situation in Vietnam demanded increasing numbers of soldiers after 1965, the rehabilitation aims of the programs got lost. The referral programs shrank, and Project 100,000 became a method to procure military manpower rather than to bolster poor men's qualifications for the civilian labor market. As the Vietnam War drew down in the early 1970s and Lyndon Johnson's successor, Richard Nixon, showed less interest in eradicating poverty, Project 100,000, which was already hated by officers up and down the line, became obsolete. In its explicit focus on preparing poor and minority men for economic citizenship, however, it had unintentionally thinned even further middle-class men's connection between military service and masculine citizenship.

CHAPTER 6

"Choice or Chance"

The Vietnam War, 1965–1973

In the spring of 1970, Harvard undergraduate James Fallows, along with a bus full of MIT and other Harvard students, arrived at the Boston Navy Yard for his preinduction physical. Like most of the other men accompanying him, Fallows received a deferment. With the help of draft counselors, he had spent much of the spring semester searching for a way to beat the military's entrance requirements, ultimately settling on starvation. His six-foot-one body weighed only 120 pounds when he arrived at the Navy Yard, placing him under the Selective Service's cutoff.[1] He joined the more than fifteen million other men of his generation who legally avoided conscription.[2]

Fallows' actions were not particularly unique, but the 1975 article he wrote for *The Washington Monthly* about their implications received wide readership and acclaim. "What Did You Do in the Class War, Daddy?" has been reprinted and cited dozens of times in anthologies and retrospectives about the war. His argument that his behavior—and that of his elite and middle-class cohort—was shameful has become one of the lasting narratives of the era.[3] The article expressed guilt that he and other men of privilege, "the mainly white, mainly well-educated children of mainly comfortable parents," did not use their bodies as a form of protest, either by fighting in Vietnam in greater numbers or by outright resisting the draft.[4] The specter of large numbers of elite men dying in battle or going to jail in protest would have jolted lawmakers into ending the war earlier, he argued.

Meanwhile, he worried that his deferment had caused the deaths of those who were drafted in his place, the "boys from Chelsea . . . the white proles of Boston." He claimed they "walked through the examination lines like so many cattle off to slaughter" right after the Cambridge men had completed their examinations. According to Fallows, "it had clearly never occurred" to these working-class boys "that there might be a way around the draft."[5] Fallows, even if he believed what he wrote, was wrong. As their lackadaisical response to the rehabilitation programs discussed in chapter 5 showed, many working-class men during the Vietnam War did look for ways to avoid the draft, just as men across social classes had during the United States' previous wars. This time, however, those in the lower echelons did not have the same tools available to them that elite and middle-class men possessed. Two-decades' worth of class-based military manpower policies had left working-class men who did not want to serve at a disadvantage.

The story of manpower policy and its effects during the Vietnam War is complicated. On one hand, the process of procuring military manpower during the Vietnam War did not differ significantly from American experiences during World War II and the Korean War. At the outset of the conflict, draft calls were low and local boards had wide latitude to grant deferments. As fighting intensified, draft calls increased, politicizing the question of deferments. Recognizing that the available manpower pool would have to be deepened, Congress held hearings to weigh the needs of various constituencies. Legislators revised the law several times, Presidents Johnson and Nixon signed executive orders, and the Selective Service issued new regulations, all with the goal of tightening deferments.

On the other hand, the Vietnam War occurred within its own specific historical context. The diplomatic, political, and social currents of the mid-1960s and early 1970s uniquely affected how it was perceived and fought. Although most Americans initially supported American engagement in Southeast Asia, their patience with Johnson's policies eroded over time. The draft became one target of protesters. In an attempt to quiet agitators, Congress, at Johnson's urging, replaced the Universal Military Training and Service Act of 1951 with the Military Selective Service Act of 1967. The new law made cosmetic changes to the conscription process, but as a political move it did not work. By 1970, the war had become deeply unpopular. Congress shifted the Selective Service to a lottery system under Richard Nixon in a bid to quell protest. Nixon hoped the change would undermine the arguments of antidraft activists, who stressed the individual's right to make his own choices about whether to serve, but he soon found that most Americans were not willing to accept the inequities they had taken for granted during the militarized peace of the previous decades.

Men's behavior followed a similar pattern as they grappled with their place in the system. In several ways, men behaved much as their forebears had. Many men, of all races and social classes, volunteered for military service, either because they genuinely wanted to serve or under pressure from the draft. Many accepted their draft notices with the same combination of resignation, fear, and anticipation that conscripts have always felt. And many looked for ways to avoid military service, primarily through legal means. As in previous wars, the draft was necessary because most American men did not wish to interrupt their lives or put themselves in harm's way.

Working-class and minority men who wanted to avoid service continued to use whatever tools they had available to them, just as men from all social classes had in earlier wars. Men from these groups questioned the purpose of the Vietnam War, often in greater numbers than their middle-class and elite counterparts. These men, however, often lived in communities that venerated the military values of "brotherhood, team work, bravery and ruggedness" and that had strong traditions of military service during wartime.[6] As a result, those men from these communities who tried to avoid service tended to operate more or less privately. They sought methods to avoid induction as individuals rather than liaising with draft counselors or antiwar organizations. They either did not feel comfortable with middle-class organizations or they did not know about the resources available to them. Unsurprisingly, they also had less success than middle-class men.

Thanks to a decade of manpower channeling, middle-class, mostly white, would-be draft avoiders were more likely than their white working-class and minority brothers to approach military service as a choice. At the outset of military escalation, would-be draft avoiders with means benefited from the Cold War military manpower policies that explicitly broadened their access to deferments. As the federal government curtailed those deferments, these men pushed back with the help of draft counselors, a phenomenon unique to the Vietnam War. They publicly sought new ways to avoid military service rather than acquiesce to the draft as their fathers had.

The Selective Service's policy of manpower channeling worked, but it had unforeseen consequences. What made sense during the militarized peace of the Cold War did not during a hot war. Men like Fallows, whom policymakers previously had identified as more valuable to national security as civilians, neither saw it as their responsibility to serve in the military nor resigned themselves to the prospect when the draft came calling, even as deferments tightened over the course of the war. Instead, with strategies learned from draft counselors, middle-class men learned to work a system designed to encourage them to see military service as a personal choice rather than as an obligation. This focus on choice, not, as Fallows argued, the Chelsea boys' inaction, is what set Fallows and other men like him apart from the working-class men of his age cohort.

When draft calls rose in 1965, Lewis B. Hershey, director of Selective Service, was sanguine. His agency had risen to the challenge of manning wars twice before under his tenure. "The present Selective Service System is not an experiment," he declared.[7] The procedures that had worked in the past were certain to work again, he figured. Hershey acknowledged public criticism, but, he reasoned, the Selective Service had faced down its critics in the past. By 1965, Hershey had been running his agency for twenty-four years. He was seventy-two years old and by all accounts out of touch with the generation of young men coming of age.[8] Hershey understood better than most how the levers of power operated on Capitol Hill, but he did not yet understand the different social and political context of this round of criticism.

As chapter 4 illustrated, conscription had come under increasing fire from some quarters even before the Vietnam buildup. Although a bill for the renewal of the Universal Military Training and Service Act had sailed through Congress in the spring of 1963—it passed the House by a vote of 378 to 3—its passage occurred amongst burgeoning criticism.[9] On the local and state levels, seemingly capricious decisions made by draft boards made good copy and alerted the public to the potential for abuse within the system.[10] Editorials and letters to the editor calling for draft reform appeared in newspapers with increasing regularity.[11]

In September of 1964, Arizona senator and Republican presidential nominee Barry Goldwater launched his campaign by vowing to end conscription.[12] Although the draft failed to become a major campaign issue, pundits and politicians, including influential *New York Times* military affairs editor Hanson W. Baldwin, called for a broader discussion.[13] Members of Congress criticized the draft almost two dozen times from the floor during the 1964 congressional session, approximately the same number of times as they had over the entire preceding decade.[14] The groundswell of discontent prompted Johnson to order Secretary of Defense Robert McNamara to initiate a full study of the draft. He wanted to know if the army still required conscription to fill its ranks.[15]

Hershey remained unperturbed. Most respondents to public opinion polls gave the Selective Service high marks. Even constituencies expected to question its operation, such as college students, approved of the draft by wide margins.[16] Sixty-four percent of Americans polled favored the draft in March 1965, and a full 90 percent held the same position in the late fall.[17] Most Americans were willing to trust the president, both to be tough on North Vietnamese communist aggressors and to use the military responsibly. The draft was a necessary feature of American life, they believed, at least until own their sons received greetings from Uncle Sam.[18]

Between 1965 and 1966, the number of young men being called into service more than tripled.[19] Unsurprisingly, given the United States' experiences in World War II and the Korean War, public discontent increased along with draft calls. Because Johnson wanted to prosecute a limited war and escalate gradually, his administration chose not to launch a public relations campaign selling American military engagement. The president hoped the conflict in Southeast Asia would remain secondary to his Great Society initiatives and that measured escalation would prevent Chinese and Soviet intervention. He did not seek a congressional declaration of war or call up the National Guard or reserves. There was no major cultural outpouring of support.

Although most Americans approved of the president's actions, a decidedly antimilitary thread ran through popular music, television shows, and films during the early years of the war. With every prowar song like Barry Sadler's "Ballad of the Green Berets" came a refutation like Barry McGuire's "Eve of Destruction."[20] Hollywood did not throw itself behind the war effort as it had during World War II. John Wayne's otherwise forgettable *The Green Berets* stands out for its pro-Vietnam War stance.[21] According to an August 1965 profile in *Life* magazine, Johnson's "problem has been to align his people behind him without creating undue alarm." Already, reported the popular weekly, there was "a strong division in America, a feeling that this [was] not our war, that real victory may be impossible."[22]

Criticism of the president's policies and the Pentagon's Vietnam strategy came from all sides. Critics on the right objected to Johnson's limited aim of a noncommunist South Vietnam. Throughout the war, they pushed the Johnson and then Nixon administrations to intensify American intervention by invading the North, lifting limits on aerial bombing, and by deploying nuclear weapons. Those on the left objected for a variety of reasons. At the outset, their protest was relatively limited. Pacifists believed that war could not solve global problems. Some liberals objected to the resources being poured into Southeast Asia that, they believed, should be used to solve domestic problems. Activists of the New Left, especially within Students for a Democratic Society (SDS), claimed that the military incursion into South Vietnam was a sign of American imperialism. By 1966, civil rights activists on the more radical end of the spectrum had expanded the New Left's critique, arguing that the United States used people of color against other people of color to further imperial aims while refusing to support democracy at home. In the words of SNCC chairman Stokely Carmichael, the war was a case of "white people sending black people to make war on yellow people in order to defend the land they stole from red people."[23]

As the war deepened, criticism of American goals and strategies expanded. Turmoil grew within the moderate wing of the civil rights movement, particularly after Martin Luther King Jr. turned on the Johnson administration's Asia policy in 1967.[24] Liberationism as an ideology spread among radicals, who began to openly support the communist National Liberation Front.[25] The AFL-CIO supported the Vietnam War until 1974, but elements of labor turned against the war effort much earlier.[26] Conservatives, meanwhile, split over the war. By 1969, members of the libertarian branch of conservatism had started arguing that the war "encouraged a fascist system in the United States," by stripping individuals of their right to dissent, forcing men to serve in the military, and increasing taxes.[27]

Perhaps most importantly, from the standpoint of the draft, war fatigue grew among nonactivist Americans. Graphic images of injured American soldiers, wounded South Vietnamese children, and burned villages combined with a lack of clear military progress led more and more American citizens to call for a negotiated peace. Polling repeatedly illustrated the instability of American public opinion. In the fall of 1965, 67 percent of respondents in a national Louis Harris poll approved of Johnson's policies, but, of the same group, the proportion of those who desired negotiations with North Vietnam was the same as those who hoped the United States would invade its enemy. By February 1968, just after the Tet Offensive, a plurality of citizens characterized U.S. involvement in South Vietnam as a mistake, but they were not ready to unilaterally pull out.[28] In fact, 70 percent of respondents in a Gallup poll that same month called for an escalation of bombing.[29] By 1971, 58 percent of Americans had crossed over to believing that the war was immoral, but even then they did not agree on how or if the United States should disengage.[30] Explained Harris, "the American people want to honor this country's commitment to the South Vietnamese, but would also like to see the war come to an honorable end as rapidly as possible." Americans were not simply "hawk[s]" or "doves," he continued. Instead, the public squabbled over "the most effective way to win our limited objective and end the fighting."[31]

Americans also squabbled over the best way to man an increasingly beleaguered military. Unsubstantiated stories about the wild lengths to which young men would go to avoid the draft began to circulate, each one more outlandish than the last. Tales abounded of men paying for braces they did not need, tattooing obscenities on their bodies, refusing to shower for weeks prior to induction exams, "fagging it up," shoving items into bodily cavities, faking suicide attempts, or even going to Tijuana for surgery to ruin knees rather than fix them.[32] Newspaper articles with headlines like, "Young Men Dream up Some Ingenious Ways to Avoid the Draft," and "Avoiding the Draft Is Becoming the Favorite Sport Among Youth," horrified Americans who believed military service should be an obligation of male citizenship.[33]

The actions of individual men could be dismissed as the result of misguided youth, but bigger structural problems emerged in articles that profiled the Selective Service System itself. Press coverage painted a portrait of an arbitrary, often disorganized system. *Life* characterized it as "random" and "scattershot."[34] State directors could not keep track of the number of eligible men in their manpower pools. Officials in Wisconsin and New York publicly called their own estimates "meaningless."[35]

Complaints of inequity dogged the system. Damning profiles emerged, including one that exposed the National Football League's practice of pulling strings to enlist players in the National Guard. In an article for *Life* magazine, Maj. Gen. George Gelston Jr. of the Maryland National Guard admitted that the Baltimore Colts had "an arrangement" with him. "When they have a player with a military problem," he explained, "they send him to us."[36] Student deferments became particularly controversial, as their entire Cold War rationale became increasingly suspect. Argued one reporter, "Certainly any system is open to question when it sends one youth into steaming jungles infested with Viet Cong but lets another stay home because he's studying English sonnets at college."[37] The uselessness of sonnets and the cushy life of the student studying them seemed obvious when set against the terrible visuals being sent home from Vietnam. Yet a record 767,935 students took the Selective Service College Qualification Test (SSCQT) after Hershey reinstituted the exam for student deferments in the spring of 1966.[38] The system's negative image only intensified after Hershey allowed protesters who had been arrested to be punitively reclassified as I-A.[39]

As previous chapters have shown, manpower planners during the decade prior to 1965 had crafted a policy that maximized inequality of service, all the while defining it as equitable; in a Cold War environment, they claimed, civilian occupations that earned deferments *were* a form of service equivalent to service in the military. The Selective Service maintained this rationale even as the war escalated through 1966. Daniel O. Omer, deputy director of Selective Service, explained, "the only and overriding consideration is whether the man can contribute more to the Nation as a civilian than he can in the military establishment." A system based on such considerations, he argued, accomplished "fairness and equity . . . between our citizenry and the Nation."[40]

The Vietnam buildup undermined Omer's stated rationale and exposed the flimsy justifications on which planners had based their reasoning. Shrinking the I-A manpower pool was not necessary during an active military conflict, when the armed forces needed more personnel. The job of defending the nation was far more dangerous in war than in peace. The notion that the defense contribution of college students, teachers, engineers, or fathers was equivalent to that of soldiers failed to resonate with the American public once soldiers mobilized into a shooting war. Rational decisions made in the early 1960s, like President Kennedy's decision to move married men without children to a secondary order of call or Hershey's choice to eliminate the SSCQT for college students, felt arbitrary.

Without question, the Vietnam era draft was inequitable. Its intent and its praxis specifically targeted certain segments of the population for military service while releasing others from the same obligation. In 1965 and 1966, this fact was no surprise to anyone familiar with the functioning of the draft. The escalation of the war shined a bright light on what policy makers, politicians, the press, and some Americans had known for years. The policy of manpower channeling, combined with the nascent rehabilitation programs, ensured that poor men were much more likely to serve in the military than affluent ones were.

It was not until 1967, however, that the New Left "discovered" channeling. In January of that year, Peter Henig of the Ann Arbor, Michigan, chapter of Students for a Democratic Society wrote a scathing article on the practice in the organization's newsletter, *New Left Notes*.[41] He quoted widely from a 1965 Selective Service memo that originally had been included in informational orientation kits put out for high school guidance counselors and other interested parties.[42] In the memo, the agency acknowledged using the "club of induction" to "drive" individuals "out of areas considered to be less important" to "areas of greater importance" by granting deferments.[43] The memo's emphasis on the system's capriciousness sparked outrage among antidraft activists at both ends of the political spectrum.[44] Their anger made sense within the context of growing draft calls and increasing evidence of gross inequity, but the practice had existed for more than a decade.

Early academic analyses backed activists' interpretation of elitism in the draft. Studies published during and immediately after the war forcefully argued that men from poorer backgrounds were more likely to serve in the

military, face combat, and die in the line of duty than their wealthier counterparts were. Researchers found that men from poor Chicago neighborhoods were three times as likely to die in combat than those from wealthier
neighborhoods, those from Boston's working-class Dorchester region were
four times as likely to die as those from the city's richer suburbs, and Long
Island's war dead hailed overwhelmingly from working-class backgrounds.[45]
Republican congressman Alvin O'Konski found that 100 percent of the
inductees surveyed from his northern Wisconsin district came from families earning less than $5,000 per year.[46] Another investigation concluded that
8 percent of American combat deaths were of men from towns with fewer
than one thousand inhabitants even though only 2 percent of the American
population resided in towns of that size.[47]

Later responses to these data took issue with the studies' small sample sizes
and lack of methodological scope. As those involved in Johnson and McNamara's rehabilitation programs had pointed out, the poorest of the poor failed
induction exams at disturbingly high rates. Those at the bottom of the socioeconomic ladder, therefore, were just as likely to avoid military service as
those at the top.[48] Military sociologists Neil Fligstein and David Segal argued
that educational attainment rather than socioeconomic status determined a
man's chances of seeing service. High school graduates were the most likely
to serve, followed by men with some high school or some college.[49] Fligstein,
in fact, argued against received wisdom, claiming that the more educated a
man's father, the higher the probability that the man would serve in the military.[50] Scholars, therefore, at the time and since, failed to agree on how deeply
class biases ran through the Selective Service or the military as a whole.

How inequitably military service was distributed is notoriously difficult
to measure. The Department of Defense did not keep records relating to soldiers' socioeconomic status during the Vietnam era.[51] Nor did it keep records
on soldiers from racial minorities other than African Americans.[52] Therefore,
most available evidence is either anecdotal or backfilled from later studies.
Which years scholars chose to study affected how they interpreted their data.
Congress made major revisions to the laws governing the draft in 1967 and
1969 with an eye both toward lessening inequity and increasing equality of
service. These changes, which will be discussed below, were partially successful. Inequity of service decreased between 1964 and 1973. But different
scholars defined their samples differently. Some studies focused solely on
draftees. Others included volunteers as well, based on the supposition that
draft-motivated enlistees could not be separated from conscripts. The picture changes based on whether one looks at the whole war or simply part of
it, the entire military or just draftees.

Scholars do agree, however, that how a man ended up in the military mattered. Conscripts were significantly more likely to be assigned to combat positions than were volunteers. Ninety percent of draftees mobilized to Vietnam at a time when the military stationed 75 percent of its personnel elsewhere around the world. Seventy percent of combat assignments went to inductees, who constituted more than 80 percent of Vietnam's infantry riflemen.[53] But, as sociologist Roger Little has shown, when one considers total military participation rather than simply those who were drafted, military representation was much more equitable. The question was one of "choice or chance," he explained. Men could either volunteer for a service branch with "minimal combat risk," as many middle- and upper-income men did in response to the options channeling created for them, or they could take their chances with induction, the most common option available to working-class men.[54]

The example of African American soldiers proves Little's point. Between 1965 and 1972, the proportion of black personnel in all branches of service hovered between 9.1 and 11.1 percent, with the highest proportion in the army. Approximately 12 percent of all American combat deaths during the war were those of black men. These statistics are generally comparable to the proportion of blacks in the American population as a whole.[55] Moreover, since African American men were much more likely than any other segment of the population to fail their induction exams, they were almost 20 percent *less* likely to serve in the armed forces than were their white counterparts. *Eligible* black men, however, were much *more* likely to be drafted than eligible white men. They were less likely to obtain deferments for education, occupation, or conscientious objection. African Americans made up almost 40 percent of Project 100,000 men, who in turn made up almost one-quarter of all military accessions.[56] Sixteen percent of all men drafted during the war were black, a statistic out of proportion with the general population.[57] Within the army alone—the branch of service that took the vast majority of conscripts—26 percent of black enlisted personnel had combat assignments, a number well out of sync with the percentage of African Americans in the American population at large. This statistic is tempered, however, by the fact that black men were more likely than white men to volunteer for dangerous assignments with better pay.[58] So, although 16 percent of combat deaths during the first part of the war were black men, it is unclear whether this disproportionately high number stemmed from racist practices, classist policies, men's own choices, or some combination of all three.[59]

Ultimately, however, the perception of inequity—or perhaps of choices inequitably distributed—fired protest more than the statistical proof of its existence. Throughout the war years, members of the African American community had the impression that black men were unfairly sent to the slaughter, even as casualty rates equalized over time.[60] Chicanos had a similar impression. The Pentagon did not create the racial identifier of "Hispanic" until 1978, although members of the community knew their men were dying in large numbers.[61] The question became what to do about the situation.

Some detractors of the Selective Service, including many who supported America's war aims, wanted to push public debate beyond the technical aspects of the draft. They focused on the very purpose of compulsory military service. National conferences that attracted scholars, policy experts, and politicians were held in 1966 and 1967 in Washington, D.C., at Antioch College in Ohio, and at the University of Chicago.[62] Academic studies critical of the Selective Service began to appear, as did similar books meant for a general audience.[63] The proposals that emerged from all these venues ran the gamut, ranging from ending the draft entirely to implementing a plan of universal service.

Most critics, however, acknowledged that the system of Selective Service could not be drastically changed while the country was in the middle of an armed conflict. If nothing else, fear of conscription spurred up to 40 percent of volunteers to join the military.[64] Department of Defense statistics indicated that the number of volunteers dropped drastically whenever the press mentioned even rumors of the end of the draft. Those parts of the 1964 Pentagon study that became public suggested that McNamara liked the idea of an all-volunteer force but found it impractical. He maintained that pay increases alone would not offset the loss of personnel if the draft were ended.[65] Realistic proposals to overhaul the Selective Service, therefore, came to focus on the questions of efficiency and equity.

Complaints about structural inefficiencies were ubiquitous. In George Q. Flynn's words, "local boards were an anachronism." They almost universally consisted of older, white, male veterans with no special qualifications other than business and political connections.[66] Regulations varied by state. In 1965, for example, Indiana deferred science and engineering graduate students while Missouri classified all graduate students as eligible.[67] In almost all cases, board members had trouble keeping track of changes in regulations. In some cases, they simply ignored the guidelines provided to them by national and state headquarters.[68]

Calling the oldest available man was inefficient. The Selective Service kept men in limbo from the day they turned eighteen until at least their twenty-sixth birthdays. The average age of induction nationwide fluctuated based on manpower needs. Local averages varied based on how many I-A men were available in any given place. Men found it hard to plan. Moreover, their classifications changed over time. Each individual's file had to be re-evaluated every time he moved, stopped or started school, changed jobs, became injured, healed, enlisted, married, divorced, or became a father. If the youngest available men were conscripted first, reasoned critics, local boards' work would become much simpler. Each man would have one or two years of prime draft liability in his late teens, but then he would be free to plan his life without the interference of the Selective Service.

Decentralization also created problems. National headquarters distributed draft quotas to state directors based on the expected number of available men in each state, a number that could not be tracked in real time, given men's constantly shifting classification status. State headquarters then assigned quotas to individual boards, which called men in the order they were available. But this meant that some localities dove more deeply into their pools than others, a phenomenon that tended to favor urban areas with more residents over sparsely populated rural counties.[69] Reformers called for centralization and computerization in order to equalize draft calls around the country.

Hershey, as director, roundly rebuffed almost all proposals for change. He hated the idea of a lottery, which he characterized as the "substitution of chance for judgment." Centralization and data processing, he argued, would eliminate the personal touch local boards provided. "I have . . . more confidence, and I am willing to put up with the mistakes of the local board . . . who can look into all the facts, than I have in a computer," he grumped to Congress. He rejected any proposal that lessened the power of local boards. That different boards in different locales would reach different conclusions in similar cases, to Hershey, was part of the appeal of the system. Local boards understood their own local conditions better than any centralized bureaucrat. Other institutions did not demand complete consistency and neither should the Selective Service. "I can't . . . find an educational institution that has the same rules in the different departments, let alone the same as other educational institutions," he opined. "Liberty and uniformity" were simply not compatible.[70]

Other stakeholders disagreed with Hershey, but they also disagreed on what should be done. In February of 1967, two federal commissions released reports on Selective Service reform. President Johnson had convened the National Advisory Commission on Selective Service the previous summer, naming as chair Burke Marshall, a former assistant attorney general and head of the Justice Department's Civil Rights Division under President Kennedy. Johnson granted him wide latitude to examine every possible alternative to conscription in the United States. Democrat L. Mendel Rivers, the chair of the House Armed Services Committee, responded by creating a second panel, the Civilian Advisory Panel on Military Manpower Procurement, headed by retired general Mark Clark. The two committees released their reports within weeks of each other. Both agreed that the United States needed Selective Service, but beyond that, they concurred on very little.

Marshall and Clark fundamentally disagreed on how the draft related to national security. The Marshall Commission, as it came to be known, advocated a massive overhaul of the Selective Service System, including more centralization, a shift to selection via lottery rather than age, and the elimination of almost all further student and occupational deferments. As the report's title, *In Pursuit of Equity: Who Serves When Not All Serve?*, illustrated, Marshall focused on how the burden of military service could be distributed more equitably throughout the young American populace.[71] To the authors of the report, security derived from a commitment to fixing America's internal divisions and inequalities. Clark, on the other hand, saw the defeat of external aggressors as more important. So long as the Selective Service could effectively deliver men into uniform, small changes would be sufficient. The Clark committee rejected centralization, selection by lottery, and the elimination of student and occupational deferments. "It is patent that any 'selective' system inherently contains inequities," Clark's report explained, and thus the defense goals of conscription needed to be paramount.[72] Its members expressed the belief that the Selective Service System already operated reasonably well in its goal of procuring military manpower.

These divisions appeared at the spring 1967 congressional hearings examining the draft. The different assumptions made by the men chairing these hearings became apparent immediately. Georgia Democrat Richard B. Russell, chair of the Senate Armed Services Committee, aligned himself with Hershey and the Clark report. He opened his proceedings by declaring it "unwise to make changes just for the sake of change" or because "there may be dissent over . . . military activities in southeast Asia." He hoped his hearings would provide a forum to find "a solution that provide[d] what the United States need[ed]" rather than a place to become "excessively preoccupied with details and alleged inequities."[73] Senator Joseph S. Clark, chair of the Subcommittee on Employment, Manpower, and Poverty of the Committee on Labor and Public Welfare, on the other hand, declared himself an ally of those who wished to use the draft for domestic purposes. He clearly preferred the Marshall Commission's report. Before turning his hearings over to Massachusetts Democrat Edward Kennedy, Senator Clark declared that the United States deserved "better than a purely military revision of the draft."

He hoped Congress could eliminate the "inequities and injustices" of the current system and help the Selective Service "make its own specific contribution to the economic health and internal strength" of the nation. Kennedy, who led the hearings, continued by emphasizing the importance of preventing the Selective Service from upsetting "the priorities imbeded [sic] in other, more broad policies for developing the capabilities" of American men.[74] In short, just as had been the case since World War II, politicians disagreed on the purpose of military service. Congress and the American populace had no shared aim to rally behind and no shared conception of the relationship between citizenship and military service.

In June, Congress replaced the Universal Military Training and Service Act with the Military Selective Service Act of 1967. The new law leaned heavily on General Clark's less controversial slate of recommendations. It prohibited reversing the order of call so that the youngest rather than oldest available man would be called first, and it did not randomize calls through a lottery or centralize draft quotas. In an effort to prevent privileged men from pyramiding deferments, it forbade anyone who had taken a student deferment from later claiming a dependency deferment. It did not, however, eliminate deferments for undergraduates or graduate students. In fact, in order to quash controversy surrounding the administration of the SSCQT, it automatically granted II-S deferments to all full-time undergraduates, regardless of test scores or class rank. It also allowed the National Security Council to make recommendations relating to deferments for graduate study. It did nothing to alter occupational or dependency deferments.

Hershey was elated.[75] He viewed the new law as a validation of his agency. To him, a few tweaks for the sake of political expediency made sense so long as the law preserved the autonomy of local boards. But the new Selective Service Act satisfied almost no one else. Its hodgepodge of reforms eliminated some uncertainty from the lives of individual men, but it provided no clear window onto American strategic priorities. The glut of available men created by the baby boom combined with Johnson's limited aims in Southeast Asia meant that neither Congress nor the Selective Service needed legislation that maximized military participation. Legislators affirmed the Selective Service's right to channel men by maintaining deferments for fathers, upholding occupational deferments for men in professional fields, and expanding the availability of undergraduate deferments. Yet it also circumscribed that right by limiting the pyramiding of certain deferments, a move that undermined the national security rationale on which channeling was based. The law, in other words, was a response to competing public complaints rather than a coherent manpower policy designed to defeat communism at home and abroad. The Military Selective Service Act of 1967 did little to limit antidraft activism.

In the years that followed, Congress, President Johnson, and then President Nixon continued to have to address complaints of inequity. Johnson had hoped that Congress would instate a lottery in 1967.[76] It did not, preferring instead the minor adjustments to the system recommended by the Clark Commission. Yet as the war became more and more unpopular, more and more men balked at the prospect of having to fight it, leading to further charges of inequity and occasionally of outright abuse. In October of 1967, following a national Stop the Draft Week, Hershey reminded local boards that any "illegal activity" that interfered with "recruiting or cause[d] refusal of duty in the military . . . could not by any stretch of the imagination be construed as being in support of the national interest." In other words, he implied that local boards should look to reclassify as available any man who participated in protest activities, not just those who broke the law by not reporting for induction or by destroying their draft cards. Activists and nonactivists alike continued to wonder why some men should have to go while others were released from that obligation. Public opinion polls on the Selective Service fluctuated by locality, but overall trends showed a populace losing faith in its draft system.[77]

Johnson and then Nixon continued to try to defuse antidraft protest. In February 1968, Johnson, at the urging of the National Security Council, eliminated graduate deferments for all men except those in the medical and allied fields starting with the 1968–69 academic year. Nixon then went on to make a number of changes. His administration, with the help of Democrats like Senator Kennedy, pushed for the diversification of local board membership. Nixon also tried to fire the seventy-five-year-old Hershey, who had become a lightning rod for criticism from antiwar and antidraft activists. But "like an embarrassing corpse in a murder mystery" that "kept falling out of closets or appearing in bathtubs to the general consternation of the host," Hershey refused to disappear gracefully.[78] He enjoyed congressional support and did not wish to retire. It took close to a year of political maneuvering to finally replace the venerable general with bureaucrat Curtis Tarr, a former academic and assistant secretary of the Air Force. Nixon suspended draft calls in November and December 1969 while Congress amended the Selective Service Act of 1967 to allow for a lottery. When the draft resumed in January 1970, the Selective Service called men based on their random sequence number (RSN), or lottery number, rather than in the chronological order of their birthdates. In the spring of 1970, Nixon ended by executive order all new occupational and fatherhood deferments except those for extreme hardship.[79]

Nixon meant these changes to sweep the legs out from underneath anti-draft protesters by eliminating the sources of their discontent. In some regards, he was successful. Equity of military service across races and social classes increased with each passing year of his administration, even as overall participation rates declined. American force levels in South Vietnam dropped with the implementation of Vietnamization, necessitating lower draft calls. Fewer men faced conscription, and those with high lottery numbers rested easy. On the other hand, the antiwar movement was much larger than simply those Americans who did not like the draft. Nixon's widening of the war into Cambodia and Laos prompted its growth and diversification.

All American men, when faced with the prospect of military service in war-time, had to figure out their place in the system. Some volunteered for the armed forces out of a general desire to support democracy and fight communism. Manuel Marin enlisted in the navy as a way of "paying off" his debt of gratitude to the United States for welcoming him from Mexico.[80] Mike Cranford of Morenci, Arizona, joined up because it was part of his "duty as a man," what he was "supposed to do."[81] Kenneth Korkow wanted to experience "the ultimate risk" after a childhood reared on John Wayne and G.I. Joe.[82] Rochester, Pennsylvania, native John Neely claimed that draft avoidance "never really even entered my mind." He chose to "make the best" of military service.[83] Danny Cruz of Tulsa, Oklahoma, stated simply, "I believed it was my duty to serve my country."[84]

Others, primarily those from working-class backgrounds, either enlisted or let themselves be drafted because they had no viable educational or occupational options in the civilian world. Sociologist Charles Moskos called unemployment the real manpower channeler. Lack of opportunity pushed men into uniform.[85] Eddie Rodriguez, a high school graduate from Corcoran, California, had no way of attending college and did not want to end up an itinerant agricultural worker. His father encouraged him to enlist.[86] A judge told Bruce Johnson that he could either go to jail or join the military, so he "just went to La Crosse [Wisconsin] and enlisted."[87] Ted A. Burton of Hawkins County, Tennessee, couldn't get a job with his I-A status, so he volunteered for the draft.[88] Stanley Goff "just succumbed." His friend, Bob Sanders, had a pregnant fiancée, which would have earned him a III-A deferment, but Sanders did not know this, so he allowed himself to be sworn in.[89] Dwight Reiland of Clarion, Iowa, and Chuck Hommes of Whitensville, Massachusetts, did not want to "run away" to Canada, which was the only option they could think of.[90] "I didn't know how else to get myself out of the mess I was in except to leave the country," explained Hommes.[91]

Hommes' dilemma characterized the experience of many working-class men. Within their communities, military service tended to be valued, and the draft—the government's call to national defense—was not something open to question. Historian Christian Appy posited that middle-class men "wrestled with the moral dilemma of whether or not to avoid the draft," but, he argued, "most working-class draftees did not see the matter as open to debate. For them, the draft notice represented an order, not a dilemma."[92] Loren Baritz contended that most working-class men "thought of the draft as an event like measles, a graduation, the weather, something that happened to people."[93] Its pull was inexorable. Yet when men like Hommes did harbor doubts, they could not marshal the same resources as middle-class men to legally avoid induction. They lacked access to the information that may have helped them gain deferments and save face within their communities.

Contrary to popular belief, many working-class men did try to avoid military service during the Vietnam War. Although they may not have considered running away an acceptable option, getting rejected by the system was another matter. But in attempting to do so, they tended to use the methods previous generations had used. In particular, they operated more or less privately or perhaps in consultation with a few friends or family members. They did not advertise their positions or work with the broader antiwar movement. Instead, they took advantage of the resources they had. Herbert De La Fuente, for example, recounted a friend's experience of going to a *curandera*, or native healer, who promised to help him fail his physical.[94] A sympathetic medical doctor might have been more effective but was not a figure available to De La Fuente's friend.

Poorer men were also much more likely than wealthier men to vanish from the Selective Service System. Because the system had no record of the names of men who turned eighteen each year, it had no way of tracking men who failed to register. Scholars have estimated that somewhere between two and three million men never identified themselves to the Selective Service.[95] Most were poor; almost half were black.[96] This option worked best for those who could operate outside of the federal bureaucracy, since prospective employers could ask about draft status and prior military service. Men under age twenty-six could be asked to produce their draft cards at job interviews, which made this option almost impossible for those seeking employment through regular channels. Men who had given up in the face of structural unemployment or who worked within a city's underground economy could risk this choice more easily.

Similarly, men already in the system frequently ignored induction orders. One 1970 Selective Service study indicated that 5.6 percent of the nearly thirty-seven thousand men called for induction nationally in April of that year failed to report. A few had legitimate excuses, such as a sudden hospitalization or car accident on the way to the induction exam, but the vast majority simply vanished.[97] In some localities, proportions of no-shows ran much higher. In such diverse locales as St. Petersburg, Florida, New York City, and the entire state of Oregon, close to half of registrants never appeared. Seventy-five percent of men called for induction in Puerto Rico failed to report. In 1968, twenty-three states could not meet their induction quotas.[98] Again, most of these men were working-class or of minority background and had less to lose from the potential consequences of going on the lam.

Aside from ignoring the Selective Service, anyone with access to a newspaper could learn how to take advantage of certain types of legal deferments, at least as long as they were available. For instance, in the summer of 1965, President Johnson issued an executive order eliminating deferments for men without children who married after August 26. As a result, couples across social classes rushed to the altar to make the deadline.[99] Men who married after that date—and many who married before it—then went on to deliberately conceive children in order to secure a paternity deferment. The birthrate for first children among young marrieds across social classes spiked significantly exactly one year after Johnson's order.[100] As previous chapters have shown, these tactics were not new.

During the Vietnam War, however, largely as a legacy of channeling, men with means could access almost all types of legal deferments much more easily than those men without means. For example, any man with a willing partner could theoretically obtain a dependency deferment, but Selective Service regulations required that a father maintain a "bona fide" relationship with his children. In other words, he had to be able to support his family financially, which was not always immediately possible for men in lowered circumstances.

Student deferments almost exclusively belonged to the more affluent. Men had to qualify for higher education and be able to pay for it. Those who sought II-S deferments had to possess the educational prerequisites to enter postsecondary programs and financial stability. Since part-time students did not receive deferments, men could not take semesters off to earn tuition money or recover from academic probation. Those men who did qualify for student deferments held on to them with both hands. The absolute number of students deferred increased by more than one million between 1965 and 1966.[101] Scholars have estimated that men trying to avoid military service drove up college attendance rates by 4 to 6 percent during the early years of the Vietnam draft.[102]

Moreover, once college men graduated, they sought jobs that would help them gain occupational deferments. In New York City, for example, male college graduates constituted 85 percent of the participants in short-term teacher training programs. Male undergraduates flooded the City University elementary education program.[103] The field of engineering saw a similar glut of qualified men.[104] Nationally, rates of graduate school attendance rose until 1968, when Johnson revoked most graduate deferments. Male enrollment then dropped again, except at medical schools and divinity schools, whose students retained their deferred status.[105] All these options required financial and educational resources. Most eligible occupations skewed toward those with college degrees, a fact that privileged middle-class white men in an era when only 5 percent of African American men attended college.[106]

The National Guard, reserves, and Reserve Officers Training Corps (ROTC) similarly served as draft havens for men with means. A 1966 Pentagon study found that 71 percent of reservists enlisted for draft-motivated reasons.[107] By 1970, it was 90 percent.[108] Waiting lists numbered more than one hundred thousand by 1968 but then vanished with the instatement of the lottery as men with high RSNs withdrew their applications.[109] In theory, any man who met requirements was eligible to enlist in the National Guard or reserves if a slot was available. In reality, however, openings overwhelmingly went to more affluent men with better connections, particularly white men. On average only 2 percent of slots went to African Americans nationwide. Numbers were worse in the South. In 1969, only one of the more than ten thousand members of the Mississippi National Guard was black in a state where 42 percent of the population was African American.[110] Since each state controlled its own National Guard selection process, those with political connections were able to pull strings. The cohort that joined the Texas Air National Guard with George W. Bush, for example, included "the son of a congressman, the sons of two U.S. Senators, and seven members of the Dallas Cowboys."[111]

ROTC was almost as elite. Although the 1964 ROTC Vitalization Act had authorized the expansion of scholarships to cadets, only men with the educational resources to be accepted into college could take advantage of these scholarships. Moreover, the law put a ceiling on the number of scholarships each branch of service could offer and limited those scholarships to men who entered ROTC as freshmen. Anyone who, for example, began their postsecondary educational career at a community college and then transferred into a four-year institution was not eligible for tuition assistance from ROTC. At least half of ROTC's enrollment during the war years came from men looking to avoid the draft. Some schools' units used the promise of

FIGURE 6.1. Student protest of ROTC. Iowa State University students turned their anger over the deaths of four students at Kent State University and their animus at the Vietnam War against ROTC cadets in a protest on May 6, 1970. Ironically, most of the cadets pictured here, like the majority of ROTC cadets nationwide, likely had signed on as a way to avoid the draft. Photo courtesy of Iowa State University Library Special Collections and University Archives.

delay to "woo . . . university students." The University of Pittsburgh's Army ROTC unit advertised itself with a poster reading, "Want to Beat the Draft? Enroll in the 2-Year ROTC Program." After the Nixon administration instituted the lottery, concluded the Pentagon, at least one-third of cadets, most with high numbers that insulated them from conscription, quit their ROTC programs, including Bill Clinton.[112] He mailed letters to his draft board and ROTC recruiter on December 3, 1969, two days after receiving a high number in the first lottery drawing.[113]

Channeling, in other words, worked, but it had unintended consequences. Between 1965 and roughly 1968, affluent men used all the avenues channeling had opened to avoid military service. They joined the reserves, the National Guard, and ROTC. They went to and stayed in college and graduate school. They married and had children. They chose professional occupations that would earn them deferments. They made choices for themselves, even if they did not always recognize their actions as independent decisions. Rodney Wayne, a 1966 graduate of a high school in a "middle-middle-class" community in coastal New Jersey, joined the Naval Reserve in 1967. Later, he reflected, "At that time you couldn't do what the hell you wanted . . . you were either in college or married or ran off to Canada or went into the service." But his decision to enlist was a *choice* he made to avoid Vietnam, a war he "did not care much for." In fact, a case study of twenty-five of Wayne's white, middle-class, male classmates revealed that ten received deferments, twelve joined the reserves or National Guard, and one enlisted in the Coast Guard. Only two served a one-year stint in Vietnam with the army, and neither were in combat positions. All of them were able to use their educations and social capital to make the choices that allowed them to stay out of combat.[114]

Prior to the escalation of the Vietnam War, the Selective Service, with the support of Congress and the presidents, lauded these men's decisions. These categories of deferments lowered the national age of induction, removed men from the eligible manpower pool, and ensured that those left as I-A faced a greater risk of induction, which, in turn, motivated eligible men to enlist, proving that Selective Service worked. Moreover, those who received these deferments supposedly served in the domestic Cold War, protecting American society by entering privileged fields and supporting a particular middle-class, breadwinning, consumerist lifestyle. As these avenues of deferment were cut off one by one, however, the middle-class men accustomed to taking advantage of such exemptions proved unwilling to give up the deferments that had been all but guaranteed during peacetime.

The focus on personal choice encouraged by the Selective Service's policy of manpower channeling enabled the draft counseling that became one of the unique hallmarks of Vietnam-era draft evasion. Between 1965 and 1967 draft counseling was a radical undertaking. Activists from the New Left and the civil rights movement, avowed pacifists, and a small group of war resisters, who hoped to challenge the Vietnam War and the Selective Service by directly and publicly refusing induction, conducted most of the counseling available.[115] After Students for a Democratic Society "discovered" channeling and the legislative revisions of 1967, however, draft counseling expanded rapidly and lost much of its radical edge. Counselors, operating within an antiwar environment but who generally held more mainstream political views, reframed the deferments guaranteed by law into a right each man deserved.

Within this context, Nixon's attempts to quell antiwar and antidraft protest—replacing Hershey, shrinking draft calls, and limiting deferments—turned out to be the equivalent of Band-Aids on a gaping wound. Unlike their fathers after deferments had tightened in 1943, affluent men of the Vietnam generation did not acquiesce to the draft. As they lost the protections that they had grown to expect, they developed new tools and strategies to avoid conscription. A handful of men, as acts of protest, destroyed their draft cards or found a way to return them to local draft boards, the Department of Justice, or the Pentagon. But many more turned to the mini "beat-the-draft" industry that emerged in the late 1960s. Some doctors and psychiatrists, sensing financial opportunity, turned their offices into letter-writing factories.[116] More commonly, as was the case for Donald Trump, family doctors and specialists wrote sympathetic letters for the men under their care.[117] Books, radio shows, courses at experimental colleges, and newspaper columns offered advice for getting out of service.[118] With the help of draft counselors trained to find and exploit loopholes in a system purposely designed to maximize means of evasion, middle- and upper-class men continued to foil the system.

Antiwar and antidraft activists established a loosely affiliated national network during the Vietnam era, opening counseling centers in church basements, civic centers, college unions, private homes, and rented office space in every state in the union. Run by pacifists, war resisters, civil rights activists, college students, and unaffiliated private citizens, these centers offered young men information on the Selective Service's policies and procedures. Trained counselors proffered advice, directed counselees to sympathetic doctors and psychiatrists, helped men fill out applications for conscientious objector status, referred men to lawyers, and connected them to refugee networks in Canada. They operated openly, advertised publicly, published pamphlets and books for those who did not live in close proximity to their services, and corresponded with young men throughout the United States and abroad. According to one survey, by the end of the war, at least 25 percent of all respondents had asked a trained counselor for advice on how to beat the draft.[119]

Much of this growth can be attributed to the Central Committee for Conscientious Objectors (CCCO). Pacifists had founded the organization in 1948, after the post–World War II reinstatement of the draft. Under the leadership of luminary A. J. Muste, the CCCO had spent the previous two decades focused on issues related to conscription, particularly helping young men without a traditionally religious upbringing.[120] It established a counseling center in Philadelphia, where it was based, started a training program for draft counselors, raised funds to bail out resisters who had been jailed, and filed legal claims challenging the constitutionality of the draft.[121] Its membership and clientele had fluctuated with political developments. It grew precipitously during the Korean War, distributing seven thousand copies of the first edition of its book, *Handbook for Conscientious Objectors*, and then contracted significantly after the armistice.[122] In

1960, CCCO counselors corresponded with 375 men seeking conscientious objector status.[123] In 1961, thanks in part to the Berlin crisis, they corresponded with 1,800.[124] In absolute numbers, however, the CCCO remained fairly small and narrowly focused on sincere conscientious objectors.

The Vietnam War provided the CCCO with new purpose. The organization opened a second office in San Francisco in 1966 to continue the direct counseling and referral services undertaken in its Philadelphia office. Its third office, renamed the Midwest Committee for Draft Counseling (MCDC), opened in Chicago in 1968. Rather than counsel clients directly, staff members at MCDC helped organize and train draft counselors throughout the Midwest. Regional offices also opened in Atlanta and Denver before the end of the war. All of these offices developed extensive outreach to individuals and organizations looking to advise registrants. By 1969, its newsletter had more than forty thousand subscribers, and the *Handbook for Conscientious Objectors* had entered its twelfth edition. More than four hundred thousand copies were in print.[125] By mid-war, the CCCO fielded more than ten thousand requests for advice annually, referring many men to the more than twelve hundred counselors it had trained by 1968.[126]

The CCCO, however, was only the tip of the iceberg. In April 1967, the Wisconsin Draft Resistance Union established a Draft Resistance Clearing House following a conference at Columbia University. Its stated purpose was to "collect, distill, and disseminate information about specific draft resistance activities and developments," especially draft counseling.[127] Members corresponded with activists around the country. A list of cooperating counseling centers included locations in every state in the union and Puerto Rico.[128] Other organizations working with draft counselors included the Fellowship of Reconciliation, the Women's International League for Peace and Freedom, the War Resisters League, the Catholic Peace Fellowship, the Episcopal Peace Fellowship, the American Friends Service Committee, the American Lutheran Church, the Jewish Peace Fellowship, Women Strike for Peace, the United Church of Christ, and the National Black Draft Resistance Union.[129] In many instances, concerned citizens or student groups simply hung out a shingle.[130] Parent activists, in locales from Des Moines to Milwaukee to New York City, advocated for the addition of draft counseling in local public high schools.[131] They succeeded in Philadelphia, San Francisco, and Great Neck and Old Bethpage, New York, and in the Diocese of Worcester, Massachusetts, where schools either hired draft counselors or provided guidance counselors with dedicated training on Selective Service regulations.[132]

As a whole, draft counselors rejected the civic republican idea that military service was an obligation of citizenship, particularly during a war they defined as immoral. "Military service is not compulsory," explained one counseling broadside. "Your country can ask you to serve but it cannot force you: personal liberty is not bought with military service, it resides in the right and obligation to choose for oneself."[133] Like critics of UMT a generation earlier, draft counselors defined the military as an institution that broke men rather than made them. It turned them into "cogs" in a militarist machine.[134] The best way to resist the "dehumanization" of the military was to secure the rights guaranteed by law "if one [knew] about them."[135] Each individual, rather than the Selective Service or government at large, had the right to decide his own future.

In order to make informed decisions, therefore, men needed to understand all the legal and extra-legal options available to them, as well as the consequences associated with each choice. By law, counselors could not advise men to avoid registration, refuse induction, fake an ailment, flee to Canada, or take any other illegal action. They could, however, make men aware that these options existed, even if choosing them might lead to arrest or exile. "We feel that no man should submit to the draft out of fear," wrote Dan Swinney of the Wisconsin Draft Resistance Union. "Every man should know all of his legal rights and alternatives, and then he should make a *decision* based on knowledge and convictions. . . . You don't jump off a bridge unless you have mighty good reasons."[136]

During the Vietnam years, much of the fight over individual rights took place within the court system, as organizations like the CCCO and their affiliated attorneys filed cases and briefs on behalf of men who felt the system violated their right to due process.[137] Because of the way Congress had constructed the laws governing Selective Service, the courts did not have jurisdiction to revise individuals' classification status. Men had to use the administrative appeal process outlined in the law for that purpose. Once administrative avenues had been exhausted, however, registrants could use the courts to try to prove that the Selective Service had not followed the law. The courts repeatedly upheld the rights of registrants in cases where local boards did not follow their own administrative procedures.[138] For example, if a man could show that he had been called for induction before someone who should have been called before him, the induction order could be voided. In one case, a local board had to drop a man's induction because it had not informed him of the availability of Selective Service advisers, a right that the 1967 law guaranteed.[139] In a bid to protect the right to free speech, the Supreme Court also ruled that men could not be punitively reclassified as I-A as a result of participating in protest activity.[140]

Two particular Supreme Court cases supported by the CCCO had an out-sized impact on middle-class men looking to avoid military service. *United States v. Seeger* challenged the Selective Service's interpretation of the portion of the Universal Military Training and Service Act of 1951 that required COs to object to all wars based on their "relation to a Supreme Being." Local boards took this to mean a belief in God and denied men CO status if they failed to relate their religious beliefs to that God. In 1965, the Supreme Court ruled that Congress had used the phrase "Supreme Being" as a synonym for "religious training and belief" and had wanted to "embrace all religions." The *Seeger* decision, therefore, meant that any man with a "sincere and meaningful" religious objection to all wars could qualify for conscientious objector status, regardless of whether or not he professed an organized religion or had been officially educated in his religion.[141]

When Congress revised the Selective Service Act in 1967, it replaced the "Supreme Being" language. Under the new law, a man could be exempted from combat service "by reason of religious training and belief," a phrase explicitly defined in the act to exclude "essentially political, sociological, or philosophical views or a merely personal moral code."[142] In the 1970 case *Welsh v. United States*, the Supreme Court found this distinction a violation of the Establishment Clause of the First Amendment as it allowed those with "theistic" beliefs exemption from military service but not those whose belief emanated "from a purely moral, ethical, or philosophical source." In other words, the law, as written, required religious belief in order to qualify as a conscientious objector.[143]

In 1971, the Supreme Court reaffirmed that conscientious objectors had to object to all wars, not just those that individuals found immoral or politically suspect, but even so, the *Seeger* and *Welsh* decisions opened the floodgates to CO claims.[144] The number of annual applications submitted rose from approximately 18,000 in 1964 to more than 40,000 in 1970.[145] During the war, more than 170,000 registrants qualified for CO status, exceeding both the World War II total and proportion of draft-eligible men.[146] In 1972, when the United States was in the midst of a drawdown in Vietnam, more men were classified as COs than were inducted into the military.[147]

More to the point, confusion as to how to interpret the Supreme Court decisions left open the possibility that local boards would become lenient or make mistakes. Counselors encouraged men to appeal their classifications in almost all cases where local boards rejected applications for deferments. They justified this flood of appeals based on the law. "The fact is," wrote activist Peter Elbow, "the same law and government which seem to condemn conscientious objection specifically invite the draft age man to plead it and sanction his doing so."[148] Appeals took time, but they were every man's right. As Arlo Tatum, the CCCO executive secretary, explained, "It is better to be confronted with 'you do not qualify' . . . than 'you are not sincere,'" as there was always a chance that a local board would accept the claim or the claim could be appealed.[149]

Even if local boards were found to have acted in good faith, appeals allowed registrants to delay induction orders, sometimes until after they had aged out of eligibility altogether. Some counselors used this as an effective strategy. The more men who appealed their classifications, the longer it took for the existing system to handle those appeals. Even if the appeals eventually failed, the process taxed the system, potentially "impeding the progress of the war . . . by keeping men away from 'the Machine.'"[150] The rate of appeals during the Vietnam War, 98 per 1,000 I-A registrants, far eclipsed the 47 per 1,000 of the Korean War and the 3 per 1,000 eligible registrants during World War II.[151] More often than not, the appeals succeeded, which in turn encouraged other men to gamble with an appeal.

Even though the Selective Service reported more than twenty thousand complaints of draft evasion per year by the late 1960s, the Department of Justice chose not to investigate all of them.[152] Half of the two hundred thousand cases the Selective Service ultimately referred avoided prosecution because local draft boards had acted improperly. Courts convicted approximately ten thousand men of draft evasion over the course of the war, but the proportion of convictions decreased every year as juries "became more sympathetic to evaders."[153] By the early 1970s, the system virtually stopped fighting the tide of protest. As the United States drew down its forces under Nixon's policy of Vietnamization, the military drafted fewer men. Since fewer men were needed, local boards and the legal system tacitly let "troublemakers" go. District attorneys dropped delinquency cases or simply failed to prosecute them. Local and appeal boards began classifying men who might be "militants" as I-Y or IV-F in order to avoid having to deal with them.[154] According to one counselor, the I-Y category in particular became "sort of a dumping ground . . . a place for guys the Army just doesn't want." Often, it was "very hard to find out why [guys] were put there."[155]

Like most other counseling strategies, however, appeals and CO classifications were prohibitively expensive for most American men. Conscientious objector status, in particular, was inordinately difficult for poorer men to attain. The onus of constructing a convincing case belonged to the applicant, and the Selective Service's CO application form was complicated. Although the Selective Service revised the form's questions over the years, all versions required men to carefully outline the "nature" of their beliefs, the source of those beliefs, the circumstances under which they found the use of force permissible, and how their beliefs restricted them from combat.[156] Essay answers needed to be clear, coherent, and well-written, a situation that privileged self-reflective men who had received excellent schooling. Draft counselor and Episcopal rector Father Elmer Sullivan of Elizabeth, New Jersey, characterized the whole process as "very cerebral." "It's definitely a middle-class, educated person's game," he explained, "and most poor people . . . don't like to play games like that."[157]

Even when working-class whites and men of color applied for CO status, they often faced the prejudices of their local boards. Local board members varied widely on their approach to conscientious objection and did not always incorporate the Supreme Court rulings into their own definition of eligibility. Regardless of the law, they tended to favor men from historical peace churches.[158] Local boards particularly rejected claimants belonging to the Nation of Islam, like boxer Muhammad Ali.[159] After Jehovah's Witnesses, members of the Nation of Islam were the second largest group of men with religious scruples to be imprisoned for noncompliance.[160]

The CCCO, American Friends Service Committee, and other draft counseling organizations maintained legal aid funds and lists of lawyers who would take cases pro bono or for reduced fees, but there were never enough to meet the need.[161] A few men forged ahead with appeals but soon found that they could not afford the lawyers they had hired. Fees could run over one thousand dollars.[162] Ultimately, only a small subsection of American men possessed the social capital, educational resources, and assets to be able to successfully claim CO status or appeal their induction order.

Draft counselors, especially those who were politically motivated, understood these race and class inequities from the start. They made a concerted effort to reach men in white working-class and minority communities. Their files are filled with proposals and plans to open counseling centers in neighborhoods far removed from the college campuses where most centers thrived.[163] But by their own acknowledgment, draft counselors had difficulty reaching their intended clientele. Middle-class white counselors had trouble finding an "in" with white working-class and minority men.[164] Sometimes they faced threats from the community itself or hostility from the community service organizations with which they wished to liaise.[165] Men of color and white working-class men were also much less likely to see military avoidance as an option. As much as counselors advertised or tried to reach out, members of these groups did not respond in large numbers to the services counselors offered.[166] Frequently, men from working-class and minority neighborhoods found the middle-class orientation and tactics of draft counselors off-putting.[167] It is for this reason that Frank Adams of the famed Highlander Research and Education Center was so excited when he was called to eastern Kentucky in 1971 to counsel a few men in Appalachia. "This is one of the first times in recent memory that really poor mountain people have asked for this sort of information," he wrote.[168]

Adams's letter highlighted another problem. Men who lived in isolated communities had difficulty accessing draft counseling even if they wanted it. Adams was willing to cross state lines to offer his services, but most rural men would have had to be the ones to travel. Counselors operated in every state in the union, but they clustered in college towns and urban centers. Counselors at the Bristol-Washington County Draft Information Service in Virginia, for example, believed theirs to be the only counseling center between Roanoke, Virginia, and Johnson City, Tennessee, and it was located on the Emory and Henry campus. Its counselors tried to "reach out to poor whites and blacks" in their community, but their reach was limited.[169]

African American activists, partially as a reaction to white counselors' failure and partially as an outgrowth of their own civil rights activities, began to open their own draft counseling centers with the explicit purpose of reaching black men. Black counselors opened centers in Philadelphia, New York, Milwaukee, Cleveland, Chicago, Louisville, Atlanta, and elsewhere, and they networked with each other.[170] Counselors at these centers universally viewed the Vietnam War as an imperial conflict and the military as a racist institution that "trapped" African American men with "the false promise of learning valuable skills and travel to other places." Instead of "learning how to kill our colored brothers the world over," exhorted Ralph Hendrix of New York's Black Anti-Draft Union, African American men needed to be able to stay in the United States "at all cost to defend our women, children, and . . . manhood."[171] They framed draft avoidance as necessary to the fight for civil rights at home, particularly since more than 30 percent of all black families lived at or below the poverty line.[172] Black men had the "right not to be drafted," especially since the promised rehabilitation training never came.[173] According to black draft counselors, military service through Project 100,000 and otherwise did not benefit black men. It did not teach useful job skills or help alleviate the unemployment rate in the African American community.[174]

Unfortunately for black men who did not wish to serve, black draft counselors had little more success in minority communities than white counselors did. Internal politics drove some organizations apart.[175] Others simply came on the scene too late. Most black draft counseling centers began operating between 1970 and 1971, a period of flux in the draft and demobilization in the war, when fewer and fewer men found themselves subject to Uncle Sam's greetings. The luxury to treat military service as a choice remained a perk of affluence.

Draft counseling flourished during the Vietnam War because the war was unpopular. In the politically charged and socially conscious environment of the late 1960s and early 1970s, the draft became a tangible target for activists from varied backgrounds. But widespread draft counseling was also an inadvertent result of manpower channeling, a policy that promised middle-class men choices about their military obligation if they played the Selective Service's game correctly. During the 1950s and early 1960s, men could either limit their obligation through special programs in the reserves or National Guard or they could avoid military service entirely if they made the right occupational or domestic choices. As Congress and the Selective Service curtailed those options—during an unpopular war no less—the men most affected by channeling's restriction turned to counselors as a way to maintain control over their lives.

Counselors, meanwhile, helped their clients by teaching them how to play the same game the Selective Service itself had started, just using new rules. They strenuously rejected military service as an obligation and shifted the conversation to one of individual rights. Clients did not necessarily agree with their counselors' political activism, but they did take advantage of the opportunities that counselors offered to beat the draft. Draft counseling thrived in an environment where the links between masculine citizenship and military service had already been substantially weakened, a feat, ironically, achieved in large measure by the policies and practices of the manpower community itself.

Draft counselors, as a group, had an outsized effect on individuals' behavior. They pushed men's already existing ambivalence toward military service into the public sphere. Where individual men during previous conflicts may have tried to avoid service on their own in order to sidestep public shaming or personal humiliation, middle-class and elite men during the Vietnam War learned that avoidance could be acceptable behavior. Counselors advertised in newspapers and on the streets. They appeared in written articles and television newscasts. College students—like James Fallows—received or heard about counseling in their dorms and from classmates. Counselors reinforced the ideas, ironically pushed originally by the Selective Service, that deferments were a right rather than an embarrassment and that service to one's country did not have to come through the military.

Counselors argued that courage stemmed from the embrace of moral conviction rather than feats of military bravery and that strength flowed from character rather than physical robustness. "True bravery," explained one CCCO pamphlet, meant "the courage to work out a better world . . . even if your decision ma[de] you unpopular."[176] To these activists and, they hoped, to the men who took their advice, acknowledging the "weakness" of a physical defect or even homosexuality was more manly than the "perverted emotions" and "obvious insecurity" that characterized military masculinity.[177] Black counselors, in particular, pointed to "meaningful employment, quality education, and decent housing"—things that had to be fought for at home rather than abroad—as the markers of manhood.[178] Counselors, therefore, gave young men a tangible connection to alternate types of masculinity.

In particular, they tapped into and reinforced a counterculture that rejected military service as a masculine responsibility. They framed their message of independent choice and personal liberty against the regimentation and hierarchy of the military. Activists handed out leaflets to men waiting for their preinduction physicals declaring the armed forces' determination to "break men." Officers emasculated recruits by forcing new inductees to shave their heads, dress in uniform, and turn their bodies over to the military to do with as it wished, including, on occasion, making

FIGURE 6.2. Protest in front of Marines poster. The claim that the Marine Corps built men held little sway for most student protesters. Photo courtesy of Fred Lonidier.

them wear diapers as punishment.[179] The physical, mental, and verbal abuse of basic training destroyed individuality. Such homogenization, explained a different handout, was nothing less than "psychological blackmail" that sardonically redefined "patriotism" as "a man who follows orders without question" and a "real man" as someone who "kills 'gooks.'"[180] Military service stripped men of their masculine dignity and autonomy. Counselors and other antiwar activists begged men not to "submit meekly like blind" mice.[181]

In their endeavors, draft counselors joined other activists of the era in promoting competing ideals of masculinity. The social movements of the late 1960s and the 1970s, particularly second-wave feminism, forced gendered paradigms into a state of flux. Masculinity as well as femininity became hard to define on a broad scale.[182] While the "Hardhat" emerged as the emblem of white, working-class male dominance, the soldier—and by extension the veteran—became a more contested symbol.[183] By the end of the Vietnam conflict, some 20 percent of American soldiers and veterans had actively engaged in protest against the war. Members of Vietnam Veterans against the War (VVAW) embraced a form of masculinity that acknowledged weakness and emotion as a way to heal the scars left by the Vietnam War. Like draft counselors, members of the VVAW thus rejected military service as the fire that forged boys into men, a truth that their own military experiences allowed them to claim.[184]

All sorts of Americans challenged these alternate versions of masculinity, of course. As this chapter has illustrated, large swaths of the American public believed military service to be a duty and a masculine rite of passage. Others, even those who disagreed with American involvement in Vietnam, rejected the notion that "draft dodging" could be a manly pursuit. The same rationale that one person used to vindicate masculine draft avoidance could sound to another as nothing more than "ladylike self-justification."[185] But the fact that Americans held these debates more or less in the public eye illustrates how contested the relationship between military service and the masculine obligations of citizenship had become since World War II.

Conclusion

The letter and newspaper clipping that Harvey J. Fischer mailed to President Johnson in 1965 and whose words opened this book expressed a fairly common refrain of the Vietnam years: male baby boomers did not understand their obligation to serve the nation in the same way that the men of the greatest generation did. In actuality, Fischer and others who thought like him overestimated the World War II generation's understanding of its responsibility to the country's military. Most men did not enlist or volunteer to be moved to the top of Selective Service's lists during World War II. They waited to be drafted. A significant proportion made occupational and domestic choices they hoped would disqualify them from the draft. Only in 1944 did the law, combined with Selective Service regulations and practice, make draft avoidance virtually impossible for men between the ages of eighteen and twenty-six. And yet, as the phenomena of "job jumping" and "farm jumping" attest, men kept trying. American men continued to take advantage of whatever loopholes they could until the draft ended in 1973.

American men's behavior during the Vietnam-era draft, therefore, was a culmination, not a rupture. Men of the baby boom generation were not less responsible or less patriotic than their fathers, uncles, or older brothers. Draft avoidance remained a constant and fairly widespread occurrence within all of the generations that faced conscription between 1940 and 1973.

Rather, the context of men's behavior changed as the nation's self-defined defense and security needs evolved during the same years.

As this book has demonstrated, military manpower policies reflected the preponderant values and demands of the historical moment in which those policies functioned. The interplay between domestic social values and national security goals shaped military manpower policy between the 1940s and 1960s. Americans during the decades of the Cold War believed that communism threatened American interests both globally and domestically. American military forces needed to be ready to contest communist enemies abroad, while everyday citizens had to project democratic, capitalist values in order to attract foreign allies and to root out the communist threat at home. Maintaining national security against an insidious internal foe moved defense planning decisively into the domestic realm.

Prior to the Cold War, attempts to use Selective Service as a form of social engineering had met significant pushback. During the father-draft controversy of 1943, Democratic representative Paul Kilday of Texas argued that Selective Service should not "indirectly" guide men's occupational choices. "Work or fight" measures left Americans cold. Organizations from the War Manpower Commission to the CIO objected to congressional plans to induct IV-F men who left essential war industries and then station them, under the auspices of the army, back into industry. Repeated attempts to draft striking workers during World War II went down in defeat. The late 1944 regulations that inducted "job jumpers" and "farm jumpers" triggered controversy.[1] More importantly, proposals for universal military training all failed. Although a significant proportion of Americans supported UMT because of the benefits universal training could provide to American manhood, a more vocal contingent rejected the plan as inappropriate in a democracy that valued free institutions and freedom of choice. American youth did not want to devote a year of their lives to military training, either in the name of national defense or internal strength. UMT would have been militarization run amok.

While its opponents deemed UMT too overt, a subtler militarization within the framework of selective conscription proved acceptable in the Cold War environment. Truman, Eisenhower, and Kennedy all maintained a much larger standing force than ever before in America's peacetime history, but none of their administrations dove so deeply into the available manpower pool that they required all eligible American men. Instead, the manpower planning apparatus, including members of Congress and Lewis B. Hershey, tacitly and then overtly agreed to use the draft as a form of social engineering. If soldiers, sailors, marines, and airmen could be deployed to protect American interests abroad, male civilians could be mobilized to protect American values and defend against enemies at home. Starting with the addition of the student deferment during the Korean War, the availability of deferments grew across the decades for those men whose civilian pursuits could be defined as in the national interest. Fathers, college students, scientists, engineers, teachers, and, at times, married men without children all gained deferments from military service because of their potential contributions to national security.

None of these categories, however, was predetermined. Instead, the choice to defer students, men in STEM occupations, teachers, and fathers at the same time that deferments for men in industrial jobs and farmers were scaled back illustrates Cold War priorities. The Selective Service ultimately defined men in STEM fields, those who might enter STEM fields, and those who could train others to enter STEM fields as Cold Warriors. From those who might conduct basic research to those who could use that research to develop sophisticated missile guidance systems, these men had the potential to contribute to the United States' technological superiority over the Soviet Union. Engineers working on new computer systems and communications networks, scientists developing new chemical compounds and medical treatments, and mathematicians seeking new algorithms were all equally categorized as working in the national interest, as their fields were mobilized in the name of defense.

Along the way, these policies and procedures militarized broad swaths of the American populace. Selective Service literature referred to the "pressurized guidance" of channeling, which "impelled" men to stay in professions they might not otherwise wish to pursue. Kilday's 1943 warning was ignored, as the Selective Service "limited" men's choices.[2] If they wanted to stay out of the armed forces, young men needed to find an occupation defined as in the national interest, support a dependent, or join the reserves. Manpower channeling, just as much as the National Defense Education Act and federal grants, militarized college campuses and primary and secondary teaching. Rehabilitation programs militarized the social services offered to underprivileged men, while Project 100,000 forayed into the militarization of welfare services.[3] Paternity deferments militarized fatherhood by directly equating it with national service.

In fact, as much as the Selective Service tried to focus on civil defense and national security in order to justify its actions, the policies, procedures, and practices that Congress, the Pentagon, and Selective Service developed between 1945 and 1965 were choices that reflected planners' cultural values as much as national defense needs. Beyond those men whose occupations clearly contributed to weapons systems and other obvious military functions,

policymakers revealed a strong commitment to ideals of breadwinner masculinity in their choices of whom to defer. Almost all of the II-A deferment
category's growth sectors required a college degree. Such deferments effectively defaulted to men with means, those men who were best positioned
to get good jobs with salaries that could support families in comfort. Men
who received occupational deferments during the 1950s and 1960s could be
trusted, as a whole, to support capitalist consumerism through their lifestyle
choices. Middle-class, breadwinner masculinity trumped martial masculinity
in an era when threats to national security came from within as well as from
without.

Such was also the underlying rationale for deferring fathers and, when
conditions allowed, childless married men. Americans across the political
spectrum believed that children and wives needed their fathers and husbands at home to provide financial support and moral guidance. The notion
that families needed their fathers was an old one. Fathers maintained their
deferred status during World War II until the requirements of total war
forced the hand of Congress and Selective Service, but the context of dependency deferments shifted during the first decade of Cold War. Amid a panic
over juvenile delinquency, overbearing mothers, and the lavender menace
of homosexuality, fatherhood took on a new importance. Social scientists
and American citizens believed that fathers acted as anchors, allowing their
families to participate in American consumer culture and helping to raise
well-adjusted, democratic children. Little ones needed their daddies, and
the military did not need all men. Deferring fathers made continued sense
within such an environment.

Those men who could not meet the standards of white, middle-class
breadwinning masculinity—and who planners deemed unlikely to ever meet
those standards—found themselves prime targets for conscription. During
the 1950s, such targeting was implicit; those men who could pass the army's
physical and mental exams usually lacked resources that would have earned
them deferments. By the early 1960s, the targeting of poor men became
explicit, as military resources were tapped to fight the War on Poverty and
the War on Poverty was used to staff the military. At first, those men who
could not pass preinduction exams found themselves referred to voluntary
programs designed to "rehabilitate" them into acceptable molds of breadwinning masculinity. After 1966, they found themselves drafted into Project
100,000 in the hopes that they would develop the skills necessary to support
a family through military service.

Ironically, however, such policies and practices exacerbated middle-class
American men's existing ambivalence toward military service. Historically,

men of all social classes equivocated when it came to service in the armed forces, especially during times of war. A few, including conscientious objectors, actively resisted conscription, but the vast majority of men worked within the system as it functioned in their historical moment. Many volunteered, most grudgingly succumbed to the draft, and many sought ways to legally avoid service, given the policies of their era. Planners' choices during the 1950s maximized the availability of deferments among middle-class men, who were valued more highly as civilians than as soldiers. The Selective Service purposely gave middle-class and affluent men more options. By the time of the Vietnam War, a significant proportion of affluent American men had come to expect their privilege. They appeared less patriotic to people like Harvey J. Fischer, but in fact they behaved quite similarly to the generations that had preceded them. They worked within the parameters established by manpower policy and Selective Service regulations, but with much greater success.

It is true that some draft avoiders, with help from counselors, internalized deferments as a right owed to them. In so doing, they tapped into contemporary political currents, as members of the libertarian right and the radical left both came to understand conscription as an infringement on liberty. But the vast majority of men who utilized draft counseling services cared only peripherally about ideology or even politics. They simply did not want to go to war. Nevertheless, by clogging up the manpower procurement system with their appeals and other forms of draft avoidance, middle-class men rejected the historical pattern of eventual acquiescence to conscription. Almost without meaning to, nonactivist draft avoiders joined forces with Vietnam-era activists. They joined James Farmer, a founder and former director of the civil rights organization Congress of Racial Equality; Norman Thomas, a cofounder of the American Civil Liberties Union and perennial presidential candidate for the Socialist Party of America; Karl Hess, an adviser and speechwriter for Republican senator and presidential candidate Barry Goldwater; Milton Friedman; and many others in advancing a liberal interpretation of citizenship with regard to military service.[4] They undermined entirely the civic republican ideal of the citizen-soldier on which conscription had been based.

The end of the draft in the twentieth-century United States is a story well told.[5] Richard Nixon, even as a candidate, knew that he could not fully halt protest against the Vietnam War or the draft. Public opinion had too tightly linked the conscription of men with the prosecution of an unpopular war. Instead, he worked to buy himself time to find "peace with honor." His decisions to advocate for a draft lottery and to end by executive order all new occupational, agricultural, and paternity deferments were part of this effort. So was his push to gradually phase out Selective Service.

In an October 1968 campaign speech, written by Columbia University economist Martin Anderson, Nixon publicly vowed to end conscription.[6] The arguments he advanced, both on the campaign trail and as chief executive, echoed those of the libertarian economists, including Anderson and Friedman, who had been arguing against the draft for years. These scholars wanted the military to compete for personnel on the open market, just like any other employer. Fair wages and other benefits would entice volunteers to join up, creating a more stable force structure and less turnover, they reasoned. In turn, an all-volunteer force (AVF) would better protect the nation and cost less than a military based on conscription. These economists characterized the draft as an unfair "time tax," exacted inequitably from conscripts but not from men who were able to avoid military service.[7]

In January 1969, President Nixon ordered the Department of Defense to study the feasibility of implementing the AVF. In March, he announced the creation of the President's Commission on an All-Volunteer Armed Force, under the chairmanship of former secretary of defense Thomas Gates Jr. Its members included Friedman and the economist Alan Greenspan. Walter Oi of the University of Chicago was one of its researchers. When the commission released its report in February 1970, it unanimously recommended transitioning to an AVF.[8] Nixon, at the urging of Secretary of Defense Melvin Laird, simultaneously called for a two-year renewal of the Military Selective Service Act when it was due to expire in 1971 and ordered the Department of Defense to begin making plans to shift to an all-volunteer force.[9] The gradual American drawdown in Vietnam combined with pay increases and other new incentives offered to volunteers created a smaller need for draftees. In January 1972, the Pentagon reduced draft calls to zero. In June, Nixon declared that conscripts would no longer be sent to Vietnam. The law authorizing the draft was allowed to expire the following summer. Conscription, at least for the foreseeable future, had ended in the United States.

The Vietnam-era draft, like so many elements of the war and the political system that supported it, scarred the collective American psyche. Americans from all walks of life grappled with how to make meaning of it. In the decade following American withdrawal from Vietnam, the federal government and the American populace struggled with reintegrating Vietnam veterans into society and debated whether diplomatic relations with Vietnam should be normalized. Americans questioned whether and how draft resisters and military deserters should be pardoned or otherwise reintegrated into American society.[10] President Jimmy Carter's 1980 decision to renew Selective Service registration, including, he hoped, for women as potential noncombatants, kicked off a round of criticism that ultimately undermined the feminist goal of an Equal Rights Amendment.[11] Reinstatement of the draft remained a political impossibility into the twenty-first century.[12] Meanwhile, the military retooled after almost thirty-five years of manpower procurement supported by a draft. The army, in particular, struggled to compete on the open market for personnel. The Vietnam War had brought it to the brink of collapse, as drug use, racial conflict, and general discontent among draftees had torn the institution apart from within. It needed to remake the soldiering ideal in order to attract volunteers.[13]

The mixed legacy of America's Vietnam War made comparisons with the nation's experience of World War II almost natural. There could only be a "good war" in American collective memory if there was a "bad" one, and vice versa. If World War II gained a reputation for bringing Americans together, the Vietnam War rent the United States' social and political fabric. It polarized the American public, destroyed the mid-century liberal consensus, and contributed to a wave of violent street clashes, arsons, fire bombings, and vandalism.[14] World War II left the United States as a global authority, able to advance a muscular foreign policy funded through unprecedented economic growth. The country's loss in Vietnam, along with other factors intimately connected to the war, created a crisis of confidence in the American political and military systems as well as a crisis of masculinity. The United States of the late 1970s seemed castrated, impotent against an inferior military force belonging to a backward country, ineffective against foreign adversaries including the Soviets and OPEC, and mired in stagflation and job loss.[15] If World War II had left the United States as a superpower, the end of the Vietnam War left Americans feeling sadly deflated.

Remilitarizing the nation, remasculinizing American men, and reclaiming the Vietnam War became massive cultural and political projects during the 1970s and 1980s. The social movements of the 1970s, particularly feminism and gay rights, lost momentum when pitted against critics' fears of a failing, feminized America. In the words of historian Michael Sherry, the New Right feared both "moral disarmament at home and military disarmament abroad," and worked tirelessly to rectify both problems.[16] President Ronald Reagan literally rearmed the nation, spending up to 10 percent of America's gross national product on defense by 1983.[17] He left his successor, George H. W. Bush, with the military tools the United States used to steamroll Iraqi forces in Kuwait in 1991, prompting Bush to declare that Americans had "kicked the Vietnam Syndrome once and for all."[18] The Gulf War succeeded in "jolt[ing] the American people out of the . . . reluctance to go to war" left by Vietnam.[19]

The cultural project of reframing the Vietnam War into something other than an American defeat was less overt. The Reagan coalition came together by co-opting discourse surrounding the family, gender roles, and citizenship, including with relation to military service. During the late 1970s and 1980s, movies, television shows, and political pronouncements erased veteran activity from the antiwar movement and constructed a militarized warrior myth: American soldiers did not lose the war, they had not been allowed to win it.[20] The "unpredictability, weakness, indeterminancy, indecisiveness," and "dependence" of an effete government bureaucracy and a feminized antiwar movement, according to the new narrative, betrayed American martial manhood.[21]

There is an irony in the conservative discourse of the 1980s. As this book has argued, the manpower system that allowed so many men to avoid military service, supposedly harming America's defense initiatives and undermining its mythical tradition of martial masculinity, was specifically justified as a means to bolster domestic masculinity and protect national security. Yet the same policies that militarized the civilian male populace ultimately undermined the civic republican citizen-soldier ideal on which World War II propaganda had capitalized, a phenomenon whose effects continue to have ramifications into the present day.[22] The manpower policies that supported the Cold War emphasis on national security ironically succeeded in undermining the already tenuous connections between military service and masculine ideals of citizenship. Context, it seems, made all the difference.

ABBREVIATIONS

CCCO	Central Committee for Conscientious Objectors Records
DCIC	Draft Counseling and Information Center Records
DDE	Dwight D. Eisenhower Library, Abilene, Kansas
HEW	Records of the Department of Health, Education, and Welfare
HGP	Harold Gauer Papers
HST	Harry S. Truman Library, Independence, Missouri
LOC	Library of Congress, Washington, D.C.
NACP	National Archives and Records Administration, College Park, Maryland
OF	Official File
PACUT	President's Advisory Commission on Universal Training
PCRW	President's Committee on Religion and Welfare in the Armed Forces
PCSE	President's Committee on Scientists and Engineers: Records, 1956–1958
RG	Record Group
SCPC	Swarthmore College Peace Collection, Swarthmore, Pennsylvania
UIC	University of Illinois Chicago, Chicago, Illinois
USAHEC	United States Army Heritage and Education Center, Carlisle, Pennsylvania
VHP	Veterans History Project
WDRU	Wisconsin Draft Resistance Union Records
WHCF	White House Central File, Harry S. Truman Papers
WHS	Wisconsin Historical Society, Madison, Wisconsin

NOTES

Introduction

1. "A Need for Patriotic Young Men," no title, n.d., attached to Harvey J. Fischer to Mr. President, September 29, 1965, Frev-Frier, box 154, Central Files, 1948–69, Records of the Selective Service, RG 147, NACP.

2. John K. Mahon, *History of the Militia and the National Guard* (New York: MacMillan Publishing Company, 1983), 67–69; Jerry Cooper, *The Militia and the National Guard in America Since Colonial Times: A Research Guide* (Westport, Conn.: Greenwood Press, 1993). For a larger discussion of exclusionary definitions of the citizen-soldier, see Eliot A. Cohen, *Citizens and Soldiers: The Dilemmas of Military Service* (Ithaca, N.Y.: Cornell University Press, 1985), chap. 5.

3. R. Claire Snyder, *Citizen-Soldiers and Manly Warriors: Military Service and Gender in the Civic Republican Tradition* (New York: Rowman & Littlefield, 1999); Karen Hagemann, Stefan Dudink, and Anna Clark, eds., *Representing Masculinity: Male Citizenship in Modern Western Culture* (New York: Palgrave MacMillan, 2007). War, itself, has also been a gendering experience. See, for example, Stefan Dudink, Karen Hagemann, and John Tosh, eds., *Masculinities in Politics and War: Gendering Modern History* (New York: Manchester University Press, 2004); Joshua S. Goldstein, *War and Gender* (New York: Cambridge University Press, 2001).

4. Amy Greenberg, *Manifest Manhood and the Antebellum American Empire* (New York: Cambridge University Press, 2005); Eleanor Hannah, *Manhood, Citizenship and the National Guard: Illinois, 1870–1914* (Columbus: Ohio State University Press, 2007); Gail Bederman, *Manliness and Civilization: A Cultural History of Gender and Race in the United States, 1880–1917* (Chicago: University of Chicago Press, 1995); Kristin L. Hoganson, *Fighting for American Manhood: How Gender Politics Provoked the Spanish-American and Philippine-American Wars* (New Haven, Conn.: Yale University Press, 1998).

5. Celia Malone Kinsbury, *For Home and Country: World War I Propaganda on the Homefront* (Lincoln: University of Nebraska Press, 2010); Christina S. Jarvis, *The Male Body at War: American Masculinity during World War II* (DeKalb: Northern Illinois University Press, 2004); Robert B. Westbrook, *Why We Fought: Forging American Obligations in World War II* (Washington, D.C.: Smithsonian Books, 2004).

6. Patrick J. Kelly, *Creating a National Home: Building the Veteran's Welfare State, 1860–1900* (New York: Oxford University Press, 2005), 7.

7. Elizabeth Mettler, *Soldiers to Citizens: The G.I. Bill and the Making of the Greatest Generation* (New York: Oxford University Press, 2005), 7.

8. Other reasons included economic necessity, adventure, and eventually survival. See, for example, Samuel Hynes, *The Soldiers' Tale: Bearing Witness to Modern*

War (New York: Penguin Books, 1997); Christopher H. Hamner, *Enduring Battle: American Soldiers in Three Wars, 1776–1945* (Lawrence: University of Kansas Press, 2011); Westbrook, *Why We Fought*, esp. chap. 2; Kenneth W. Noe, *Reluctant Rebels: The Confederates Who Joined the Army after 1861* (Chapel Hill: University of North Carolina Press, 2010); Christian G. Appy, *Working-Class War: American Combat Soldiers and Vietnam* (Chapel Hill: University of North Carolina Press, 1993).

9. Conscription was used much more sparingly during the Civil War than during the wars of the twentieth century. It is estimated that the Union Army drafted only 8 percent of its strength and the Confederacy somewhere between 10 and 21 percent of its. Seventy-one percent of the American force during World War I was drafted. See Jennifer D. Keene, *Doughboys, the Great War, and the Making of America* (Baltimore: Johns Hopkins University Press, 2001), 2. For an overview on the history of the draft, see David R. Segal, *Recruiting for Uncle Sam: Citizenship and Military Manpower Policy* (Lawrence: University Press of Kansas, 1989), 17–38. On the New York City draft riots, see Iver Bernstein, *The New York City Draft Riots: Their Significance for American Society and Politics in the Age of the Civil War* (New York: Oxford University Press, 1990). For a description of opposition to the draft and the problems it presented the U.S. government during World War I, see Christopher Capozzola, *Uncle Sam Wants You: World War I and the Making of the Modern American Citizen* (New York: Oxford University Press, 2008), chaps. 1–2; and Jeanette Keith, *Rich Man's War, Poor Man's Fight: Race, Class, and Power in the Rural South during the First World War* (Chapel Hill: University of North Carolina Press, 2004). On the draft from World War II, see William A. Taylor, *Military Service and American Democracy: From World War II to the Iraq and Afghanistan Wars* (Lawrence: University Press of Kansas, 2016).

10. John Whiteclay Chambers II, "Conscientious Objectors and the American State from Colonial Times to the Present," in *The New Conscientious Objection: From Sacred to Secular Resistance*, ed. Charles C. Moskos and John Whiteclay Chambers II (New York: Oxford University Press, 1993), 23–46.

11. Michael S. Foley, *Confronting the War Machine: Draft Resistance During the Vietnam War* (Chapel Hill: University of North Carolina Press, 2003), 11–13.

12. Thomas Paine, "The Crisis," in *Thomas Paine: Collected Writings*, ed. Eric Foner (New York: Library of America, 1995), 91.

13. Lawrence M. Baskir and Willam A. Strauss estimated that approximately 570,000 men broke the law to avoid the draft. In contrast, 15,410,000 were deferred, exempted, or disqualified from military service. Baskir and Strauss, *Chance and Circumstance: The Draft, the War, and the Vietnam Generation* (New York: Knopf, 1978), 5.

14. Chambers, "Conscientious Objectors and the American State," 40.

15. Baskir and Strauss, *Chance and Circumstance*, xviii, 7.

16. It should be noted that the survey cited asked men to list *all* of the methods they used to evade the draft, and, on average, those respondents who took action to avoid military service tried 2.3 different methods. Thus, the percentages of men who tried the various methods add up to greater than 100 percent of respondents. See G. David Curry, *Sunshine Patriots: Punishment and the Vietnam Offender* (Notre Dame, Ind.: University of Notre Dame Press, 1985), 65–66.

17. This is not to say, of course, that no draft avoiders had their masculinity questioned, just that it was less likely to happen than during previous conflicts. For example, one counterprotester at a public draft card burning in New York City in October

1965 explicitly challenged draft avoiders' masculinity in a sign that read, "Thanks pinkos, queers, cowards, draft dodgers [signed] Mao Tse-Tung." See Michael Ferber and Staughton Lynd, *The Resistance* (Boston: Beacon Press, 1971), 24.

18. Robert O. Self, *All in the Family: The Realignment of American Democracy since the 1960s* (New York: Hill and Wang, 2012); Margot Canaday, *The Straight State: Sexuality and Citizenship in Twentieth-Century America* (Princeton, N.J.: Princeton University Press, 2009); Peggy Pascoe, *What Comes Naturally: Miscegenation Law and the Making of Race in America* (New York: Oxford University Press, 2009); Barbara Young Welke, *Law and the Borders of Belonging in the Long Nineteenth Century United States* (New York: Cambridge University Press, 2010).

19. Alice Kessler-Harris, *In Pursuit of Equity: Women, Men, and the Quest for Economic Citizenship in Twentieth-Century America* (New York: Oxford University Press, 2001); Meg Jacobs, *Pocketbook Politics: Economic Citizenship in Twentieth-Century America* (Princeton, N.J.: Princeton University Press, 2005).

20. Meredith H. Lair, *Armed with Abundance: Consumerism and Soldiering in the Vietnam War* (Chapel Hill: University of North Carolina Press, 2011).

21. Andrea Friedman, *Citizenship in Cold War America: The National Security State and the Possibilities of Dissent* (Amherst: University of Massachusetts Press, 2014), 108–18.

22. Civil rights activists made a parallel argument in their fight for equal rights for African Americans. See, for example, Mary L. Dudziak, *Cold War Civil Rights: Race and the Image of American Democracy* (Princeton, N.J.: Princeton University Press, 2000); Thomas Borstelmann, *The Cold War and the Color Line: American Race Relations in the Global Arena* (Cambridge, Mass.: Harvard University Press, 2001); Penny M. Von Eschen, *Race against Empire: Black Americans and Anticolonialism, 1937–1957* (Ithaca, N.Y.: Cornell University Press, 1997); Jonathan Rosenberg, *How Far the Promised Land? World Affairs and the American Civil Rights Movement from the First World War to Vietnam* (Princeton, N.J.: Princeton University Press, 2006).

23. For more on militarization during the Cold War, see Andrew D. Grossman, *Neither Dead nor Red: Civilian Defense and American Political Development during the Early Cold War* (New York: Routledge, 2001); Stuart W. Leslie, *The Cold War and American Science: The Military-Industrial-Academic Complex at MIT and Stanford* (New York: Columbia University Press, 1994); Elaine Tyler May, *Homeward Bound: American Families in the Cold War Era* (New York: Basic Books, 1988); Laura McEnaney, *Civil Defense Begins at Home: Militarization Meets Everyday Life in the Fifties* (Princeton, N.J.: Princeton University Press, 2000); Guy Oakes, *The Imaginary War: Civil Defense and American Cold War Culture* (New York: Oxford University Press, 1994).

24. Lisa M. Mundey, *American Militarism and Anti-Militarism in Popular Media, 1945–1970* (Jefferson, N.C.: McFarland and Company, 2012), 7.

25. Richard H. Kohn, "The Danger of Militarization in an Endless 'War' on Terrorism," *Journal of Military History* 73, no. 1 (Jan. 2009): 182.

26. Michael S. Sherry, *In the Shadow of War: The United States since the 1930s* (New Haven, Conn.: Yale University Press, 1995), xi.

27. Kohn, "The Danger of Militarization in an Endless 'War' on Terrorism," 182.

28. Aaron L. Friedberg, *In the Shadow of the Garrison State: America's Anti-Statism and Its Cold War Grand Strategy* (Princeton, N.J.: Princeton University Press, 2000).

29. Tom Englehardt, *The End of Victory Culture: Cold War America and the Disillusioning of a Generation* (Amherst: University of Massachusetts Press, 1995), 69–89; Lawrence H. Suid, *Guts and Glory: The Making of the American Military Image in Film*, rev. and expanded ed. (Lexington: University Press of Kentucky, 2002), 5.

30. On the many ways to be a man, see James Gilbert, *Men in the Middle: Searching for Masculinity in the 1950s* (Chicago: University of Chicago Press, 2005). On ambivalent war stories, see Mundey, *American Militarism and Anti-Militarism*; and Andrew J. Huebner, *The Warrior Image: Soldiers in American Culture from the Second World War to the Vietnam Era* (Chapel Hill: University of North Carolina Press, 2008).

31. Anne Deighton, "Did the Cold War Matter," plenary session, LSE-GWU-UCSB Graduate Conference on the Cold War, London School of Economics, London, United Kingdom, April 2012. Matthew Farish made a similar argument in "The Ordinary Cold War: The Ground Observer Corps and Midcentury Militarization in the United States," *Journal of American History* 103, no. 3 (2016): 629–55.

32. Armed Forces Examination Stations are sometimes referred to as Armed Forces Examining and Induction Stations (AFEISs) or Armed Forces Examining and Entrance Stations (AFEESs). For the sake of consistency, this work will use the acronym AFES.

33. Between 1950 and 1972, men took the Armed Forces Qualification Test (AFQT), which included sections that measured verbal ability, mathematical ability, and spatial reasoning.

Chapter 1. "Digging for Deferments"

1. Carlton S. Dargusch to General Donovan, November 25, 1941, 330 Class III-Dependency Def-Ala.-Wyo., 1941, box 139, Selective Service Central Files, 1940–41, entry 1, Records of the Selective Service, RG 147, NACP.

2. See, for example, C. G. Parker Jr. to Colonel Thomson, September 24, 1941, 330 Class III-Dependency Def-Ala.-Wyo., 1941, box 139, entry 1, RG 147, NACP.

3. Memorandum for General Hershey, March 5, 1941, 330 Class III Dependency Def-General, 1941, box 139, entry 1, RG 147, NACP.

4. Robert A. Bier to Maj. Walter Mendelson, August 12, 1943, 331 Class III-A-General, entry 1, RG 147, NACP.

5. Suzanne Mettler, *From Soldiers to Citizens: The G.I. Bill and the Making of the Greatest Generation* (New York: Oxford University Press, 2005), 7.

6. The most famous example is Tom Brokaw's *The Greatest Generation* (New York: Random House, 1998). The term, as coined by Brokaw, has become so ubiquitous when describing the World War II generation that a Google search yields hundreds of relevant results, including http://greatestgeneration.tumblr.com; http://www.artofmanliness.com/2009/04/30/7-lessons-in-manliness-from-the-greatest-generation/; http://www.delcotimes.com/opinion/20150605/darts-laurels-remembering-the-greatest-generation; http://www.allprodad.com/greatest-generation-characteristics-and-what-you-can-learn/ (accessed June 5, 2017).

7. See, for example, Brokaw, *The Greatest Generation*, introduction; Stephen E. Ambrose, *Citizen Soldiers: The U.S. Army from the Normandy Beaches to the Bulge to the Surrender of Germany, June 7, 1944 to May 7, 1945* (New York: Simon & Schuster, 1998), chap. 1; Mettler, *From Soldiers to Citizens*.

8. Thomas Bruscino, *A Nation Forged in War: How World War II Taught Americans to Get Along* (Knoxville: University of Tennessee Press, 2010), 178.

9. See, for example, John Morton Blum, *V Was For Victory: Politics and American Culture during World War II* (New York: Harcourt Brace Jovanovich, 1976); William L. O'Neill, *A Democracy at War: America's Fight at Home and Abroad in World War II* (Cambridge, Mass.: Harvard University Press, 1993); Bruscino, *A Nation Forged in War*.

10. See, for example, Studs Terkel, *"The Good War": An Oral History of World War II* (New York: The New Press, 1984); Michael C. C. Adams, *The Best War Ever: America and World War II* (Baltimore: Johns Hopkins University Press, 1994); John Bodnar, *The "Good War" in American Memory* (Baltimore: Johns Hopkins University Press, 2010); Kenneth D. Rose, *Myth and the Greatest Generation: A Social History of Americans in World War II* (New York: Routledge Press, 2007).

11. Bodnar, *The "Good War" in American Memory,* 10.

12. Edward M. Coffman, *The Regulars: The American Army, 1898–1941* (Cambridge, Mass.: The Belknap Press, 2004), 96–98, 292–93; Brian McAllister Linn, *Elvis's Army: Cold War GIs and the Atomic Battlefield* (Cambridge, Mass.; Harvard University Press, 2016), 14–15.

13. S. the Von to Dear Mag, July 7, 1942, folder 1, box 1, Accession M93-076, HGP, WHS.

14. Christina S. Jarvis, *The Male Body at War: American Masculinity during World War II* (DeKalb: Northern Illinois University Press, 2004); James T. Sparrow, *Warfare State: World War II Americans and the Age of Big Government* (New York: Oxford University Press, 2011).

15. S. the Von to Dear Mag, July 7, 1942.

16. Robert B. Westbrook, *Why We Fought: Forging American Obligations in World War II* (Washington, D.C.: Smithsonian Books, 2004), esp. chap. 2.

17. Christian G. Appy, "'We'll Follow the Old Man': The Strains of Sentimental Militarism in Popular Films of the Fifties," in *Rethinking Cold War Culture*, ed. Peter J. Kuznick and James Gilbert (Washington, D.C.: Smithsonian Institution Press, 2001), 74–105.

18. Michael S. Shull and David Edward Wilt, *Hollywood War Films, 1937–1945: An Exhaustive Filmography of American Feature-Length Motion Pictures Relating to World War II* (Jefferson, N.C.: McFarland & Company, Inc., 1996), 170–72, 258–60.

19. Sparrow, *Warfare State*, chap. 5; Jarvis, *The Male Body at War*, 60. See Cartoon, n.d., 800 Publicity and Public Relations, Selective Service System-Planning Council, box 69, Selective Service System Planning Council Files, entry 3, RG 147, NACP.

20. Sparrow, *Warfare State*, 6, 161.

21. Terkel, *"The Good War,"* 39.

22. Terkel, *"The Good War,"* 174.

23. Terkel, *"The Good War,"* 179.

24. Robert M. McClure (AFC 2001/001/45005), Audio Recording (SR02), VHP, American Folklife Center, LOC.

25. Ralph W. Chase, Jr. (AFC 2001/001/76158), Transcript (MS02), VHP, LOC.

26. Timothy Stewart-Winter, "Not a Soldier, Not a Slacker: Conscientious Objectors and Male Citizenship during the Second World War," *Gender and History* 19, no. 3 (2007): 519–42.

27. John L. McRee (AFC 2001/001/72401), Video Recording (MV02), VHP, LOC.

28. Lt. James T. Gibson to Brig. Gen. Ben M. Smith, January 22, 1941, 320 Class II-Occupational Def.-Ala.-Wyo., box 138, entry 1, RG 147, NACP.

29. See, for example, Morgan the Inorganic to Dear Boss, March 2, 1942; Harold to Dear Bob, April 4, 1942; and Walter Lippman to Sir, n.d., all in folder 1, box 1, M93–076, HGP, WHS.

30. S. the Von to Dear Mag, July 19, 1942, folder 1, box 1, M93–076, HGP, WHS.

31. Linn, *Elvis's Army*, 25.

32. Bodnar, *The "Good War" in American Memory*, 4.

33. John O'Sullivan, *From Voluntarism to Conscription: Congress and Selective Service, 1940–1945* (New York: Garland Publishing, Inc., 1982), 2–3.

34. On pacifist opposition to the bill, see J. Garry Clifford and Samuel R. Spencer, *The First Peacetime Draft* (Lawrence: University Press of Kansas, 1986), chap. 8.

35. For more on the legislative debates over the law, see O'Sullivan, *From Voluntarism to Conscription*, chap. 2–3.

36. On the problems of the Civil War draft and how the legislation creating the World War I draft responded to these problems, see John Whiteclay Chambers II, *To Raise an Army: The Draft Comes to Modern America* (New York: The Free Press, 1987), 47–65, 142–44, 172–77.

37. For more on Hershey's childhood influences, see George Q. Flynn, *Lewis B. Hershey: Mr. Selective Service* (Chapel Hill: University of North Carolina Press, 1985), chap. 1–2. On his civic republicanism, see also Nicholas A. Krehbiel, *General Lewis B. Hershey and Conscientious Objection during World War II* (Columbia: University of Missouri Press, 2011), chap. 2; James W. Davis Jr. and Kenneth M. Dolbeare, *Little Groups of Neighbors: The Selective Service System* (Chicago: Markham Publishing Co., 1968).

38. *Selective Service in Peacetime: First Report of the Director of Selective Service, 1940–1941* (Washington, D.C.: GPO, 1942), 3.

39. *Selective Service as the Tide of War Turns: Third Report of the Director of Selective Service, 1943–1944* (Washington, D.C.: GPO, 1945), 404.

40. *Selective Service in Peacetime*, 54; George Q. Flynn, *The Draft, 1940–1973* (Lawrence: University Press of Kansas, 1993), 58.

41. *Selective Service in Victory: The Fourth Report of the Director of Selective Service, 1944–1945, With a Special Supplement for 1946–1947* (Washington, D.C.: GPO, 1948), 422.

42. See appendix 1 of *Selective Service in Victory*, 359–360.

43. Anne Yoder, Military Classifications for Draftees, Swarthmore College Peace Collection, available at http://www.swarthmore.edu/library/peace/conscientious objection/MilitaryClassifications.htm (accessed June 5, 2017).

44. On the Civil War draft, see James W. Geary, *We Need Men: The Union Draft in the Civil War* (DeKalb: Northern Illinois University Press, 1991) and Kenneth W. Noe, *Reluctant Rebels: The Confederates Who Joined the Army after 1861* (Chapel Hill: University of North Carolina Press, 2010). On the World War I draft, see Chambers, *To Raise an Army*.

45. Selective Draft Act of 1917, Public Law 65-12, *United States Statutes at Large* 40, part I, (1919), 79.

46. Paul T. Murray, "Blacks and the Draft: A History of Institutional Racism," *Journal of Black Studies* 2, no. 1 (Sep. 1971): 62.

47. John Whiteclay Chambers II, "Conscientious Objectors and the American State from Colonial Times to the Present," in *The New Conscientious Objection: From Sacred to Secular Resistance*, ed. Charles C. Moskos and John Whiteclay Chambers II (New York: Oxford University Press, 1993), 23–46.

48. Selective Draft Act of 1917, *United States Statutes at Large*, 79.

49. Christopher Capozzola, *Uncle Sam Wants You: World War I and the Making of the Modern American Citizen* (New York: Oxford University Press, 2008), 30–31.

50. Capozzola, *Uncle Sam Wants You*, 37.

51. Jeannette Keith, *Rich Man's War, Poor Man's Fight: Race, Class, and Power in the Rural South during the First World War* (Chapel Hill: University of North Carolina Press, 2004), 1; Dorit Geva, "Different and Unequal: Breadwinning, Dependency Deferments, and the Gendered Origins of the U.S. Selective Service System," *Armed Forces and Society* 37 (Fall 2011): 606–9.

52. Capozzola, *Uncle Sam Wants You*, 30–31.

53. Keith, *Rich Man's War*, 113–16; Gerald E. Shenk, *"Work or Fight!" Race, Gender, and the Draft in World War I* (New York: Palgrave MacMillan, 2005), 49–51, 77–79, 101–3.

54. Capozzola, *Uncle Sam Wants You*, 37–38.

55. *Selective Service in Peacetime*, 137.

56. "Quotes Backing on Draft View," *New York Times*, Jan. 22, 1941.

57. Memorandum for Col. Hershey Re: The Marital Status as a Basis of Deferment, Sept. 21, 1940, 322 Class III Dependency Deferments, General, box 36, entry 1, RG 147, NACP.

58. See, for example, J. Paul Kuhn to Mr. Armstrong, November 7, 1941, William F. Hanley to Lewis B. Hershey, July 12, 1941, and Selective Service, New York City Headquarters, Bulletin No. 22, April 18, 1941, all in 330 Class III-Dependency Def-Ala.-Wyo., 1941, box 139, entry 1, RG 147, NACP.

59. Census Data Relative to the Percentage of Married Males by Age Groups, July 31, 1941, 330 Class III-Dependency Def-General, 1941, box 139, entry 1, RG 147, NACP.

60. Paul G. Armstrong to Brig. Gen. Lewis B. Hershey, December 10, 1941, 330 Class III-Dependency Def-Ala-Wyo., 1941, box 139, entry 1, RG 147, NACP.

61. Late Marriages, n.d., 330 Class III-Dependency Def-General, 1941, box 139, entry 1, RG 147, NACP.

62. See, for example, the letters contained in 322 Class III-Dependency Deferments-Ala. to Wyo., 1940, box 36, entry 1, RG 147, NACP.

63. See, for example, Lewis B. Hershey to General Byrd, Dec. 2, 1940, 322 Class III-Dependency Deferments-Ala. to Wyo., 1940, box 36, entry 1, RG 147, NACP.

64. Newspaper clipping, n.d., attached to memo from Major Shattuck to Colonel Langston, July 2, 1941, Dependency Deferments, box 68, entry 3, RG 147, NACP. See also Doyle Young to Hon. John J. Sparkman, n.d., attached to Director to Mr. Sparkman, May 6, 1942, and Ward Johnson to Gen. Lewis B. Hershey, August 7, 1942, attached to LBH to Mr. Johnson, Aug. 17, both in 330 Class III-Dependency Def-Ala.-Hawaii, 1942, box 443, entry 1, RG 147, NACP; D. D. Hatcher to Sir, Nov. 30, 1942, attached to Ford K. Brown to Mr. Hatcher, Feb. 26, 1943, 331 Class III-A-Dependents-Ohio, box 838, entry 1, RG 147, NACP.

65. Memo from Major Shattuck to Colonel Langston, July 2, 1941, Dependency Deferments, box 68, entry 3, RG 147, NACP.

66. Bulletin No. 22, New York City Headquarters, April 8, 1941, Class III-Dependency Def-Ala.-Wyo., 1941, box 139, entry 1, RG 147, NACP.

67. Memorandum for General Hershey, March 5, 1941, 330 Class III-Dependency Def-General, 1941, box 139, entry 1, RG 147, NACP.

68. Memorandum to the Operations Group, January 31, 1941, 330 Class III-Dependency Def-General, 1941, box 139, entry 1, RG 147, NACP.

69. Spencer Bidwell King Jr., *Selective Service in North Carolina in World War II* (Chapel Hill: University of North Carolina Press, 1949), 196.

70. *Selective Service in Wartime: Second Report of the Director of Selective Service, 1941–1942* (Washington, D.C.: GPO, 1943), 139–40.

71. *Selective Service in Wartime*, 141.

72. *Selective Service in Wartime*, 142.

73. Flynn, *The Draft*, 70.

74. US Department of Commerce, Bureau of the Census, *Vital Statistics of the United States, 1940, Part I* (Washington, D.C.: GPO, 1940), 6, available at http://www.cdc.gov/nchs/data/vsus/vsus_1940_1.pdf; US Department of Commerce, Bureau of the Census, *Vital Statistics of the United States, 1943, Part I* (Washington, D.C.: GPO, 1943), 6, available at http://www.cdc.gov/nchs/data/vsus/VSUS_1943_1.pdf.

75. Public Reactions to the Draft and Selective Service, Memo no. 46, Jan. 9, 1943, Confidential Planning Council, box 67, entry 3, RG 147, NACP.

76. Grantland Rice, "Logic Given for Baseball during War," *Hartford Courant*, April 1, 1942; "Nyvall Jr., Who Battled Draft, Plans to Marry," *Chicago Tribune*, June 7, 1942; Sally Joy Brown, "Friend of the Yank's Kin," *Chicago Tribune*, Sept. 2, 1942.

77. George Gallup, "Public Favors Drafting Fathers Last," *Atlanta Constitution*, Sept. 6, 1942.

78. "Teen Age Draft Problems Seen for Colleges," *Atlanta Constitution*, Oct. 18, 1942; "Lower Draft Held Blow to Colleges," *New York Times*, Oct. 16, 1942.

79. See statements inserted into the record, House Committee on Military Affairs, *Lowering Draft Age to 18 Years: Hearings Before the Committee on Military Affairs*, 77th Cong., 2d sess., 1942, 161–65.

80. George Q. Flynn, *The Mess in Washington: Manpower Mobilization in World War II* (Westport, Conn.: Greenwood Press, 1979), 188; *Selective Service and Victory*, 592.

81. Flynn, *The Mess in Washington*, 39–40.

82. See, for example, telegram to Brig. Gen. Lewis B. Hershey, Aug. 26, 1942, 330 Class II-C Agriculture-Iowa-Nev., 1942, box 438, entry 1, RG 147, NACP; Flynn, *The Mess in Washington*, 201. For more on the Tydings Amendment, see Albert A. Blum, "The Farmer, the Army, and the Draft," *Agricultural History* 38, no. 1 (Jan. 1964): 34–42.

83. Cited in Dean J. Kotlowski, *Paul V. McNutt and the Age of FDR* (Bloomington: Indiana University Press, 2015), 341, 364.

84. Executive Order 9279, December 5, 1942, cited in Kotlowski, *Paul V. McNutt and the Age of FDR*, 353–54.

85. For more on McNutt and the WMC, see Kotlowski, *Paul V. McNutt and the Age of FDR*, chap. 13 and Flynn, *The Mess in Washington*. For more on "work or fight," see Albert A. Blum, "Work or Fight: The Use of the Draft as a Manpower Sanction

During the Second World War," *Industrial and Labor Relations Review* 16, no. 3 (April 1963): 366–80.

86. Quoted in Blum, "Work or Fight," 363.

87. "Kilday's Bill Would Block Father Draft," *Hartford Courant*, Feb. 6, 1943; "Father-Draft Rider Seen on Farm Bill," *Washington Post*, March 3, 1943.

88. "Father Draft in Immediate Future Likely," *Hartford Courant*, May 14, 1943.

89. "Fathers to be Drafted Oct. 1 to Meet Quotas," *Los Angeles Times*, Aug. 3, 1943.

90. Memo re: Bona Fide Family Relationship, Jan. 9, 1943, attached to Lieutenant Commander Winston to Lieutenant Colonel Parker, June 24, 1943, 331 Class III-A-General, box 838, entry 1, RG 147, NACP.

91. "Dire Results from Father Draft Seen," *Los Angeles Times*, Aug. 28, 1943.

92. "Protests Father Draft," *New York Times*, Sept. 7, 1943; "Explains Draft Ouster," *New York Times*, Sept. 9, 1943; "3 Quit Mobile Board over Father Draft," *Washington Post*, Sept. 17, 1943; "Father Draft Protest Made in Circulars," *Washington Post*, Nov. 18, 1943; Ben W. Gilbert, "McNutt Firm on Drafting Fathers as Revolt Brews," *Washington Post*, Aug. 7, 1943; "Quits Over Father Draft," *New York Times*, Aug. 17, 1943; Memorandum, Sept. 3, 1943, 331 Class III-A-General, box 838, entry 1, RG 147, NACP.

93. Tokyo in Spanish at 7:15 EWT to Latin America, Aug. 22, 1943, 331 Class III-A-General, box 838, entry 1, Selective Service Central Files, RG 147, NACP.

94. George Gallup, "Draft of Fathers Opposed by Public," *New York Times*, Sept. 15, 1943.

95. "Father Draft Stay Voted in Committee," *Hartford Courant*, July 3, 1943; "Review of Draft Quotas Urged by House Group," *Christian Science Monitor*, Aug. 6, 1943; "Stampede of Fathers to War Jobs Seen," *Los Angeles Times*, Aug. 8, 1943; "Senate to Seek Showdown on Father Draft," *Chicago Tribune*, Aug. 22, 1943; C. P. Trussell, "Roosevelt Backs Draft of Fathers," *New York Times*, Sept. 15, 1943; C. P. Trussell, "Father Draft Plunges Congress into a Crisis," *New York Times*, Sept. 19, 1943; C. P. Trussell, "Taft Plan Is Rival of Wheeler Bill," *New York Times*, Sept. 22, 1943.

96. The overwhelming message from testimony at congressional hearings was that married men and fathers should be drafted. See Senate Committee on Military Affairs, *Married Men Exemption [Drafting of Fathers]: Hearings Before the Committee on Military Affairs*, 78th Cong., 1st sess., 1943, 3–420.

97. Robert C. Albright, "Father Draft Delay Plan Is Approved," *Washington Post*, Nov. 17, 1943.

98. *Selective Service and Victory*, 116 [emphasis in original].

99. *Selective Service as the Tide of War Turns*, 138.

100. *Selective Service and Victory*, 116.

101. See, for example, Tom Brokaw, *The Greatest Generation Speaks: Letters and Reflections* (New York: Random House, 1999), conclusion.

102. *Selective Service and Victory*, 133–34, 136–37.

103. Flynn, *The Draft*, 60.

104. House Committee on Military Affairs, *H.R. 1908, Investigation of the National War Effort: Second General Report of the Committee on Military Affairs, House of Representatives*, 78th Cong., 2d sess., September 19, 1944, 38–39.

105. King, *Selective Service in North Carolina*, 109.

106. "Draft Appeals for Deferment Hit New Low," *Washington Post*, Sept. 14, 1944.

107. Committee on Military Affairs, House of Representatives, Release Afternoon Papers, July 31, 1945, Deferments in General, box 68, entry 3, RG 147, NACP.

108. King, *Selective Service in North Carolina*, 123.

109. See, for example, King, *Selective Service in North Carolina*, 342; Flynn, *The Draft*, 68; Deferment of Agricultural Workers, November 1942–March 1945, Agriculture Selective Service System, Presidential Appeals, box 67, entry 3, RG 147, NACP; "'Back to the Farm' Movement Grows," *Christian Science Monitor*, March 22, 1943.

110. *Selective Service and Victory*, 97.

111. See, for example, "Draft to Take 5000 'Shifters' Each Month," *Washington Post*, Feb. 6, 1945; "Father of Nine Inducted," *Hartford Courant*, May 25, 1945; "Begin Drafting of Job Jumpers in Illinois," *DuPage County* [Illinois] *Register*, April 6, 1945; "Coast Manpower Crisis Blamed on Job Jumping," *Los Angeles Times*, Aug. 1, 1945.

112. Historical Sketch, Local Board no. 1, Sumner County, Kansas, Aug. 1, 1946, and Historical Sketch, Local Board no. 1, Thomas County, Kansas, Sept. 1, 1946, both in Universal Military Training, Conscientious Objectors, Lewis B. Hershey Papers, United States Army War College Library and Archives, USAHEC.

113. See, for example, Theda Skocpol, *Protecting Soldiers and Mothers: The Political Origins of Social Policy in the United States* (Cambridge, Mass.: Harvard University Press, 1992) and Alice Kessler-Harris, *In Pursuit of Equity: Women, Men, and the Quest for Economic Citizenship in Twentieth-Century America* (New York: Oxford University Press, 2001).

114. Public Reactions to the Draft and Selective Service, memorandum No. 46, Jan. 9, 1943, Confidential Planning Council, box 67, entry 3, RG 147, NACP.

115. *Selective Service and Victory*, 70–71, 111–13.

116. On African Americans and the fight for equality in the armed forces and the implications of soldiering, see Christine Knauer, *Let Us Fight as Free Men: Black Soldiers and Civil Rights* (Philadelphia: University of Pennsylvania Press, 2014), chap. 1; Kimberley L. Phillips, *War! What Is It Good For? Black Freedom Struggles and the U.S. Military from World War II to Iraq* (Chapel Hill: University of North Carolina Press, 2012), chap. 1; Stephen Tuck, "'You Can Sing and Punch . . . But You Can't Be a Soldier or a Man:' African American Struggles for a New Place in Popular Culture," in *Fog of War: The Second World War and the Civil Rights Movement*, ed. Kevin M. Kruse and Stephen Tuck (New York: Oxford University Press, 2012), 103–25.

Chapter 2. "To Rub Smooth the Sharp Edges"

1. See, for example, letters contained in boxes 610–640, WHCF, OF 109, and boxes 845–848, WHCF, OF 245, Harry S. Truman Papers, HST.

2. Fred Barnard to President Truman, June 3, 1945, "B" [1945–49] [Misc. Pro.], box 612, WHCF, OF 109, HST [emphasis in the original].

3. Gilbert Blair to the Honorable Harry S. Truman, Sept. 7, 1945, "B" [1945–49] [Misc. Pro.], box 612, and Eugene Lankford to Hon. Harry S. Truman, Oct. 18, 1945, "L" [1945–49] [Misc. Pro.], box 614, both WHCF, OF 109, HST.

4. Hazel D. Leeft to President Truman, Oct. 26, 1945, "L" [1945–49] [Misc. Pro.], box 614; R. McD. Smith to My Dear Mr. President, Oct. 23, 1945, "S" [1945–49] [Misc.

Pro.], box 616; and Robert P. Skinner to Mr. President, Oct. 25, 1945, "S" [1945–49] [Misc. Pro.], box 616, all in WHCF, OF 109, HST.

5. S. Ira Arnold to Mr. Truman, Dec. 23, 1946, "A" [1946–1949] [Misc. Con], box 617; Mr. and Mrs. Homer W. Arnold to President Harry S. Truman, April 24, 1945, "A" [1945] [Misc. Con], box 617; Lisbeth Frantz to My Dear Mr. President, Jan. 31, 1952, "F" [1950–53] [Misc. Con] [2 of 2], box 623; Rev. and Mrs. Neil F. Bintz to President Truman, Jan. 29, 1952, "F" [1950–53] [Misc. Con] [2 of 2], box 623; Corda L. Anderson to Mr. Harry S. Truman, Dec. 30, 1945, "A" [1945] [Misc. Con.] box 617, all in WHCF, OF 109, HST.

6. Suzanne Mettler, *Soldiers to Citizens: The G.I. Bill and the Making of the Greatest Generation* (New York: Oxford University Press, 2005); John Grant Porter, "Concepts of Reserve Officers Training Corps Held by Advisers" (MS thesis: Iowa State University, 1967), 43.

7. John Gary Clifford, *The Citizen Soldiers: The Plattsburg Training Camp Movement, 1913–1920* (Lexington: University Press of Kentucky, 1972), 60–66, 152.

8. Chase C. Mooney and Martha E. Layman, "Some Phases of the Compulsory Military Training Movement, 1914–1920," *Mississippi Valley Historical Review* 38, no. 4 (March 1952): 655.

9. Clifford, *The Citizen Soldiers*, 296.

10. Transcript, "Comments on Universal Military Training at the Meeting of Religious Leaders—3 May 1945 by General George C. Marshall, Chief of Staff," May 3, 1945, 020 Chief of Staff, Plans and Policy Office, UMT Decimal File (1944–48), Records of the Legislative and Liaison Division, Records of the War Department General and Special Staffs, RG 165, NACP, quoted in Michael S. Sherry, *Preparing for the Next War: American Plans for Postwar Defense, 1941–1945* (New Haven, Conn.: Yale University Press, 1977), 3.

11. Marshall's Remarks to the Academy of Political Science in New York City, November 10, 1942, excerpts attached to memorandum, Marshall to General Ray Porter, October 21, 1945, file 353, RG 165, NACP, in Sherry, *Preparing for the Next War*, 4.

12. See William A. Taylor, *Every Citizen a Soldier: The Campaign for Universal Military Training after World War II* (College Station: Texas A&M University Press, 2014), esp. chaps. 3–5.

13. John McAuley Palmer, "General Marshall Wants a Citizen Army," *Saturday Evening Post*, Dec. 23, 1944, 9–10, 56; Henry L. Hopkins, "Tomorrow's Army and Your Boy," *The American*, March 1945, 20–21, 101–2, 104; Henry L. Stimson, "Should Universal Military Training Be Made Obligatory: Henry L. Stimson's Response," *The Nation's Schools* 34, no. 5 (Nov. 1944): 27; Walter L. Weible, "The War Department and the Program for Universal Military Training," *Bulletin of the American Association of University Professors* 30, no. 4 (Winter 1944): 491–99.

14. "A Real Military Training," *Washington Times-Herald*, Sept. 18, 1944; "Eisenhower's Letter on Youth Training," *New York Times*, June 16, 1945; "Arm or Die, Marshall Tells U.S.," [Pittsburgh] *Post Gazette*, Oct. 10, 1945; Taylor, *Every Citizen a Soldier*, 42–47.

15. Taylor, *Every Citizen a Soldier*, 47–49.

16. "Opinion Survey: Universal Military Training," Digest Prepared by Analysis Branch, War Department Bureau of Public Relations, March, 2, 1945, Opinion

Survey: Universal Military Training, Weekly Surveys of Newspaper Opinion Concerning Universal Military Training and the Postwar Military Establishment, 1944–1945, entry 52, volumes 1 and 2, Records of the Secretary of War, RG 107, NACP.

17. House Select Committee on Postwar Military Policy, *Universal Military Training*, H. Rpt. 857, 79th Cong., 1st sess., 1945.

18. Randall Jacobs, House Select Committee on Postwar Military Policy, *Universal Military Training: Hearings Before the Select Committee on Postwar Military Policy*, 79th Cong., 1st sess., June 1945, 533–34 [hereafter Woodrum Committee Hearings]. See also testimonies of John MacAuley Palmer, 489–93; James Forrestal, 525–28; Dwight D. Eisenhower, 486–89; and Chester Nimitz, 528–29.

19. See the testimony of Joseph C. Grew, 1–6; Henry Stimson, 481; and James Forrestal, 526, Woodrum Committee Hearings.

20. See the testimony of William F. Tompkins, 498, and Dwight Eisenhower, 487, Woodrum Committee Hearings.

21. See the testimony of James Forrestal, 527; Charles G. Bolte, 23; George Fielding Eliot, 29–30; Dorothy K. Funn, 348; Henry Stimson, 480; and John MacAuley Palmer, 492, Woodrum Committee Hearings.

22. Woodrum Committee Hearings, 529, 533.

23. Woodrum Committee Hearings, 39.

24. Woodrum Committee Hearings, 6; Taylor, *Every Citizen a Soldier*, 47–53.

25. John M. Swomley Jr., "A Study of the Universal Military Training Campaign, 1944–1952" (PhD diss., University of Colorado, 1959), 324.

26. See, for example, the testimony of Franklin Clarke Fry, 17–18; A. J. Brumbaugh, 91–107; William J. Miller, 107–11; Gould Wickey, 117–21; Thomasina W. Johnson, 197–209; and Ernest Angell, 209–12, Woodrum Committee Hearings.

27. Testimony of George F. Zook, House Military Affairs Committee, *Universal Military Training: Hearings on H.R. 515*, Part I, 79th Cong., 1st sess., November 20, 1945, 180 [hereafter May Committee Hearings, 1945].

28. Woodrum Committee Hearings, 112.

29. George Q. Flynn, *The Draft, 1940–1973* (Lawrence: University Press of Kansas, 1993), 91.

30. Flynn, *The Draft*, 92, 96.

31. Samuel P. Huntington, *The Common Defense: Strategic Programs in National Defense* (New York: Columbia University Press, 1961), 240.

32. According to "Poll of Women Favors Military Duty for Boys," *New York Herald Tribune*, Dec. 4, 1944, a poll in *The Woman's Home Companion* found that 83 percent of readers favored UMT.

33. Sherry, *Preparing for the Next War*, 75.

34. See "Summary of Public Opinion Polls Relating to Universal Military Training and National Security," May 6, 1947, Poll Results, box 2, PACUT, Records of Temporary Committees, Commissions, and Boards, RG 220, HST.

35. See, for example, "Statement on Compulsory Military Training, Adopted by the Council of Bishops of the Methodist Church at Buck Hill Falls Inn, Pennsylvania, Dec. 5, 1945," reprinted in the *Congressional Record*, 79th Cong., 2d sess., 1946, vol. 92, pt. 1, 555, and " 'Why the Haste? Can't We Wait on Peacetime Conscription until Peace Conference?' radio address by William T. Evjue," Jan. 7, 1945, reprinted in the *Congressional Record*, 79th Cong., 1st sess., 1945, vol. 91, pt. 10, A155.

36. See, for example, 78 H.R. 1806, 78 H.R. 3947, 79 S. 1473, and 79 S. 1749.

37. "Text of Truman Plea for Year's Army Training," *Chicago Tribune*, Oct. 24, 1945.

38. Representative Frederick Smith, Oct. 24, 1945, *Congressional Record*, 91, pt. 8, 10008.

39. Flynn, *The Draft*, 91, 96–97.

40. Taylor, *Every Citizen A Soldier*, 102.

41. "Sees End of Hyphen in Universal Drill," *New York Times*, May 19, 1916.

42. Senate Committee on Armed Services, *Reorganization of the Army: Hearings Before the Subcommittee of the Committee on Military Affairs*, 66th Cong., 1st sess., 1919, 827–828.

43. For examples of women and organizations that objected based on the exclusion of women, see Leila M. Murray, commander, The American Association of WACS, to Mr. President, October 26, 1945, "A" [1945–49] [misc. pro] 1 of 2, box 612, WHCF, OF 109, HST; Frieda S. Miller, Director, Women's Bureau, to Wilbur Cohen, Research Director, PACUT, April 16, 1947, Commission Kit—13th Meeting, 4-18/19-47, box 4, PACUT, RG 220, HST; The Place of Women in a Universal Training Program, n.d., folder 2, box 2, PACUT, RG 220, HST; Report of the Committee on Manpower to the Association of American Universities, n.d., Universal Military Service and Training, box 164, Principal File, Eisenhower Pre-Presidential Papers, DDE. Even those who otherwise supported the equal rights of women did not critique UMT for excluding women. For example, congresswoman Frances Bolton, a Republican from Ohio, chided the Woodrum Committee for failing to include any women members but did not mention women and universal military training or women and citizenship in her testimony other than to state that during World War II women showed themselves equal to all tasks placed in front of them. See testimony of Frances Bolton, Woodrum Committee Hearings, 583–88.

44. See Lizabeth Cohen, *A Consumers' Republic: The Politics of Mass Consumption in Postwar America* (New York: Vintage, 2003), 137–47; and Margot Canaday, *The Straight State: Sexuality and Citizenship in Twentieth-Century America* (Princeton, N.J.: Princeton University Press, 2011), chap. 4.

45. See, for example, appendix 7, "Women and National Security," in President's Advisory Commission on Universal Training, *A Program for National Security* (Washington, D.C.: GPO, 1947), 209–24.

46. Woodrum Committee Hearings, 529.

47. Woodrum Committee Hearings, 588.

48. Testimony of John Thomas Taylor, Woodrum Committee Hearings, 47.

49. Testimony of Henry Stimson, Woodrum Committee Hearings, 483. See also the testimonies of John Thomas Taylor, 35–49, and Robert Patterson, 16, Woodrum Committee Hearings; and the testimonies of Mrs. LaFell Dickinson, 124; Lula E. Bachman, 136–37; S. Stanwood Menken, 301; and Dunlap C. Clark, 334–35, all in May Committee Hearings, 1945.

50. Testimony of Thomasina W. Johnson, Woodrum Committee Hearings, 203.

51. Testimony of Samuel L. Harrison, House Military Affairs Committee, *Universal Military Training: Hearings on H.R. 515*, Part II, 79th Cong., 1st sess., February 21, 1946, 994 [hereafter May Committee Hearings, 1946]. See also the testimony of Edward C. M. Richards, Woodrum Committee Hearings, 387.

52. May Committee Hearings, 1945, 307.

53. Testimony of Huber F. Klemme, Woodrum Committee Hearings, 160.

54. Woodrum Committee Hearings, 107.

55. Woodrum Committee Hearings, 329.

56. Woodrum Committee Hearings, 325.

57. See, for example, the testimony of Sam Morris, May Committee Hearings, 1946, 958–60, and the testimony of Charles R. Bell Jr., Woodrum Committee Hearings, 700.

58. Testimony of Ralph McDonald, May Committee Hearings, 1945, 420. See also the testimony of Daniel L. Marsh, May Committee Hearings, 1945, 325.

59. Informal Remarks of the President to his Advisory Commission on Universal Training, Dec. 20, 1946, Commission Kit—2nd Meeting, 12-28-46, box 3, PACUT, RG 220, HST.

60. See the testimony of Karl T. Compton, 191–97, and Daniel A. Poling, 508–18, Woodrum Committee Hearings; and the testimony of Compton, May Committee Hearings, 1945, 207–23.

61. See Swomley, "A Study of the Universal Military Training Campaign," 209–11.

62. See Report of the First Meeting of the President's Advisory Commission on Universal Training, December 20, 1946, box 10, PACUT, RG 220, HST.

63. Report of the First Meeting of the President's Advisory Commission on Universal Training, 22.

64. Report of the First Meeting of the President's Advisory Commission on Universal Training, 6.

65. Report of the First Meeting of the President's Advisory Commission on Universal Training, 7.

66. Report of the First Meeting of the President's Advisory Commission on Universal Training, 8.

67. For a complete list, see President's Advisory Commission on Universal Training, A Program for National Security, 104–10.

68. President's Advisory Commission on Universal Training, A Program for National Security, 2.

69. President's Advisory Commission on Universal Training, A Program for National Security, 3.

70. President's Advisory Commission on Universal Training, A Program for National Security, 13.

71. President's Advisory Commission on Universal Training, A Program for National Security, 14.

72. President's Advisory Commission on Universal Training, A Program for National Security, 20.

73. President's Advisory Commission on Universal Training, A Program for National Security, 20–21.

74. President's Advisory Commission on Universal Training, A Program for National Security, 39–40.

75. "The AGF UMT Experimental Unit, Fort Knox, Kentucky," n.d., Staff Studies—Fort Knox, Ky., box 8, PACUT, RG 220, HST.

76. House Committee on Expenditures in the Executive Departments, Investigation of Participation of Federal Officials of the War Department in Publicity and Propaganda,

as it Relates to Universal Military Training, Fourth Intermediate Report of the Committee on Expenditures in the Executive Departments, 80th Cong., 1st sess., July 1947, 6.

77. "The AGF UMT Experimental Unit," PACUT, RG 220, HST, 5.

78. "The Fort Knox Experiment," n.d., Staff Studies—Fort Knox, Ky., box 8, PACUT, RG 220, HST, 1.

79. "The AGF UMT Experimental Unit," PACUT, RG 220, HST, 6.

80. "The AGF UMT Experimental Unit," PACUT, RG 220, HST, 4.

81. "The AGF UMT Experimental Unit," PACUT, RG 220, HST, 5.

82. See Taylor, *Every Citizen a Soldier,* 103–6.

83. House Subcommittee on Publicity and Propaganda, Committee on Expenditures in the Executive Departments, *Investigation of War Department Publicity and Propaganda in Relation to Universal Military Training: Hearings Before the Subcommittee on Publicity and Propaganda,* 80th Cong., 2nd sess., 1948, 13; House Committee on Expenditures in the Executive Departments, *Investigation of Participation of Federal Officials of the Department of the Army in Publicity and Propaganda, as it Relates to Universal Military Training,* Supplemental Report to the Fourth Intermediate Report of the Committee on Expenditures in the Executive Departments, 80th Cong., 2nd sess., March 4, 1948, 3.

84. United States Army Field Forces, Universal Military Training Experimental Unit, *Interim Report: U.M.T. Experimental Unit,* Fort Knox, Kentucky, 1 August 1947, 45.

85. "The AGF UMT Experimental Unit," PACUT, RG 220, HST, 45.

86. "Universal Military Training," n.d., Universal Military Training, box 3672, Publications "P" Files, 1946–51, Document Library Branch, Assistant Chief of Staff (G-2), Intelligence, Administrative Div., Records of the Army Staff, RG 319, NACP, 24.

87. "The Fort Knox Experiment," PACUT, RG 220, HST, 3.

88. "Universal Military Training," RG 319, NACP, 12.

89. "Universal Military Training," RG 319, NACP, 1.

90. A Jewish chaplain from the larger installation at Fort Knox was available for the few Jewish volunteers, and Jewish worship services were also available. "The AGF UMT Experimental Unit," 33.

91. A secular lecture on ethics was made available, but only one volunteer took advantage of this option during the first training group. See "The Fort Knox Experiment," n.d., Universal Military Training, Compton Committee, box 41, PCRW, RG 220, HST, 10.

92. "The Fort Knox Experiment," PCRW, RG 220, HST, 6.

93. "The Fort Knox Experiment," PCRW, RG 220, HST, 10.

94. "Universal Military Training," RG 319, NACP, 22–23.

95. Report on the Activities and Program of the Protestant Chaplain, UMT Exper. Unit, 18 March 1947, Staff Studies—Fort Knox, Ky., box 8, PACUT, RG 220, HST; Universal Military Training Experimental Unit, *Interim Report: U.M.T. Experimental Unit,* 25.

96. "The Fort Knox Experiment," PACUT, RG 220, HST, 6.

97. Universal Military Training Experimental Unit, *Interim Report: U.M.T. Experimental Unit,* 11.

98. Dave Bennett, "Blue and Gold Revue: Trainee Diary," *UMT Pioneer,* Feb. 8, 1947, in Commission Kit, 9th mtg., 2-14-47, box 3, PACUT, RG 220, HST.

99. "The Fort Knox Experiment," PACUT, RG 220, HST, 1.

100. "Universal Military Training," RG 319, NACP, 5–6.

101. "The AGF UMT Experimental Unit," PACUT, RG 220, HST, 18.

102. "The Fort Knox Experiment," PACUT, RG 220, HST, 3.

103. "Universal Military Training," RG 319, NACP, 42.

104. Memorandum on Public Opinion Polls Relating to Universal Military Training, February 19, 1947, Commission Kit—10th mtg., 2-21-47, box 3, PACUT, RG 220, HST.

105. PACUT and Truman received 2,750 letters in this period. Of these, 1,850 expressed a favorable opinion of UMT. See Analysis of Correspondence, December 20, 1946–February 6, 1947, Commission Kit—10th mtg., 2-21-47, box 3, PACUT, RG 220, HST.

106. Hanson W. Baldwin, "Army's Youth Unit Called a Success," *New York Times*, May 18, 1947.

107. Analysis of Correspondence, December 20, 1946–February 6, 1947.

108. Taylor, *Every Citizen a Soldier*, 112.

109. Analysis of Correspondence, December 20, 1946–February 6, 1947.

110. Summary of Public Opinion Polls Relating to Universal Military Training and National Security, May 6, 1947, Poll Results, box 2, PACUT, RG 220, HST.

111. House Committee on Armed Services, *Universal Military Training*, H. Rpt. No. 1107, Report to accompany H.R. 4278, 80th Cong., 1st sess., July 1947, 7.

112. House Committee on Armed Services, *Subcommittee Hearings on Universal Military Training: Hearings on H.R. 4121*, 80th Cong., 1st sess., July 1947, 4443.

113. See Clarence E. Wunderlin, *Robert A. Taft: Ideas, Tradition, and Party in U.S. Foreign Policy* (New York: Rowman & Littlefield, 2005), 131–32.

114. James M. Gerhardt, *The Draft and Public Policy: Issues in Military Manpower Procurement, 1945–1970* (Columbus: Ohio State University Press, 1971), 71.

115. See House Committee on Expenditures in the Executive Departments, *Investigation of Participation of Federal Officials of the War Department in Publicity and Propaganda, as it Relates to Universal Military Training*, Fourth Intermediate Report, 80th Cong., 1st sess., July 1947, and House Committee on Expenditures in the Executive Departments, *Investigation of Participation of Federal Officials of the Department of the Army in Publicity and Propaganda, as it Relates to Universal Military Training*, Supplemental Report to the Fourth Intermediate Report, 80th Cong., 2d sess. March 1948.

116. James Gilbert, *Redeeming Culture: American Religion in an Age of Science* (Chicago: University of Chicago Press, 1997), 110.

117. Gerhardt, *The Draft and Public Policy*, 84–85.

118. Secretary of State Marshall, quoted in "Secretary Is Firm," *New York Times*, March 19, 1948.

119. "The Text of President Truman's Address to the Joint Session of the Congress," *New York Times*, March 18, 1948.

120. Gerhardt, *The Draft and Public Policy*, 87.

121. "The Text of President Truman's Address to the Joint Session of the Congress."

122. Gerhardt, *The Draft and Public Policy*, 90; Wunderlin, *Robert A. Taft*, 131–32.

123. See the testimonies of William Greene, 840–51; George F. Zook, 891–97; and Herbert W. Voorhees, 138–44, Senate Committee on Armed Services, *Universal Military Training*, 80th Cong., 2d sess., 1948.

124. See the testimony of Grant Reynolds, 676–85, and A. Philip Randolph, 685–95, Senate Committee on Armed Services, *Universal Military Training*.

125. Christine Knauer, *Let Us Fight as Free Men: Black Soldiers and Civil Rights* (Philadelphia: University of Pennsylvania Press, 2014), 93.

126. Paula E. Pfeffer, *A. Philip Randolph: Pioneer of the Civil Rights Movement* (Baton Rouge: Louisiana State University Press, 1990), chap. 4.

127. For further discussion, see Mary L. Dudziak, *Cold War Civil Rights: Race and the Image of American Democracy* (Princeton, N.J.: Princeton University Press, 2002), chap. 3; Pfeffer, *A. Philip Randolph*, chap. 4.

128. Swomley, "A Study of the Universal Military Training Campaign," 131.

129. "Race Segregation Still a Live Issue in Draft Program," *New York Times*, May 13, 1948.

130. See Gerhardt, *The Draft and Public Policy*, 166–67.

131. Senate Committee on Armed Services, *Universal Military Training*, 32.

132. House Committee on Armed Services, *Selective Service: Hearings on Sundry Legislation*, H. Rept. 265, 80th Cong., 2d sess., April 8, 1948, 6138, as quoted in Gerhardt, *The Draft and Public Policy*, 100.

133. Ray T. Maddocks, *Universal Military Training as Applied in the 3d Armored Division*, Armored School, Fort Knox, Ky., 1948; Gilbert, *Redeeming Culture*, chap. 5.

134. Baldwin, "Army's Youth Unit Called a Success."

135. Alexander Stewart, "Is 'UMTee' the Answer?" *Christian Century*, reprinted in House Committee on Armed Services, *Full Committee Hearings on Universal Military Training*, 80th Cong., 1st sess., June 1947, 4276.

136. "The Army's Kid-Glove Rookies," *Life*, March 10, 1947, 43–46.

Chapter 3. "Really First-Class Men"

1. The Selective Training and Service Act of 1940 is widely considered the United States' first peacetime draft by both scholars and the legislators who crafted it. It is clear, however, that the 1940 act was passed with an eye toward America's entrance into World War II. For more on the fuzzy edges of wartime in the United States, see Mary L. Dudziak, *War Time: An Idea, Its History, Its Consequences* (New York: Oxford University Press, 2012).

2. Selective Service Act of 1948, Public Law 80-759, *United States Statutes at Large* 62, part 1 (1948), 605.

3. Newton D. Baker to Woodrow Wilson, May 26, 1917, box 4, Newton D. Baker Papers, LOC, as quoted in John Whiteclay Chambers III, *To Raise an Army: The Draft Comes to Modern America* (New York: The Free Press, 1987), 190.

4. Chambers, *To Raise an Army*, 233.

5. "Widens Deferment for Men in College," *New York Times*, March 5, 1943.

6. George Q. Flynn, *The Draft, 1940–1973* (Lawrence: University Press of Kansas, 1993), 79.

7. President's Scientific Research Board, *Science and Public Policy*, vol. 3, Administration for Research (Washington, D.C.: GPO, 1947), 2–3.

8. Alan I. Marcus and Amy Sue Bix, *The Future Is Now: Science and Technology Policy since 1950* (Amherst, N.Y.: Humanity Books, 2007), 14–23; Irvin Stewart, *Organizing Scientific Research for War: The Administrative History of the Office of Scientific Research and Development* (Boston: Little, Brown, and Co., 1948), esp. 35–51, 143. Available online at http://openlibrary.org/books/OL6026526M/Organizing_scientific_research_for_war.

9. Vannevar Bush, *Science: The Endless Frontier* (Washington, D.C.: GPO, 1945), available online at http://www.nsf.gov/od/lpa/nsf50/vbush1945.htm#summary (accessed Sept. 16, 2017).

10. Bush, *Science*.

11. Laura Micheletti Puaca, *Searching for Scientific Womanpower: Technocratic Feminism and the Politics of National Security, 1940–1980* (Chapel Hill: University of North Carolina Press, 2014), 28–31.

12. Puaca, *Searching for Scientific Womanpower*, esp. chap. 2 and 3, and Amy Sue Bix, *Girls Coming to Tech: A History of American Engineering Education for Women* (Cambridge, Mass.: MIT Press, 2013).

13. President's Scientific Research Board, *Science and Public Policy*, vol. 1. A Program for the Nation (Washington, D.C.: GPO, 1947), III.

14. Aaron Lecklider, *Inventing the Egghead: The Battle over Brainpower in American Culture* (Philadelphia: University of Pennsylvania Press, 2013), chap. 7; Paul Boyer, *By the Bomb's Early Light: American Thought and Culture at the Dawn of the Atomic Age* (New York: Pantheon Books, 1985).

15. Stuart W. Leslie, *The Cold War and American Science: The Military-Industrial-Academic Complex at MIT and Stanford* (New York: Columbia University Press, 1993).

16. Lecklider, *Inventing the Egghead*, chap. 6, esp. p. 169; President's Scientific Research Board, *Science and Public Policy*, vol. 1, 3.

17. President's Scientific Research Board, *Science and Public Policy*, vol. 4. Manpower for Research, 13.

18. President's Scientific Research Board, *Science and Public Policy*, vol. 4, 3.

19. President's Scientific Research Board, *Science and Public Policy*, vol. 4, 27.

20. President's Scientific Research Board, *Science and Public Policy*, vol. 4, 27.

21. President's Scientific Research Board, *Science and Public Policy*, vol. 4, 6.

22. President's Scientific Research Board, *Science and Public Policy*, vol. 4, 3.

23. President's Scientific Research Board, *Science and Public Policy*, vol. 4, 6–7.

24. President's Scientific Research Board, *Science and Public Policy*, vol. 1, 7.

25. President's Scientific Research Board, *Science and Public Policy*, vol. 1, 5, 12.

26. President's Scientific Research Board, *Science and Public Policy*, vol. 1, 13.

27. United States Selective Service System, *Annual Report of the Director of Selective Service for the Fiscal Year 1951 to the Congress of the United States pursuant to the Universal Military Training and Service Act as Amended* (Washington, D.C.: GPO, 1952), 18 [hereafter *Annual Report*, (year)].

28. Preparedness Subcommittee of the Senate Committee on Armed Services, *Universal Military Training and Service Act of 1951: Hearings before the Preparedness Subcommittee of the Committee on Armed Services*, 82d Cong., 1st sess., Jan. 1951, 78.

29. For more information, see M. H. Trytten, *Student Deferment in Selective Service: A Vital Factor in National Security* (Minneapolis: University of Minnesota Press, 1952), 7–11.

30. See Meeting of Scientific Committees, November 4 and 5, 1948, and Meeting of Scientific Committees, December 9 and 10, 1948, both in box 71, Papers of the Planning Office, 1947–1963, entry UD 24, Records of the Selective Service System, RG 147, NACP.

31. Meeting of Scientific Committees, December 9 and 10, 1948, 115.

32. Meeting of Scientific Committees, December 9 and 10, 1948, 117.

33. Meeting of Scientific Committees, December 9 and 10, 1948, 117–18.

34. For a complete transcript of this discussion, see Meeting of Scientific Committees, December 9 and 10, 1948, 107–35.

35. See "Reports of the Scientific Advisory Committees" in Trytten, *Student Deferment in Selective Service*, 81–91.

36. Meeting of Scientific Committees, December 9 and 10, 1948, 114.

37. For a discussion of this debate, see Brian McAllister Linn, *Elvis's Army: Cold War GIs and the Atomic Battlefield* (Cambridge, Mass.: Harvard University Press, 2016), 52.

38. Preparedness Subcommittee of the Senate Committee on Armed Services, *Universal Military Training and Service Act of 1951*, 137–38.

39. See "A Report to the National Security Council—NSC-68." April 12, 1950, President's Secretary's File, Truman Papers, http://www.trumanlibrary.org/whistlestop/study_collections/coldwar/documents/pdf/10-1.pdf.

40. *Annual Report, 1952*, 63.

41. *Annual Report, 1951*, 11.

42. See Meeting of Advisory Committee on Specialized Personnel, Washington D.C., December 3, 1951, box 71, entry UD 24, RG 147, NACP, 25–31.

43. Testimony of Anna Rosenberg, Preparedness Subcommittee of the Senate Committee on Armed Services, *Universal Military Training and Service Act of 1951*, 37–66; Senate Committee on Armed Services, *Universal Military and Service Act: Report of the Committee on Armed Services to Accompany S. 1*, Report No. 117, 82d Cong., 1st sess., February 1951, 8–9 [hereafter Senate Report 117]; James M. Gerhardt, *The Draft and Public Policy: Issues in Military Manpower Procurement, 1945–1970* (Columbus: Ohio State University Press, 1971), 148.

44. See Report of the Meeting of the Combined Scientific Committees with the Healing Arts Educational Advisory Committee, July 31, 1950, and Walter R. Krill to Colonel Eanes, September 26, 1950, both in 105 Advisory Committee (Gen), 1950–48, box 34, Central Files, 1948–69, RG 147, NACP.

45. "Reports of the Scientific Advisory Committees," in Trytten, *Student Deferment in Selective Service*, 92.

46. Report to the Director of the Selective Service System by the Six Committees on Scientific, Professional, and Specialized Personnel, n.d., Statements and Reco's, Oct. 5, 1950, Office Files, 1950s: Scientific Advisory Committee, ca. 1950–1957, Lewis B. Hershey Papers, United States Army War College Library and Archives, USAHEC.

47. Report to the Director of the Selective Service System by the Six Committees on Scientific, Professional, and Specialized Personnel, 20.

48. Report to the Director of the Selective Service System by the Six Committees on Scientific, Professional, and Specialized Personnel, 43.

49. Scientific Advisory Committees Minutes of Public Meeting, December 18, 1950, box 71, UD 24, RG 147, NACP, 14.

50. Senate Preparedness Subcommittee of the Committee on Armed Services, *Universal Military Training and Service Act of 1951*, 508.

51. Senate Preparedness Subcommittee of the Committee on Armed Services, *Universal Military Training and Service Act of 1951*, 23.

52. House Committee on Armed Services, *Universal Military Training: Hearings before the Committee on Armed Services*, 82d Cong., 1st sess., Jan. 1951, 62.

53. Senate Committee on Armed Services, *Report of Proceedings: Hearing Held Before Committee on Armed Services, Executive Session*, 82d Cong., 1st sess., Feb. 1951, 120, 123.

54. See Senate Report 117, 7.

55. Senate Preparedness Subcommittee of the Committee on Armed Services, *Universal Military Training and Service Act of 1951*, 627, 667.

56. Senate Report 117, 6; Testimony of Anna Rosenberg, Senate Preparedness Subcommittee of the Committee on Armed Services, *Universal Military Training and Service Act of 1951*, 69.

57. Senate Preparedness Subcommittee of the Committee on Armed Services, *Universal Military Training and Service Act of 1951*, 68–70.

58. House Committee on Armed Services, *Universal Military Training*, 143.

59. House Committee on Armed Services, *Universal Military Training*, 172.

60. House Committee on Armed Services, *Universal Military Training*, 9, 345.

61. Senate Preparedness Subcommittee of the Committee on Armed Services, *Universal Military Training and Service Act of 1951*, 1203.

62. See, for example, the testimonies of Ezra Ellis, Robert W. Lyon, J. Raymond Schmidt, Ruth Bleier, Sidney Aberman, and John M. Swomley Jr., all excerpted in Senate Report 117, 29–31.

63. Senate Report 117, 30.

64. Senate Report 117, 29.

65. Senate Report 117, 30.

66. Testimony of Ralph W. McDonald, as quoted in Senate Report 117, 27.

67. See also Paul E. Elicker, Senate Report 117, 28.

68. See the testimonies of Elicker and Edgar Fuller, excerpted in Senate Report 117, 28.

69. For examples, see the letters contained in boxes 988–991, WHCF, OF 245 Misc., Harry S. Truman Papers, HST. Within these boxes, three folders contain letters in favor of drafting eighteen-year-olds and twenty-five contain letters against.

70. Eighteen Year Old Draft, n.d. and Random Sample, n.d., both in 18-yr-old-boys, box 988, WHCF, OF 245-Misc., HST.

71. See, for example, letters contained in 1950–June 1951, box 845, WHCF, OF 245-Misc., HST.

72. Mrs. Bennett M. Groisser to My Dear Mr. President, Feb. 5, 1951, 1950–June 1951, box 845, WHCF, OF 245-Misc., HST.

73. Mrs. Martin Rabinowitz to the President of the United States, Feb. 5, 1951, and Warren Rinda to Mr. President, February 15, 1951, both in 1950–June 1951, box 845, WHCF, OF 245-Misc., HST.

74. Mrs. Joseph Pepe to Dear President, February 6, 1951, 1950–June 1951, box 845, WHCF, OF 245-Misc., HST [emphasis mine].

75. See Nancy Woloch, *Women and the American Experience: A Concise History*, 2nd Edition (Boston: McGraw Hill Higher Education, 2002), 343.

76. See Jessica Weiss, *To Have and To Hold: Marriage, the Baby Boom, and Social Change* (Chicago: University of Chicago Press, 2000), esp. chap. 4; Otis Lee Weise, "Live the Life of *McCall's*," *McCall's*, May 1954, 27.

77. "More Children Equal Less Divorce," *Look*, Feb. 13, 1951, 80; "Married Women Live Longer," *Look*, March 13, 1951, 21.

78. O. Spurgeon English and Constance J. Foster, "How to Be a Good Father," *Parents Magazine*, June 1950, 84.

79. Philip Wylie, *Generation of Vipers* (New York: Rhinehart and Company, Inc., 1942), 203; Michael Rogin, "Kiss Me Deadly: Communism, Motherhood, and Cold War Movies," *Representations* 6 (Spring 1984): 6.

80. Sheldon Glueck and Eleanor Glueck, *Unraveling Juvenile Delinquency* (Cambridge, Mass., Harvard University Press, 1950), 125.

81. For more, see Elaine Tyler May, *Homeward Bound: American Families in the Cold War Era* (New York: Basic Books, 1988), 146–49; Jessica Weiss, *To Have and To Hold*, esp. chap. 3; James Gilbert, *Men in the Middle: Searching for Masculinity in the 1950s* (Chicago: University of Chicago Press, 2005), esp. chap. 7; Ralph LaRossa, *Of War and Men: World War II in the Lives of Fathers and their Families* (Chicago: University of Chicago Press, 2011), esp. parts III and IV.

82. See, for example, Nina Mackert, "'But Recall the Kind of Parents We Have to Deal With': Juvenile Delinquency, Interdependent Masculinity, and the Government of Families in the Postwar U.S.," in *Inventing the Modern American Family: Family Values and Social Change in 20th Century United States,* ed. Isabel Heinemann (New York: Campus Verlag, 2012), 201–4; Olaf Stieglitz, "Is Mom to Blame? Anti-Communist Law Enforcement and the Representation of Motherhood in Early Cold War U.S. Film," in *Inventing the Modern American Family*, 244–64; James Gilbert, *A Cycle of Outrage: America's Reaction to the Juvenile Delinquent in the 1950s* (New York: Oxford University Press, 1986), 73–78.

83. J. Edgar Hoover, "Juvenile Delinquency," *Southwest Review* 32, no. 4 (Autumn 1947): 388.

84. Glueck and Glueck, *Unraveling Juvenile Delinquency*, 287.

85. Donald W. Wyatt to Lyndon B. Johnson, January 17, 1951, published in Senate Preparedness Subcommittee of the Committee on Armed Services, *Universal Military Training and Service Act of 1951*, 1137.

86. See the testimonies of Omar Bradley, Forrest Sherman, James P. Baxter III, Karl B. Compton, Detley W. Bronk, Harold W. Dodds, and the representatives of the American Legion, the Veterans of Foreign Wars of the United States, the Disabled American Veterans, AMVETS, the American Veteran's Committee, and the Jewish War Veterans of the United States of America, Senate Preparedness Subcommittee of the Committee on Armed Services, *Universal Military Training and Service Act of 1951*.

87. Senate Report 117, 72; Universal Military Training and Service Act of 1951, Public Law 82-51, *United States Statutes at Large 65*, part 1 (1951), 88–89.

88. Senate Report 117, 48.

89. Testimony of Maurice J. Tobin, Senate Preparedness Subcommittee of the Committee on Armed Services, *Universal Military Training and Service Act of 1951*, 328–33, 336–39.

90. Lewis B. Hershey to the President, March 3, 1949, 105 Advisory Committee (Gen), 1950-48, box 34, Central Files, 1948-69, RG 147, NACP.

91. Henry Chauncy, "The Use of the Selective Service College Qualification Test in the Deferment of College Students," *Science*, July 25, 1952, 73.

92. Trytten, *Student Deferment in Selective Service*, 65.

93. Trytten, *Student Deferment in Selective Service*, 68.

94. Edward A. Suchman, Robin M. Williams, and Rose K. Goldsen, "Student Reaction to Impending Military Service," *American Sociological Review* 18, no. 3 (June 1953): 293–304.

95. See, for example, Leonard Carmichael and Leonard C. Mead, eds., *The Selection of Military Manpower: A Symposium* (National Academy of Sciences—National Research Council, 1951); Robert A. Walker, ed., *America's Manpower Crisis: The Report of the Institute on Manpower Utilization and Government Personnel, Stanford University, August 22, 23, and 24, 1951* (Chicago: Public Administration Service, 1952); National Manpower Council, *Student Deferment and National Manpower Policy* (New York: Columbia University Press, 1952); National Manpower Council, *Proceedings of a Conference on the Utilization of Scientific and Professional Manpower, Held October 7–11, 1953* (New York: Columbia University Press, 1954).

96. "Students and the Draft," *Scientific American*, Sept. 1951, 48.

97. *Annual Report*, 1953, 18.

98. See "Deferment Plan Scored," *New York Times*, May 12, 1951; "Conant and Dodds Assail Deferment on Student Marks," *New York Times*, April 9, 1951; and B. R. Stanerson to General Hershey, May 4, 1953, American [C], box 82, Central Files, 1948-69, RG 147, NACP.

99. Flynn, *The Draft*, 143.

100. See *Annual Report*, 1953, 55–57.

101. Press Release, August 3, 1951, 002.40, 1963-48, box 26, Central Files, 1948–69, RG 147, NACP.

102. Press Release, August 3, 1951.

103. George Gallup, "Draft Deferments for College Men, Fathers Favored," *Daily Boston Globe*, June 1, 1952.

104. See, for example, "Wealthy Men Dodging Draft, Senators Told," *Chicago Daily Tribune*, Feb. 5, 1953; "Why Korea Is Called 'Poor Man's War,'" *U.S. News and World Report*, Feb. 20, 1953, 18–20; "Board Quits; Claims Draft Favors Rich," *Washington Post*, July 10, 1953; "Lawmaker's Son Deferred; Draft Board Resigns," *Los Angeles Times*, July 15, 1953; "Drafting Fathers," *The States-Graphic*, Aug. 28, 1953, Fathers, box 819, Hershey Papers, USAHEC.

105. Psychology professor Everett L. Kelly of the University of Michigan brought up the possibility at the November 1948 meeting as did economics professor John Kenneth Galbraith of Harvard at the December meeting. Trytten dismissed both of their concerns by making a joke. See Meeting of Scientific Committees, November 4 and 5, 1948, 65, and Meeting of Scientific Committees, December 9 and 10, 1948, 36–37. See also Untitled Report, n.d., ETS Test, Steno Report of Meeting, 11/22/50, Office Files, 1950s, Scientific Advisory Committee, ca. 1950–1957, Hershey Papers, USAHEC, 16–18.

106. *Annual Report*, 1954, 20; Irving C. Whitmore to Delmar Leighton, Feb. 5, 1953, Student Deferment Correspondence, box 627, Hershey Papers, USAHEC.

107. Harold H. Martin, "Why Ike Had to Draft Fathers," *Saturday Evening Post,* Aug. 29, 1953, 27; "To End Uncertainties and Inequities in the Draft," *Philadelphia Inquirer,* March 30, 1953.

108. Scientific Advisory Committee on Specialized Personnel Statement and Recommendations, August 18, 1952, 105 Advisory Committee (Gen.), 1952–51, box 34, Central Files, 1948–69, RG 147, NACP.

109. National Manpower Council, *Student Deferment and National Manpower Policy,* 3.

110. Daniel O. Omer to Roger W. Jones, June 1, 1953, attached to Daniel O. Omer to Roger W. Jones, June 5, 1953, 110 General, 1954–1950, box 35, Central Files, 1948–69, RG 147, NACP.

111. Flynn, *The Draft,* 138; National Manpower Council, *Student Deferment and National Manpower Policy.*

112. "Planning Nation's Man Power for 10 Years Ahead," *U.S. News and World Report,* Jan. 4, 1952, 32.

113. Bulletin to the Advisory Committee on Specialized Personnel, No. 10, November 15, 1952, 105, Advisory Committee (Gen.), 1952-51, box 34, Central Files, 1948–69, RG 147, NACP.

114. Premises Underlying Manpower Policies, November 30, 1951, attached to Meeting of Advisory Committee on Specialized Personnel, Washington D.C., December 3, 1951, box 71, UD 24, RG 147, NACP.

Chapter 4. "A Draft-Dodging Business"

1. Lewis B. Hershey to Honorable William H. Avery, February 4, 1958, and attachments, Bala thru Bald, box 82, Central Files, 1948–69, Records of the Selective Service, RG 147, NACP.

2. Lewis B. Hershey, "Altered Role, Continuing Need for Draft Stressed," *Selective Service,* March 1958, 1–2.

3. Subcommittee on Independent Offices, House Appropriations Committee, *Independent Offices Appropriations for 1959: Hearings before the Subcommittee of the Committee on Appropriations, House of Representatives,* 85th Cong., 2d sess., Jan. 1958, 200.

4. Hershey, "Altered Role, Continuing Need for Draft Stressed," 2.

5. Subcommittee on Independent Offices, *Independent Offices Appropriations for 1959,* 197–211.

6. Selective Service System, "Channeling," *Orientation Kit,* 1965, 1.

7. George C. Herring, *From Colony to Superpower: U.S. Foreign Relations Since 1776* (New York: Oxford University Press, 2008), 653; Robert R. Bowie and Richard H. Immerman, *Waging Peace: How Eisenhower Shaped an Enduring Cold War Strategy* (New York: Oxford University Press, 1998), 178.

8. For a detailed description of the New Look Policy, see Bowie and Immerman, *Waging Peace,* esp. chap. 12.

9. Herring, *From Colony to Superpower,* 660.

10. James M. Gerhardt, *The Draft and Public Policy: Issues in Military Manpower Procurement, 1945–1970* (Columbus: Ohio State University Press, 1971), 192; Brian McAllister Linn, *Elvis's Army: Cold War GIs and the Atomic Bomb* (Cambridge, Mass.: Harvard University Press, 2016), 85–86.

11. Senate Committee on Armed Services, *Career Incentive Act of 1955*, S. Rept. No. 125, March 29, 1955, 84th Cong., 1st sess., 1955, 5.

12. Senate Committee on Armed Services, S. Rept. No. 125, 3; Gerhardt, *The Draft and Public Policy*, 214.

13. House Armed Services Committee, *Review of the Administration and Operation of the Selective Service System: Hearings before the Committee on Armed Services, House of Representatives*, 89th Cong., 2d. sess., 1966, 10003.

14. United States Selective Service System, *Annual Report of the Director of Selective Service for the Fiscal Year 1953 to the Congress of the United States pursuant to the Universal Military Training and Service Act as Amended* (Washington, D.C.: GPO, 1953), 67 [hereafter *Annual Report*, (year)]; *Annual Report*, 1957, 74; *Annual Report*, 1961, 58.

15. Gerhardt, *The Draft and Public Policy*, 217.

16. Selective Service, Induction Statistics, http://www.selectiveservice.us/military-draft/8-induction.shtml (accessed Feb. 18, 2018).

17. Commencement of Classification, August 1, 1955, attached to R. T. Finks to Major General Lewis B. Hershey, August 8, 1955, 300 Classification-Gen. & Ala.-Nev. 1963-1948, box 61, Central Files, RG 147, NACP.

18. See Chester A. Furbish to General Hershey, March 29, 1955, attached to Bernard T. Franck III to Colonel Furbish, April 26, 1955, 127 General Mass. 1963-1955, box 47; and Lewis B. Hershey to Colonel Armstrong, January 5, 1956, and attachments, 127 General Ill. 1963-1953, box 46, both in Central Files, RG 147, NACP.

19. See, for example, the statements of Charles E. Wilson and Arthur Bradford, Senate Committee on Armed Services, *1955 Amendments to the Universal Military Training and Service Act, Hearings Before the Committee on Armed Services, United States Senate on H.R. 3005, H.R. 6057, and S. 1467*, 84th Cong., 1st sess., June 1955, 182–85.

20. Senate Committee on Armed Services, *1955 Amendments to the Universal Military Training and Service Act*, 199.

21. See the testimony of Lewis B. Hershey, Senate Committee on Armed Services, *1955 Amendments to the Universal Military Training and Service Act*, 225.

22. William M. Brucker to Everett R. Hopper, Jan. 9, 1959, Interoffice Memos (Admin. Corres.) 1958, box 109, Training and Conference Files, RG 147, NACP.

23. Testimony of Lewis B. Hershey, Senate Committee on Armed Services, *1955 Amendments to the Universal Military Training and Service Act*, 229.

24. See "Legion Head Says Draft Is Unfair," *Baltimore Sun*, March 28, 1955; David Lawrence, "Young Men Can Relax Again," *U.S. News and World Report*, Jan. 6, 1956, 52–53.

25. John G. Norris, "Answer to Lagging Reserve Program is 3-Fold," *Washington Post*, Dec. 5, 1955.

26. Edward A. Suchman, Robin M. Williams, and Rose K. Goldsen, "Student Reaction to Impending Military Service," *American Sociological Review* 18, no. 3 (1953): 293–304.

27. See Oliver LaVerne Rapp, "Military Problems Facing High School Boys" (EdD diss., University of Illinois, Urbana, 1956), 46, 90.

28. "The Chance of Being Drafted Now," *U.S. News and World Report*, Jan. 21, 1955, 32; "Draft to Go On—Who'll Be Called," *U.S. News and World Report*, Feb. 18, 1955, 32.

29. Lawrence, "Young Men Can Relax Again," 52.

30. John H. Greenaway to General Hershey, January 6, 1955 [*sic*], attached to Bernard T. Franck III to Mr. Greenaway, January 30, 1956, 127 General N.H. 1963-1948, box 48, Central Files, RG 147, NACP.

31. Subcommittee No. 1, House Armed Services Committee, *Review of Reserve Program by Subcommittee No. 1*, Serial No. 41, Jan. 5, 1956, 84th Cong., 2d sess., 4914–15. See also Bernard T. Franck III to Mr. Greenaway, January 30, 1956.

32. Hershey, "Public Reaction to Settle Fate of Reserve Program," *Selective Service*, Feb. 1956, 2.

33. *Annual Report*, 1956, 65.

34. "Proposal to Ease Draft Is Offered," *New York Times*, Sept. 23, 1955. See also Gerhardt, *The Draft and Public Policy*, 228–29.

35. John E. Walsh to Maj. Gen. Lewis B. Hershey, July 13, 1955, attached to Dee Ingold to General Walsh, July 26, 1955, 127 General Idaho, 1955-1948, box 46, Central Files, RG 147, NACP.

36. William P. Averill to General Hershey, June 10, 1955, 311-General Military Service (I-A), box 63, Central Files, RG 147, NACP.

37. Paul G. Armstrong to My Associates in Selective Service, n.d., attached to Lewis B. Hershey to Colonel Armstrong, January 5, 1956, 127 General Ill. 1963-1953, box 46, Central Files, RG 147, NACP.

38. Dee Ingold to General Walsh, July 26, 1955, 127 General Idaho, 1955-1948; and Lewis B. Hershey to Colonel Armstrong, January 5, 1956, and attachments, 127 General Ill. 1963-1953, all in box 46, Central Files, RG 147, NACP.

39. R. T. Finks to Maj. Gen. Lewis B. Hershey, August 8, 1955, 300 Classification—Gen. & Ala.-Nev. 1963-1948, box 61, Central Files, RG 147, NACP.

40. *Annual Report*, 1958, 5.

41. Subcommittee on Independent Offices, *Independent Offices Appropriations for 1959*, 221. New York was the only exception, as it possessed two state headquarters, one that administered New York City and one that handled the rest of the state.

42. In fiscal 1958, only 14.3 percent of the system's total employees were paid. *Annual Report*, 1958, 4.

43. Subcommittee on Independent Offices, *Independent Offices Appropriations for 1959*, 197, 209–10.

44. Subcommittee on Independent Offices, *Independent Offices Appropriations for 1959*, 65; National Science Foundation, *Ninth Annual Report for the Fiscal Year Ended June 30, 1959* (Washington, D.C.: GPO, 1960), 134. Available online at http://www.nsf.gov/pubs/1959/annualreports/start.htm.

45. James W. Davis Jr. and Kenneth M. Dolbeare, *Little Groups of Neighbors: The Selective Service System* (Chicago: Markham Publishing Company, 1968), 42–46. See also Gary Lee Wamsley, "Selective Service and American Political Culture: The Maintenance of Equilibrium between Demands of Function and Political Culture by an Institution of Civil Military Justice" (PhD diss., University of Pittsburgh, 1968), 164–68, 364–81.

46. Diary of Lewis B. Hershey, March 12, 1917, and June 7, 1917, personal papers of Gilbert Hershey, Jacksonville, North Carolina, cited in George Q. Flynn, *Lewis B. Hershey: Mr. Selective Service* (Chapel Hill: University of North Carolina Press, 1985), 23.

47. Flynn, *Lewis B. Hershey*, 188.

48. *Annual Report*, 1957, 61.

49. Gerhardt, *The Draft and Public Policy*, 240–41.

50. Selective Service: Present and Future, January 5, 1949, 032-GEN, 1963-1948, box 26, Central Files, RG 147, NACP; *Annual Report*, 1955, 17; *Annual Report*, 1957, 61–62.

51. "Community Defense Emphasized," *Selective Service*, Oct. 1956, 4.

52. *Annual Report*, 1957, 61.

53. Hershey, "Storekeeper of Manpower," *Selective Service*, July 1956, 1–2.

54. Hershey, "Selective Service Obligations," *Army Digest*, Nov. 1959, 36–37.

55. Hershey, "Probabilities and Possibilities—1957," *Selective Service*, Jan. 1957, 1–2.

56. Hershey, "Selective Service Obligations," 36; Hershey, "Probabilities and Possibilities—1957," 27.

57. See *Annual Report*, 1958, 51.

58. Charles Finucane to General Hershey, July 31, 1959, orientation course, box 71, Papers of the Planning Office, RG 147, NACP.

59. "Defense, Civilian Officials Attend Sessions on Manpower Held at National Headquarters," *Selective Service*, Feb. 1960, 1–2.

60. Charles H. Grahl to General Hershey, January 14, 1959, orientation course, box 71, Papers of the Planning Office, RG 147, NACP.

61. Joel D. Griffing to Colonel Grahl, Dec. 16, 1959, orientation course, box 71, Papers of the Planning Office, RG 147, NACP.

62. Lieutenant Colonel Rankin to Colonel Griffing, December 11, 1959, orientation course, box 71, Papers of the Planning Office, RG 147, NACP.

63. The Emergency Role of Selective Service, n.d. attached to Joel D. Griffing to Col. Grahl, Dec. 16, 1959, orientation course, box 71, Papers of the Planning Office, RG 147, NACP.

64. Flynn, *The Draft, 1940–1973* (Lawrence: University Press of Kansas, 1993), 209; Gerhardt, *The Draft and Public Policy*, 229.

65. Hershey, "Selective Service Obligations," 32.

66. John Michael Kendall, "An Inflexible Response: United States Army Manpower Mobilization Policies, 1945–1957" (PhD diss.: Duke University, 1982), 183 note 1.

67. For more on the mobilization of the reserves and National Guard during the Korean War, see Gerhardt, *The Draft and Public Policy*, 162; Michael D. Doubler, *The National Guard and Reserve: A Reference Handbook* (Westport, Conn.: Praeger Security International, 2008), 33–34; Kendall, "An Inflexible Response," 180–83, 206–9.

68. Kendall, "An Inflexible Response," 246–47.

69. Kendall, "An Inflexible Response," 248; Gerhardt, *The Draft and Public Policy*, 200–201.

70. House Committee on Armed Services, *Reserve Forces Legislation: A Legislative History of the Reserve Forces Act of 1955*, Hearings and Papers No. 82, 84th Cong., 2d sess., 1956, 7525, 7530–31.

71. Dwight Eisenhower, "Message on Military Security," January 13, 1955, reprinted in House Committee on Armed Services, *Reserve Forces Legislation*, 7523–26; *Annual Report*, 1957, 62.

72. Text of the Reserve Forces Act of 1955, Public Law 305, 84th Congress, reprinted in House Committee on Armed Services, *Reserve Forces Legislation*, 7575.

73. For more information on these programs, see Gerhardt, *The Draft and Public Policy*, 203–6.

74. For discussion of the exclusion of the Army National Guard and Air National Guard from the final bill, see "Compulsory Service Bill Near Death," *Los Angeles Times*, June 5, 1955; "Ike's Military Reserves Bill Passes House," *Chicago Daily Tribune*, July 2, 1955; "Ike Flays Congress, Powell Flays Ike, Military Bill is OK'd," *Cleveland Call and Post*, Aug. 27, 1955; Gerhardt, *The Draft and Public Policy*, 201–2.

75. See Gerhardt, *The Draft and Public Policy*, 208–9; *Annual Report*, 1963, 24; Stephen S. Jackson to General Hershey, June 10, 1960, 314.1 Gen., 1962-1961-1960; E. L. Keenan to J. F. C. Hyde Jr., December 4, 1959, 314.1 Gen., 1959-1958-1957; Statement of Policy, Engineering Manpower Commission, Engineers Joint Council, November 1959, attached to Roy Wheelock to Col. E. D. Ingold, November 2, 1959, all in box 67, Central Files, RG 147, NACP.

76. Public Relations for the Reserve Forces Act of 1955, n.d., box 70, Public Relations Society of America records, WHS.

77. National Security Training Commission, *Annual Report to the Congress* (Washington, D.C.: GPO, 1956), 21–22, 31–32. See pp. 20–41 for the full scope of recruitment efforts from all branches of service.

78. See box 70, Public Relations Society of America, WHS.

79. "Answer to Lagging Reserve Program Is 3-Fold," *Washington Post*, Dec. 5, 1955.

80. Hershey, "Public Reaction to Settle Fate of Reserve Program," *Selective Service*, Feb. 1956, 1–2.

81. "Military in Poor Favor, Poll Shows," *Los Angeles Times*, Jan. 1, 1956.

82. See "Army 'Tough Guy' Thing of Past, Youth Forum Told," *Hartford Courant*, Dec. 4, 1955.

83. "Is Birth Rate Making Draft a Clumsy Injustice," *Washington Post*, Jan. 6, 1957.

84. "Reservists Like 6-Month Program," *Selective Service*, April 1956, 1, 4.

85. See Gerhardt, *The Draft and Public Policy*, 208; and U.S. House of Representatives, *Extending the Special Enlistment Programs Provided by Section 262 of the Armed Forces Reserve Act of 1952, As Amended*, Rpt. No. 84, 86th Cong., 1st sess., Feb. 1959, 3.

86. "Are You 'Draft' Bait, n.d., attached to Louis H. Renfrow to Ellard A. Walsh, June 21, 1956, 314.1 General, 1956-1954, box 67, Central Files, RG 147, NACP [emphasis in the original].

87. "Draft Dodgers?" *Democratic Digest*, March 1957, 6; Gerhardt, *The Draft and Public Policy*, 207–8.

88. House Committee on Armed Services, Subcommittee No. 1, *Review of the Reserve Program*, Hearings and Papers No. 35, 85th Cong., 1st sess., 1957, 1409, as quoted in Gerhardt, *The Draft and Public Policy*, 209.

89. House Committee on Armed Services, Subcommittee No. 3, *Consideration of H.R. 3368, A Bill to Extend the Special Enlistment Programs Provided by Section 262 of the Armed Forces Reserve Act of 1952, as Amended*, Hearings and Papers, No. 7, 86th Cong., 1st sess., 1959, 419, as quoted in Gerhardt, *The Draft and Public Policy*, 210.

90. Gerhardt, *The Draft and Public Policy*, 230, 266.

91. As quoted in House of Representatives, *Extending the Special Enlistment Programs Provided by Section 262 of the Armed Forces Reserve Act of 1952, As Amended*, Rpt. No. 84, 86th Cong., 1st sess., Feb. 1959, 5.

92. Gerhardt, *The Draft and Public Policy*, 255; Beth Bailey, *America's Army: Making the All-Volunteer Force* (Cambridge, Mass.: Belknap Press, 2009), 15.

93. See, for example, "Inquiries on Draft Status Swamp Selective Service," *Washington Post*, July 27, 1961; Uncle Dudley, "To Active Duty," *Boston Globe*, Oct. 2, 1961; "Questions and Answers on Caught in the Draft are Numerous," *Chicago Daily Defender*, Aug. 31, 1961.

94. "Army's New Reserve Program," *Selective Service*, June 1956, 4, reprinted from *The Portsmouth* [N.H.] *Herald*, April 27, 1956.

95. See Aaron L. Friedberg, "Science, the Cold War, and the American State," Review Essay, *Diplomatic History* 20, no. 1 (1996): 107–18.

96. Linn, *Elvis's Army*, 84.

97. President's Committee on Scientists and Engineers, *Final Report to the President*, December 1958, Final Report to the President, box 35, PCSE, DDE.

98. First Interim Report of the National Committee for the Development of Scientists and Engineers, n.d., First Interim Report to the President, box 35, PCSE, DDE.

99. President's Committee on Scientists and Engineers, *Second Interim Report to the President*, October 4, 1957, Second Interim Report to the President, box 35, PCSE, DDE.

100. President's Committee on Scientists and Engineers, The United States Program of Public Education on the Shortage of Scientists & Engineers, September 18, 1957, Public Relations, box 35, PCSE, DDE, 6; press release, March 31, 1957, Donnelley—Committee Clippings, box 36, PCSE, DDE.

101. President's Committee on Scientists and Engineers, *Final Report to the President*, December 1958.

102. Eisenhower announced the creation of the President's Science Advisory Committee on November 27, 1957. See Zuoyue Wang, *In Sputnik's Shadow: The President's Science Advisory Committee and Cold War America* (New Brunswick, N.J.: Rutgers University Press, 2008), 82.

103. Josephine Ripley, "The Challenge in the Classroom: An Intimate Message from Washington," *Christian Science Monitor*, Nov. 27, 1957.

104. See for example, C. C. Furness, "Why Did the U.S. Lose the Race? Critics Speak Up," *Life*, Oct. 21, 1957, 22–23; "U.S. Tries Hard to Catch Up," *Life*, Nov. 4, 1957; Robert Wallace, "All Russian Science," *Life*, Dec. 16, 1957, 109–22. Quote from George R. Price, "Arguing the Case for Being Panicky," *Life*, Nov. 18, 1957, 126.

105. David Halberstam, *The Fifties* (New York: Villard Books, 1993), 626. See also, for example, Hyman Rickover, *Education and Freedom* (New York: Dutton, 1959); David C. Greenwood, *Solving the Scientist Shortage* (Washington, D.C.: Public Affairs Press, 1958); Grant S. McClellan, *America's Educational Needs* (New York: H. W. Wilson Co., 1958).

106. Ripley, "The Challenge in the Classroom"; "Text of Speech by Secretary Dulles," *Washington Post*, January 17, 1958, as quoted in Barbara Barksdale Clowse, *Brainpower for the Cold War: The Sputnik Crisis and National Defense Education Act of 1958* (Westport, Conn.: Greenwood Press, 1981), 9.

107. Paul O'Neil, "U.S. Change of Mind," *Life*, March 3, 1958, 92.

108. Subcommittee on Research and Development, Joint Committee on Atomic Energy, *Shortage of Scientific and Engineering Manpower: Hearings before the Subcommittee on Research and Development of the Joint Committee on Atomic Energy*, 84th Cong., 2d sess., April–May 1956.

109. Dwight Eisenhower, "Address at the National Education Association Centennial," *Public Papers of the Presidents of the United States*, Dwight D. Eisenhower (Washington, D.C.: Office of the *Federal Register*, National Archives and Records Service, 1953–), 265, as quoted in Clowse, *Brainpower for the Cold War*, 27.

110. Eisenhower signed P.L. 85-864 on September 2, 1958. For a summary of the law's major provisions, see Clowse, *Brainpower for the Cold War*, 162–67.

111. Fact Sheet on the 1964 Amendments to the National Defense Education Act, October 16, 1964, attached to Legislative Notes, Office of Education, U.S. Department of Health, Education, and Welfare, October 19, 1964, National Defense Education Act, box 1, entry UD-UP 3, HEW, RG 235, NACP.

112. See "List of Essential Activities," Appendix 12, *Annual Report*, 1955, 87.

113. See, for example, "Slash Draft Exemptions: Farmers Now Eligible," *Detroit Times*, March 2, 1955.

114. Lewis B. Hershey to Colonel Holmes, March 8, 1955, 127 General Mich., 1963-1955, box 47, Central Files, RG 147, NACP.

115. Memo re: Meeting No. 28, Committee on Specialized Personnel, August 17, 1954, Committee on Specialized Personnel—Minutes, etc., box 71, Papers of the Planning Office, RG 147, NACP; *Annual Report*, 1955, 86–87.

116. National Science Foundation, *Comparisons of Earned Degrees Awarded, 1901–1962: With Projections to 2000*, NSF-64 (Washington, D.C.: National Science Foundation, 1964), 10. Available at http://babel.hathitrust.org.

117. National Science Foundation, *Comparisons of Earned Degrees Awarded*, 20, 30.

118. National Science Foundation, *Comparisons of Earned Degrees Awarded*, 1–2.

119. See *Annual Report*, 1955, 22; *Annual Report*, 1963, 11; Dee Ingold to the Director and attachments, February 13, 1958, 105 Advisory Committee (Ala.-Wyoming), 1963-48, box 34; and Memo, re: Amendments to Selective Service Regulations, November 16, 1962, 110 General, 1963-1955, box 35, both in Central Files, RG 147, NACP.

120. William S. Perry [Lt. Col. AGC] to Colonel Bossidy, February 3, 1958, Committee on Specialized Personnel—Minutes, etc., box 71, Papers of the Planning Office, RG 147, NACP.

121. National Science Foundation, *Comparisons of Earned Degrees Awarded*, 13.

122. Bernard T. Franck III to Charles A. Quattlebaum, January 15, 1958, 321 Deferments 1963-1954, box 70, Central Files, RG 147, NACP.

123. "1955 Teacher Deferment Bulletin Is Rescinded," *Selective Service*, July 1960, 2.

124. "New Occupation, Activity Lists Issued to Boards for Reference," *Selective Service*, Nov. 1962, 1.

125. Wamsley, "Selective Service and American Political Culture," 242–49. See also Davis and Dolbeare, *Little Groups of Neighbors*, 79–88.

126. "II-S Criteria Deleted from Regulations," *Selective Service*, Feb. 1962, 1; "Simplified, Flexible System of Reporting on Status of Student Registrations Adopted, *Selective Service*, May 1963, 3.

127. Gerhardt, *The Draft and Public Policy*, 270.

128. See Lewis B. Hershey to Dean Bowman, February 21, 1961, 321 Deferments 1963-1954, box 70; and Bernard T. Franck III to George H. Link, June 7, 1961, 321 General Occup. Def. Ala.-Maine, box 71, both in Central Files, RG 147, NACP.

129. Memo: Peace Corps, July 21, 1961, 321 Deferments 1963-1954, box 70, Central Files, 1948-69, RG 147, NACP.

130. Selective Service Quarterly Report, October–December 1960, attached to Lewis B. Hershey to Leo A. Hoegh, December 21, 1960, 100 General, 1961-60, box 29, Central Files, RG 147, NACP.

131. "Data Disclose U.S. Student, Teacher Status," *Selective Service*, April 1958, 3.

132. Bernard T. Franck III to Charles A. Quattlebaum, January 15, 1958, 321 Deferments 1963-1954, box 70, Central Files, RG 147, NACP.

133. *Annual Report*, 1961, 11.

134. See Jeffrey M. Schevitz, *The Weaponsmakers: Personal and Professional Crisis During the Vietnam War* (Cambridge, Mass.: Schenkman Publishing Company, 1979), esp. 75, 84. "Russ" and "Pete" both admit to being channeled.

135. See also John C. Esty Jr., "The Draft Dilemma: A Way Out," *Nation*, March 14, 1959, 223–26.

136. *Annual Report*, 1955, 16; *Annual Report*, 1965, 17.

137. Elaine Tyler May, *Homeward Bound: American Families in the Cold War Era* (New York: Basic Books, 1988); Laura McEnaney, *Civil Defense Begins at Home: Militarization Meets Everyday Life in the 1950s* (Princeton, N.J.: Princeton University Press, 2000); Guy Oakes, *The Imaginary War: Civil Defense and American Cold War Culture* (New York: Oxford University Press, 1994).

138. *Annual Report*, 1956, 28.

139. Only one article appeared in the *New York Times*, for example, and it ran without commentary. See "Younger Men Placed First in Revised Rules for Draft," *New York Times*, Feb. 17, 1956.

140. *Annual Report*, 1957, 3.

141. *Annual Report*, 1957, 26.

142. Memo: Liable Registrants, Age 18 to 35, May 16, 1961, 311-General Military Service (I-A), box 63, Central Files, RG 147, NACP.

143. *Annual Report*, 1963, 13.

144. "Many Fathers Move into III-A from Class I-A," *Selective Service*, Dec. 1959, 2.

145. Memorandum for Director Selective Service, August 19, 1963; and Enclosure, Lewis B. Hershey to the President, August 30, 1963, both at JFKPOF-087-008, President's Office Files, Presidential Papers, Papers of John F. Kennedy, http://www.jfklibrary.org/Asset-Viewer/Archives/JFKPOF-087-008.aspx, (Accessed December 19, 2018).

146. Gilbert H. Winter to Colonel Higgins, July 17, 1963, 311-General Military Service (I-A), box 63, Central Files, RG 147, NACP.

147. Bernard T. Franck III to Colonel Traver, November 15, 1963, 314 General, box 64, Central Files, RG 147, NACP.

148. Appendix 1, House Armed Services Committee, *Review of the Administration and Operation of the Selective Service System*, June 1966, 10014.

149. "Manpower for Defense," *Indianapolis Star*, Nov. 10, 1958, 14, in 020 Gen., 1963–1948, box 27, Central Files, RG 147, NACP.

150. "Draft Seen to Guide Science, Teaching," *Washington Post*, April 23, 1958.

151. How to Beat the Draft, n.d., attached to Paul Akst to Daniel Omer, April 8, 1963, 127 General N.Y. City, 1963-1956, box 49, Central Files, RG 147, NACP.

152. Orill L. Alward, Leo C. Friend, and Tell Thompson to General Hershey, January 16, 1963, attached to Daniel O. Omer to Gentlemen, February 5, 1963, 300—Classification—New Hampshire-Wyo. 1963-1948, box 61, Central Files, RG 147, NACP.

153. "Playing the Odds," *Toledo Blade*, Nov. 24, 1962.

154. John G. Esty Jr., "The Draft: Many Threatened, Few Chosen," *New York Times*, October 20, 1963. See also, "Another Look at UMT," *The American Legion Magazine*, October 1962; "The Draft—Campus to Chaos," *Newsweek*, April 4, 1960.

Chapter 5. "The Most Important Human Salvage Operation in the History of Our Country"

1. Senate Committee on Labor and Public Welfare, *Manpower Implications of Selective Service: Hearings Before the Subcommittee on Employment, Manpower, and Poverty of the Committee on Labor and Public Welfare*, 90th Cong., 1st sess., 1967, 84.

2. See Robert H. Haveman, "Introduction: Poverty and Social Policy in the 1960s and 1970s—an Overview and Some Speculations," in *A Decade of Federal Antipoverty Programs: Achievements, Failures, and Lessons*, ed. Robert H. Haveman (New York: Academic Press, 1977), 4; Charles Brecher, *The Impact of Federal Antipoverty Policies* (New York: Praeger Press, 1973), 19–24; John A. Andrew III, *Lyndon Johnson and the Great Society* (Chicago: Ivan R. Dee, 1998), 57.

3. Lyndon B. Johnson, "Annual Message to the Congress on the State of the Union," January 8, 1964. Online by Gerhard Peters and John T. Woolley, *The American Presidency Project*. http://www.presidency.ucsb.edu/ws/?pid=26787 (accessed Feb. 18, 2018).

4. Senate Committee on Labor and Public Welfare, *Manpower Implications of Selective Service*, 83.

5. Gareth Davies, "War on Dependency: Liberal Individualism and the Economic Opportunity Act of 1964," *Journal of American Studies* 26, no. 2 (Aug. 1992): 205–31.

6. See Jennifer S. Light, *From Warfare to Welfare: Defense Intellectuals and Urban Problems in Cold War America* (Baltimore: Johns Hopkins University Press, 2003). The relationship between the social sciences in general and the military was complicated during the Cold War, as each influenced the other. See Joy Rohde, *Armed with Expertise: The Militarization of American Social Research during the Cold War* (Ithaca, N.Y.: Cornell University Press, 2013); Mark Solovey, *Shaky Foundations: The Politics-Patronage-Social Science Nexus in Cold War America* (New Brunswick, N.J.: Rutgers University Press, 2013).

7. Robert O. Self, *All in the Family: The Realignment of American Democracy since the 1960s* (New York: Hill and Wang, 2012), 4.

8. *Congressional Record*, Aug. 5. 1964 (Washington, D.C.: GPO, 1965), 18302, quoted in Davies, "War on Dependency," 222.

9. See, for example, T. J. Jackson Lears, *No Place of Grace: Antimodernism and the Transformation of American Culture, 1880–1920* (New York: Pantheon Books, 1981); David Axeen, "'Heroes of the Engine Room': American 'Civilization' and the War with Spain," *American Quarterly* 36, no. 4 (Autumn 1984): 481–502; E. Anthony

Rotundo, *American Manhood: Transformations in Masculinity from the Revolution to the Modern Era* (New York: Basic Books, 1993), chap. 10; Michael Kimmel, *Manhood in America: A Cultural History* (New York: Free Press, 1996), chap. 4.

10. Gail Bederman, *Manliness and Civilization: A Cultural History of Gender and Race in the United States, 1880–1917* (Chicago: University of Chicago Press, 1995), 27.

11. Kristin L. Hoganson, *Fighting for American Manhood: How Gender Politics Provoked the Spanish-American and Philippine-American Wars* (New Haven, Conn.: Yale University Press, 1998).

12. J. Howard Beard, "Physical Rejection for Military Service: Some Problems in Reconstruction," *Scientific Monthly* 9, no. 1 (July 1919): 5.

13. John Whiteclay Chambers II, *To Raise an Army: The Draft Comes to Modern America* (New York: Free Press, 1987), 251; Daniel J. Kevles, "Testing the Army's Intelligence: Psychologists and the Military in World War I," *Journal of American History* 55, no. 3 (Dec. 1968): 565–81.

14. Christina S. Jarvis, *The Male Body at War: American Masculinity during World War II* (DeKalb: Northern Illinois University Press, 2004), 19, 61–63.

15. James M. Gerhardt, *The Draft and Public Policy: Issues in Military Manpower Procurement, 1945–1970* (Columbus: Ohio State University Press, 1971), 46–47; Janice H. Laurence and Peter F. Ramsberger, *Low-Aptitude Men in the Military: Who Profits? Who Pays?* (Westport, Conn.: Praeger, 1991), 20.

16. For more information, see Rachel Louise Moran, *Governing Bodies: American Politics and the Shaping of the Modern Physique* (Philadelphia: University of Pennsylvania Press, 2018), 62–63, 75; Michael W. Sherraden, "Military Participation in a Youth Employment Program: The Civilian Conservation Corps," *Armed Forces and Society* 7, no. 2 (Winter 1980): 227–45.

17. Richard H. Hanes to James A. Crabtree, March 2, 1949, 002 National Security Resources Board, 1948-63, box 21, Central Files, 1948–1969, Records of the Selective Service, RG 147, NACP; "Former Rehabilitation Programs Recalled in Which Selective Service Played a Role," *Selective Service*, Aug. 1964, 4.

18. See, for example, Betty Birmingham Moorehead, "The Work of a Family Welfare Agency in Investigations for Selective Service Boards Where Deferment Is Requested because of Family Problems" (MSSS thesis: Boston University School of Social Work, 1944).

19. Cooperative Relationship Memorandum No. 9 (Revised), February 18, 1949, attached to Phyllis W. Francis to Richard H. Eanes, July 11, 1958, 002 National Security Resources Board, 1948-63, box 21, Central Files, RG 147, NACP.

20. State Director Advice No. 73, February 9, 1949, attached to Phyllis W. Francis to Richard H. Eanes.

21. The Office of Vocational Rehabilitation was moved to the Department of Health, Education, and Welfare when the new cabinet position was created in 1953. Cooperative Relationship Memorandum No. 9 (Revised); Dear General Hershey, December 2, 1963, attached to memo card, Miss Switzer to Mr. Nestingen, 12-3-63, Selective Service Rejectees, box 2, entry UD-UP 3, HEW, RG 235, NACP.

22. Robert M. Collins, "Growth Liberalism in the Sixties," in *The Sixties: From Memory to History*, ed. David Farber (Chapel Hill: University of North Carolina Press, 1994), 13; Gladys Roth Kremen, "MDTA: The Origins of the Manpower Development and

Training Act of 1962," available online at United States Department of Labor, http://www.dol.gov/oasam/programs/history/mono-mdtatext.htm (accessed Feb. 18, 2018).

23. Bernard D. Karpinos, "Fitness of American Youth for Military Service," *The Milbank Memorial Fund Quarterly* 38, no. 3 (July 1960): 213–67.

24. Virginia Pasley, *21 Stayed: The Story of the American GI's who Chose Communist China: Who They Were and Why They Stayed* (New York: Farrar, Straus, and Cudahy, 1955); H. H. Wubben, "American Prisoners of War in Korea: A Second Look at the 'Something New in History' Theme," *American Quarterly* 22, no. 1 (Spring 1970): 3–19; Colin Flint, "Mobilizing Civil Society for the Hegemonic State: The Korean War and the Construction of Soldiercitizens in the United States," in *War, Citizenship, Territory*, ed. Deborah Cowen and Emily Gilbert (New York: Routledge, 2008), 345–61.

25. For more on the existential crisis of the 1950s, see James Gilbert, *Men in the Middle: Searching for Masculinity in the 1950s* (Chicago: University of Chicago Press, 2005); Elaine Tyler May, *Homeward Bound: American Families in the Cold War Era* (New York: Basic Books, 1988); Tom Englehardt, *The End of Victory Culture: Cold War America and the Disillusioning of a Generation* (New York: Basic Books, 1995); Robert Corber, *Homosexuality in Cold War America: Resistance and the Crisis of Masculinity* (Durham, N.C.: Duke University Press, 1997); David K. Johnson, *The Lavender Scare: The Cold War Persecution of Gays and Lesbians in the Federal Government* (Chicago: University of Chicago Press, 1994); Carolyn Herbst Lewis, *Prescription for Heterosexuality: Sexual Citizenship in the Cold War Era* (Chapel Hill: University of North Carolina Press, 2010).

26. K. A. Cuordileone, *Manhood and American Political Culture in the Cold War* (New York: Routledge, 2005); Donald J. Mrozek, "The Cult and Ritual of Toughness in Cold War America," in *Sport in America: From Wicked Amusement to National Obsession*, ed. David K. Wiggins (Champaign, Ill.: Human Kinetics, 1995), 257–67; Robert D. Dean, "Masculinity as Ideology: John F. Kennedy and the Domestic Politics of Foreign Policy," *Diplomatic History* 22, no. 1 (Winter 1998): 29–62; Jeffrey Montez de Oca, "'As Our Muscles Get Softer, Our Missile Race Becomes Harder': Cultural Citizenship and the 'Muscle Gap,'" *Journal of Historical Sociology* 18, no. 3 (Sept. 2005): 145–72.

27. Christopher A. Preble, *John F. Kennedy and the Missile Gap* (DeKalb: Northern Illinois University Press), 7.

28. John F. Kennedy, Speech, Fairgrounds, Bangor, Maine, September 2, 1960, available at Woolley and Peters, *The American Presidency Project*, http://www.presidency.ucsb.edu/ws/index.php?pid=25911; John F. Kennedy, remarks at San Francisco International Airport, San Francisco, California (Advance Release Text), September 3, 1960, available at Woolley and Peters, *The American Presidency Project*, http://www.presidency.ucsb.edu/ws/index.php?pid=25941 (both accessed Feb. 18, 2018).

29. Kennedy, speech at high school auditorium, Pocatello, Idaho, September 6, 1960, available at Woolley and Peters, *The American Presidency Project*, http://www.presidency.ucsb.edu/ws/index.php?pid=25650 (accessed Feb. 18, 2018).

30. Robert D. Dean, *Imperial Brotherhood: Gender and the Making of Cold War Foreign Policy* (Amherst: University of Massachusetts Press, 2001); and Cuordileone, *Manhood and American Political Culture*.

31. National Committee for Children and Youth, *Experimental and Demonstration Manpower Project for Recruitment, Training, Placement, and Followup of Rejected Armed*

Forces Volunteers in Baltimore, Maryland and Washington, D.C.: Final Report, March 1, 1965, to June 30, 1966, 2.

32. Katherine Oettinger to F. Robert Meier, October 3, 1963, Selective Service Rejectees, and Manpower Conservation for Selective Service Rejectees: Program Operations, and Preliminary Estimates for DHEW (FY 1964–65), both in box 2, entry UD-UP 3, RG 235, NACP.

33. Phillips Cutright, Pilot Study of Factors in Economic Success or Failure: Based on Selective Service and Social Security Records, United States Department of Health, Education, and Welfare, Social Security Administration, Division of Research and Statistics, 1964, folder 838.9, Pilot Study–Maryland, box 278, Lewis B. Hershey Papers, United States Army War College Library and Archives, USAHEC.

34. Milton H. Maier, *Military Aptitude Testing: The Past Fifty Years*, DMDC Technical Report 93-007, Defense Manpower Data Center, Personnel Testing Division, June 1993, 67–70, available at http://www.dtic.mil/cgi-bin/GetTRDoc?AD=ADA269818 (accessed Feb. 18, 2018).

35. Memorandum to the President, September 10, 1963, attached to Secretary Wirtz's Proposal to Work with the Selective Service System in Identifying and Training a Large Group of Young Men Rejected for Military Service because of "Mental Reasons," September 23, 1963, Selective Service Rejectees, box 2, entry UD-UP 3, RG 235, NACP.

36. John F. Kennedy, "Statement by the President on the Need for Training or Rehabilitation of Selective Service Rejectees," September 30, 1963, available at Peters and Woolley, *The American Presidency Project*, http://www.presidency.ucsb.edu/ws/?pid=9446 (accessed Feb. 18, 2018).

37. "Dismal Fact: 1 Out of 2 Draftees Rejected," *Boston Globe*, Oct. 1, 1963.

38. "Draft Study Ordered on Rejections," *Hartford Courant*, Oct. 1, 1963.

39. John F. Kennedy, "The Soft American," *Sports Illustrated*, December 26, 1960, 14–17, available at *Sports Illustrated* Vault, https://www.si.com/vault/issue/43278/20/2 (accessed Feb. 18, 2018).

40. Volunteers, because they self-selected and because of the initial screening, failed their induction exams at a much lower rate than draftees. President's Task Force on Manpower Conservation, *One-Third of a Nation: A Report on Young Men Found Unqualified for Military Service*, January 1, 1964, 7–8, 11, Selective Service Rejectees, box 2, entry UD-UP 3, RG 235, NACP.

41. President's Task Force on Manpower Conservation, *One-Third of a Nation*, 25.

42. President's Task Force on Manpower Conservation, *One-Third of a Nation*, 13.

43. President's Task Force on Manpower Conservation, *One-Third of a Nation*, 16.

44. President's Task Force on Manpower Conservation, *One-Third of a Nation*, 16, 17.

45. President's Task Force on Manpower Conservation, *One-Third of a Nation*, 20.

46. President's Task Force on Manpower Conservation, *One-Third of a Nation*, 15, 16.

47. President's Task Force on Manpower Conservation, *One-Third of a Nation*, A-7, 16.

48. President's Task Force on Manpower Conservation, *One-Third of a Nation*, 18.

49. President's Task Force on Manpower Conservation, *One-Third of a Nation*, i.

50. President's Task Force on Manpower Conservation, *One-Third of a Nation: A Report on Young Men Found Unqualified for Military Service*, January 1, 1964, 20, 22, digitized version available at Hathi Trust Digital Library, http://babel.hathitrust.org/cgi/pt?id=mdp.39015035832677;seq=30;view=1up;num=20 (accessed Feb. 18, 2018).

51. President's Task Force on Manpower Conservation, *One-Third of a Nation*, 29.

52. President's Task Force on Manpower Conservation, *One-Third of a Nation*, 4.

53. President's Task Force on Manpower Conservation, *One-Third of a Nation*, 33–35.

54. President's Task Force on Manpower Conservation, *One-Third of a Nation*, 33.

55. President's Task Force on Manpower Conservation, *One-Third of a Nation*, 29.

56. See text of Johnson's statement announcing the release of the report, reprinted at "Examination at Age 18 Ordered by President," *Selective Service*, Feb. 1964, 3–4.

57. President's Task Force on Manpower Conservation, *One-Third of a Nation*, 29.

58. Self, *All in the Family*, 37–41.

59. For the way the policy community approached the problem of poverty among women, see Jennifer Mittelstadt, *From Welfare to Workfare: The Unintended Consequences of Liberal Reform, 1945–1965* (Chapel Hill: University of North Carolina Press, 2005); Lisa Levenstein, *A Movement Without Marches: African American Women and the Politics of Poverty in Postwar Philadelphia* (Chapel Hill: University of North Carolina Press, 2009); Marisa Chappell, *The War on Welfare: Family, Poverty, and Politics in Modern America* (Philadelphia: University of Pennsylvania Press, 2010).

60. Anthony Celebrezze to Governor, December 7, 1964, Selective Service Rejectees, box 2, entry UD-UP 3, RG 235, NACP; "Examination at Age 18 Ordered by President."

61. Francis Keppel to Ivan A. Nestingen, March 10, 1964, attached to Francis Keppel to Ivan A. Nestingen, June 2, 1964, Selective Service Rejectees, box 2, entry UD-UP 3, RG 235, NACP.

62. "Salvaging Young Americans," *Washington Daily News*, Jan. 15, 1964, in News Items, January 16, 1964, Poverty (Economic Opportunity Act), box 1, entry UD-UP 3, RG 235, NACP.

63. John F. Henning to Ivan A. Nestingen, February 19, 1964, attached to Ivan A. Nestingen to John F. Henning, March 20, 1964, Selective Service Rejectees, box 2, entry UD-UP 3, RG 235, NACP.

64. Department of Health, Education, and Welfare and Department of Labor Coordinating Committee Meeting, March 2, 1964, MDTA-DHEW-Labor Coordinating Committee (Minutes of Meetings), box 4, entry UD-UP 3, RG 235, NACP.

65. Department of Health, Education, and Welfare and Department of Labor Coordinating Committee Meeting, March 2, 1964; Minutes of DHEW-BES-OMAT Coordinating Committee Meeting, March 16, 1964, MDTA-DHEW-Labor Coordinating Committee (Minutes of Meetings), box 4, entry UD-UP 3, RG 235, NACP.

66. Rhode Island Division of Vocational Rehabilitation, *Why I-Y: A Research Study of the Rehabilitation of Selective Service Rejectees in Rhode Island* (Providence, R.I.: Rhode Island Division of Vocational Rehabilitation, 1967), 2, 5.

67. See, for example, Cyrus Mayshark and Ralph Balyeat, *Analysis of Selective Service Health Referral Patterns in Tennessee* (Knoxville: University of Tennessee, 1967), 5.

68. National Manpower Council, *Improving Work Skills of the Nation: Proceedings of a Conference on Skilled Manpower* (New York: Columbia University Press, 1955), 149, quoted in Kremen, "MDTA."

69. Brecher, *The Impact of Federal Antipoverty Policies*, 32.

70. U.S. House of Representatives, *Amendments of Manpower Development and Training Act of 1962*, H. Rpt. 861, 88th Cong., 1st sess., October 18, 1963, 1–3.

71. Institute of Management and Labor Relations, *The Selection of Trainees under MDTA* (New Brunswick, N.J.: Rutgers University, 1966), 2.

72. National Committee for Children and Youth, *NCCY Youth Services Project: Final Report to the Office of Manpower Policy, Evaluation and Research, United States Department of Labor* (Washington, D.C.: National Committee for Children and Youth, 1967), v, 75–81.

73. John F. Henning to Ivan A. Nestingen, February 19, 1964.

74. Rhode Island Division of Vocational Rehabilitation, "Why I-Y," 10–11.

75. Hubert M. Clements, Jack A. Duncan, and Richard E. Hardy, *The Unfit Majority: A Research Study of the Rehabilitation of Selective Service Rejectees in South Carolina* (Columbia, S.C.: South Carolina Vocational Rehabilitation Department, 1967), 10, 25–26.

76. Clements, Duncan, and Hardy, *The Unfit Majority*, foreword; Rhode Island Division of Vocational Rehabilitation, "Why I-Y," 8–9.

77. Clements, Duncan, and Hardy, *The Unfit Majority*, 33.

78. Rhode Island Division of Vocational Rehabilitation, "Why I-Y," 10, 31.

79. Mayshark and Balyeat, *Analysis of Selective Service Health Referral Patterns in Tennessee*, 6–7, 31–32, 64–65.

80. "July Examinations of 18-Year-Olds," *Selective Service*, Sept. 1965, 3.

81. Rehabilitation programs through AFES are not mentioned in U.S. Department of Labor, *Index to Publications of the Manpower Administration, Jan. 1969 through June 1974* (Washington, D.C.: GPO, 1974).

82. See also Gerald Robert Gill, "Afro-American Opposition to the United States' Wars of the Twentieth Century: Dissent, Discontent, and Disinterest" (PhD diss: Howard University, 1985), 212–31.

83. Lewis B. Hershey, "The Need of a Yardstick," *Selective Service*, Sept. 1956, 2.

84. Summary, n.d., attached to Ted Reardon to the President, August 9, 1961, Council on Youth Fitness, February 1961–November 1962, series 07, Departments and Agencies, President's Office Files, Presidential Papers, Papers of John F. Kennedy, John F. Kennedy Library Online, Digital Identifier JFKPOF-094-001, http://www.jfklibrary.org/Asset-Viewer/Archives/JFKPOF-094-001.aspx (accessed Feb. 18, 2018).

85. See Senate Appropriations Committee, *Supplemental Appropriation Bill, 1965*, S. Rpt. 1604, 88th Cong., 2d sess., September 29, 1964, 11.

86. Report of the State Directors Meeting, Region III, September 23–24, 1964, Region III Correspondence (Training) 1960; John W. Barber to William Kizer, June 18, 1965, Conference One–Region VI-10-24, July 1965; and memo, Regions V and VI, June 11, 1965, Conference One–Region VI-10-24, July 1965, all in box 109, Training and Conference Files, Entry UD 20, RG 147, NACP; "State Directors View Role of System in Poverty War," *Selective Service*, April 1965, 4.

87. "President Creates Committee on Manpower Needs, Resources," *Selective Service*, May 1965, 3–4.

88. Lewis B. Hershey, "SS Personnel are Invited to Join Poverty War," *Selective Service*, Jan. 1965, 1–2; "Efforts of Selective Service in Poverty War Are Extensive," *Selective Service*, March 1965, 1, 4. Answers from Selective Service personnel can be found in box 1035, Hershey Papers, USAHEC.

89. "Efforts of Selective Service in Poverty War Are Extensive," 1; "Summer Jobs Being Sought for Ages 16–21," *Selective Service*, June 1966, 3.

90. George Q. Flynn, *Lewis B. Hershey: Mr. Selective Service* (Chapel Hill: University of North Carolina Press, 1985), 227, 232.

91. Hershey, "SS Personnel Are Invited to Join Poverty War."

92. See, for example, Michael J. Hogan, *A Cross of Iron: Harry S. Truman and the Origins of the National Security State, 1945–1954* (New York: Cambridge University Press, 1998); Aaron L. Friedberg, *In the Shadow of the Garrison State: America's Anti-Statism and its Cold War Grand Strategy* (Princeton, N.J.: Princeton University Press, 2000); David A. Horowitz, *Beyond Left and Right: Insurgency and the Establishment* (Urbana: University of Illinois Press, 1997), chap. 10; Michael Brenes, "For Right and Might: The Cold War and the Making of Big-Government Conservatism" (PhD diss., City University of New York, 2013).

93. Hershey, "Storekeeper of Manpower," *Selective Service*, July 1956, 2.

94. "IV-F Review Puts 41 Percent in 'Y' Category," *Selective Service*, February 1961, 1; Gerhardt, *The Draft and Public Policy*, 268.

95. Lewis B. Hershey, "Induction for Rehabilitation, Citizenship Training of Disqualified Personnel," *Selective Service*, Feb. 1964, 1–2.

96. Hershey, "Induction for Rehabilitation."

97. Memo: Secretary Wirtz' Proposal to Work with the Selective Service System in Identifying and Training a Large Group of Young Men Rejected for Military Service because of 'Mental Reasons,'" September 23, 1963, Selective Service Rejectees, box 2, entry UD-UP 3, RG 235, NACP.

98. See Douglas Kinnard, "McNamara at the Pentagon," *Parameters* 10, no. 3 (1980): 22–31.

99. Fred Richard Bahr, "The Expanding Role of the Department of Defense as an Instrument of Social Change" (DBA diss.: George Washington University, 1970), 12; Robert S. McNamara, *The Essence of Security: Reflections in Office* (New York: Harper and Row, 1968), chap. 8, xi, 123.

100. Edward J. Drea, *McNamara, Clifford, and the Burdens of Vietnam, 1965–1969*, Secretaries of Defense Historical Series, vol. 6 (Washington, D.C.: Historical Office, Office of the Secretary of Defense, 2011), 266; Senate Subcommittee of the Committee on Appropriations, *Department of Defense Reprogramming, 1965: Hearings before the Subcommittee of the Committee on Appropriations, United States Senate, on the Department of the Army Special Training Enlistment Program (STEP)*, 89th Cong., 1st sess., January 1965, 9, 23–25. This was not the first time the American military had flirted with rehabilitation within the ranks. See the essays contained in Sanders Marble, ed., *Scraping the Barrel: The Military Use of Substandard Manpower, 1860–1960* (New York: Fordham University Press, 2012).

101. Michael Beschloss, ed., *Reaching for Glory: Lyndon Johnson's Secret White House Tapes, 1964–1965* (New York: Simon and Schuster, 2001), 141.

102. Drea, *McNamara, Clifford, and the Burdens of Vietnam*, 266; Beschloss, *Reaching for Glory*, 141.

103. Senate Subcommittee of the Committee on Appropriations, *Department of Defense Reprogramming, 1965*, 13, 17, 20.

104. U.S. House of Representatives, *Department of Defense Appropriation Bill, 1966: Conference Report*, H. Rpt. 1006, 89th Cong., 1st sess., September 15, 1965, 2, 6.

105. McNamara, *The Essence of Security*, 128, 131.

106. Laurence and Ramsberger, *Low-Aptitude Men in the Military*, 23–24; Thomas G. Sticht et al., *Cast-Off Youth: Policy and Training Methods from the Military Experience* (Westport, Conn.: Praeger, 1987), 42; Drea, *McNamara, Clifford, and the Burdens of Vietnam*, 268.

107. Drea, *McNamara, Clifford, and the Burdens of Vietnam*, 266–67; Laurence and Ramsberger, *Low-Aptitude Men in the Military*, 20.

108. "Excerpts from Address by McNamara," *New York Times*, Aug. 24, 1966; "M'Namara Plans to 'Salvage' 40,000 Rejected in Draft," *New York Times*, Aug. 24, 1966.

109. Sticht et al., *Cast-Off Youth*, 42.

110. Drea, *McNamara, Clifford, and the Burdens of Vietnam*, 268–270; Sticht et al., *Cast-Off Youth*, 41.

111. Sticht et al., *Cast-Off Youth*, 40–41.

112. Mr. Greenberg to Mr. Moskowitz, Feb. 27, 1967, Project 100,000, box 2, entry 14, UD-04W, Records of the Secretary of Defense, RG 330, NACP [emphasis in original].

113. "Army Studies Capabilities of Soldiers," *Selective Service*, Dec. 1966, 1.

114. See Subcommittee on Oversight and Investigations of the House Veterans' Affairs Committee, *Readjustment of Project 100,000 Veterans: Hearing before the Subcommittee on Oversight and Investigations of the Committee on Veterans' Affairs, House of Representatives*, Serial 101-38, 101st Cong., 1st sess., February 28, 1990, 1.

115. Lisa Hsiao, "Project 100,000: The Great Society's Answer to Military Manpower Needs in Vietnam," *Vietnam Generation* 1, no. 2 (Spring 1989): 16.

116. Lawrence M. Baskir and William Strauss, *Chance and Circumstance: The Draft, The War, and the Vietnam Generation* (New York: Vintage Books, 1978), 129.

117. Drea, *McNamara, Clifford, and the Burdens of Vietnam*, 269.

118. Baskir and Strauss, *Chance and Circumstance*, 128.

119. Informal Memorandum for Mr. Moskowitz, Feb. 6, 1967, Project 100,000, box 2, entry 14, UD-O4W, Records of the Office of the Secretary of Defense, RG 330, NACP.

120. Office of Policy Planning and Research, United States Department of Labor, *The Negro Family: The Case for National Action*, March 1965, 29, 42. The report's assumption that families headed by African American women were pathological had far-reaching policy consequences. See Self, *All in the Family*, 26–32.

121. Daniel P. Moynihan, "Who Gets in the Army?" *New Republic*, Nov. 5, 1966, 21, 22 [emphasis in original].

122. Quoted in Drea, *McNamara, Clifford, and the Burdens of Vietnam*, 266.

123. Hsiao, "Project 100,000," 24–25.

124. Robert S. McNamara, "Social Inequities: Urban Racial Ills," Nov. 7, 1967, reprinted in *Vital Speeches of the Day* 34, no. 4 (December 1, 1967): 101.

125. "Defense Reports 'Project 100,000' Proves Successful," no publication, n.d., attached to Memo: New Mental Standards Effective December 1, 1966, December 2,

1966, box 126, entry UD 20, RG 147, NACP. See also Nancy Hicks, "Mentally 'Unfit' Helping Military," *New York Times*, Feb. 17, 1969; "Lower Standards Satisfy Military," *New York Times*, Jan. 27, 1970; George W. Ashworth, "'Marginal' Servicemen Rescued: Extra Training Applauded," *Christian Science Monitor*, Oct. 7, 1967; Ralph H. Kennan, "New Program in Military Aids Rejects," *Baltimore Sun*, Oct. 27, 1968; "Once Rejects, They're Now Good Soldiers," *Los Angeles Times*, Dec. 10, 1968; Donald H. May, "U.S. Training its 'Rejects' for Military," *Chicago Tribune*, Jan. 7, 1968.

126. Hamilton Gregory, *McNamara's Folly: The Use of Low-IQ Troops in the Vietnam War* (West Conshohocken, Pa.: Infinity Publishing, 2015), 3–8, 12–15, 40–41.

127. Drea, *McNamara, Clifford, and the Burdens of Vietnam*, 270.

128. Hanson W. Baldwin, "Men Once Rejected for Low Aptitudes Adapt to Military," *New York Times*, Nov. 19, 1967.

129. Office of the Secretary of Defense, Assistant Secretary of Defense (Manpower and Reserve Affairs), "Project 100,000: Characteristics and Performance of 'New Standards' Men," June 1968, attached to memo: New Mental Standards Effective December 1, 1966, Dec. 2, 1966, box 126, entry UD 20, RG 147, NACP.

130. "Lower Standards Satisfy Military," *New York Times*, Jan. 27, 1970; Drea, *McNamara, Clifford, and the Burdens of Vietnam*, 269.

131. The statistic was not discussed in either the official history of the Department of Defense or at congressional hearings reviewing the program that were convened in 1990. See Drea, *McNamara, Clifford, and the Burdens of Vietnam*; House Subcommittee on Oversight and Investigations of the Committee on Veterans' Affairs, *Readjustment of Project 100,000 Veterans*.

132. "13 Percent Draft Fiscal Year 1966 Were Nonwhites," *Selective Service*, Sept. 1967, 1; "Data for 1967 Reveal 8.9% Negro," *Selective Service*, Oct. 1968, 2.

133. "More Negroes Passed Tests Report Shows," *Selective Service*, July 1967, 1.

134. In fiscal 1966, for example, 8 percent of all volunteers were black, but 13 percent of all draftees were. See "13 Percent Draft Fiscal Year 1966 Were Nonwhites," *Selective Service*, Sept. 1967, 1.

135. Drea, *McNamara, Clifford, and the Burdens of Vietnam*, 271.

136. "Rights Leaders Deplore Plan to 'Salvage' Military Rejects," *New York Times*, Aug. 26, 1966.

137. Dick Edwards, "US Army Draft Called Institutional Racism," *New York Amsterdam News*, March 27, 1971.

138. Longitudinal studies of Project 100,000 veterans indicate that the program had mixed results. See Sticht et al., *Cast-Off Youth*, 37–65; Laurence and Ramsberger, *Low-Aptitude Men in the Military*, 55–61, 94–100, 109–23; Subcommittee on Oversight and Investigations of the House Veterans' Affairs Committee, *Readjustment of Project 100,000 Veterans*.

139. Baskir and Strauss, *Chance and Circumstance*, 127.

140. Hsiao, "Project 100,000," 17–19.

141. "Lower Standards Satisfy Military," *New York Times*, Jan. 27, 1970; Subcommittee on Oversight and Investigations of the House Veterans' Affairs Committee, *Readjustment of Project 100,000 Veterans*, 9, 12.

142. John L. Ward, *Moron Corps: A Vietnam Veteran's Case for Action* (Houston: Strategic Book Publishing and Rights Co., 2012), 13.

143. "Pentagon to Phase Out Project 100,000," *Boston Globe*, March 26, 1971.

144. "Low-IQ Recruit Plan Stirs Complaints," *Washington Post*, June 29, 1969; Hsaio, "Project "100,000," 20; Baskir and Strauss, *Chance and Circumstance*, 127–128.

145. "McNamara's Salvation Army," *New Republic*, Sept. 10, 1966, 13–14; Bob Horton, "Long-Range Study to Decide the Effect of Now Accepting Some Service Rejectees," *Muscatine* [Iowa] *Journal*, Dec. 13, 1967.

146. "Clifford Tells Ghetto Aid Plan," *Chicago Tribune*, Sept. 27, 1968.

147. Michael Harrington, *The Other America: Poverty in the United States* (New York: MacMillan Press, 1962).

148. John E. Eslinger, "Rejected by the Services," *Evening Sun*, Oct. 25, 1965, reprinted in National Committee for Children and Youth, *Experimental and Demonstration Manpower Project for Recruitment, Training, Placement, and Followup of Rejected Armed Forces Volunteers in Baltimore, Maryland and Washington, D.C.: Final Report*, 145.

149. Isolde Weinberg, "He's in the Army Now—and Happy to Be There," *Washington Post*, Dec. 12, 1965.

150. "States Examine First Groups of 18-Year-Olds," *Selective Service*, July 1964, 4

151. See, for example, Office of the Secretary of Defense, Assistant Secretary of Defense (Manpower and Reserve Affairs), "Project 100,000: Characteristics and Performance of 'New Standards' Men," June 1968, attached to memo: New Mental Standards Effected December 1, 1966, December 2, 1966, box 126, entry UD 20, RG 147, NACP; Project One Hundred Thousand, attached Mr. Greenberg to Mr. Moskowitz; Hershey, "SS Personnel Are Invited to Join Poverty War."

Chapter 6. "Choice or Chance"

1. James Fallows, "What Did You Do in the Class War, Daddy?" *The Washington Monthly* 7, no. 8 (October 1975): 5–14.

2. Lawrence M. Baskir and William Strauss, *Chance and Circumstance: The Draft, the War, and the Vietnam Generation* (New York: Vintage Books, 1978), 30.

3. A Google Scholar search conducted on Jan. 11, 2018, yielded sixty-six citations. See also Penny Lewis, *Hardhats, Hippies, and Hawks: The Vietnam Antiwar Movement as Myth and Memory* (Ithaca, N.Y.: Cornell University Press, 2013), 26.

4. Fallows, "What Did You Do in the Class War, Daddy?" 7.

5. Fallows, "What Did You Do in the Class War, Daddy?" 7.

6. Lewis, *Hardhats, Hippies, and Hawks*, 74. See also Lorena Oropeza, ¡Raza Sí! ¡Guerra No! Chicano Protest and Patriotism During the Viet Nam War (Berkeley: University of California Press, 2005), chap. 1.

7. Selective Service System, *Memorandum from General Lewis Hershey, Director of the Selective Service System, on Present Operations of the System and Local Draft Boards* (Washington, D.C.: GPO, 1966), 4.

8. George Q. Flynn, *Lewis B. Hershey: Mr. Selective Service* (Chapel Hill: University of North Carolina Press, 1985), 237–42.

9. "House Votes 378 to 3 to Keep Draft," *Baltimore Sun*, March 12, 1963. For a description of the renewal process, including congressional hearings, see Harry A. Marmion, *Selective Service: Conflict and Compromise* (New York: John Wiley and Sons, 1968), 1–2.

10. See, for example, James Howard, "5 Quit Draft Board in Row," *Chicago Tribune*, Nov. 1, 1962; "A Congressman Can Be Too Obliging," Editorial, *Chicago Tribune*,

Nov. 2, 1962; Robert Howard, "Inject Spoils Politics into State Draft," *Chicago Tribune*, May 17, 1962; Martin Nolan, "He's Married . . . And Drafted," *Boston Globe*, Sept. 15, 1963; "City and U.S. Vary on Draft Rejects," *New York Times*, Jan. 5, 1964.

11. See, for example, John K. Arnot, "End the Draft," *Chicago Tribune*, Jan. 1, 1963; Hanson Baldwin, "New Attitude on Peacetime Draft," *New York Times*, March 8, 1963; B. D. Ayres Jr., "Manpower Excess Seen Causing Stress in Nation's Draft System," *Washington Post*, Jan. 13, 1964; Jack Anderson, "Are We Becoming a Nation of Draft Dodgers," *Boston Globe*, Jan. 19, 1964; Kathryn R. Strom, "End the Draft," *Chicago Tribune*, Feb. 2, 1964; Uncle Dudley, "Overhaul the Draft," *Boston Globe*, April 20, 1964.

12. See Rick Perlstein, *Before the Storm: Barry Goldwater and the Unmaking of the American Consensus* (New York: Hill and Wang, 2001), 409–11.

13. Hanson W. Baldwin, "Should We End the Draft?" *New York Times Magazine*, Sept. 27, 1964.

14. See James M. Gerhardt, *The Draft and Public Policy: Issues in Military Manpower Procurement, 1945–1975* (Columbus: Ohio State University Press, 1971), 286.

15. "Johnson Asks Study of Way to End Draft," *Chicago Tribune*, April 19, 1964; "Johnson Orders Study to Assess Need for Draft," *New York Times*, April 19, 1964; Gerhardt, *The Draft and Public Policy*, 286–87, 362.

16. Flynn, *Lewis B. Hershey*, 234, 243.

17. Louis Harris and Associates, "Public Opinion and the Draft," in *Dialogue on the Draft: Report of the National Conference on the Draft*, ed. June A. Willenz (Washington, D.C.: American Veterans Committee, 1966), 64; Howard James, "Draft Dodging: Is it Growing?" *Christian Science Monitor*, Sept. 1, 1965.

18. William L. Lunch and Peter W. Sperlich, "American Public Opinion and the War in Vietnam," *The Western Political Quarterly* 32, no. 1 (March 1979): 25.

19. George Q. Flynn, *The Draft, 1940–1973* (Lawrence: University Press of Kansas, 1993), 170; United States Selective Service System, *Semi-Annual Report of the Director of Selective Service for the Period July 1 to December 31, 1968* (Washington, D.C.: GPO, 1969), 13.

20. Barry Sadler, *Ballad of the Green Berets* (New York: RCA Victor, 1966); Barry McGuire, *Eve of Destruction* (Los Angeles: Dunhill Records, 1965).

21. Renata Adler, " 'Green Berets' as Viewed by John Wayne: War Movie Arrives at the Warner Theater," *New York Times*, June 20, 1968, available at *The New York Times* online, http://www.nytimes.com/movie/review?res=990ce1d8163ae134bc48 51dfb0668383679ede (accessed Feb. 13, 2018).

22. "Doubling the Draft: When they Tag You 1-A," *Life*, August 20, 1965, 24.

23. Quoted in Charles DeBenedetti and Charles Chatfield, *An American Ordeal: The Antiwar Movement of the Vietnam Era* (Syracuse, N.Y.: Syracuse University Press, 1990), 158.

24. Simon Hall, *Peace and Freedom: The Civil Rights and Antiwar Movements of the 1960s* (Philadelphia: University of Pennsylvania Press, 2005), chap. 3.

25. Oropeza, *¡Raza Sí!, ¡Guerra No!*, 92–102; Daryl J. Maeda, *Chains of Babylon: The Rise of Asian America* (Minneapolis: University of Minnesota Press, 2009), esp. chap. 4; Judy Tzu-Chun Wu, *Radicals on the Road: Internationalism, Orientalism, and Feminism during the Vietnam Era* (Ithaca, N.Y.: Cornell University Press, 2013), esp. part II.

26. Lewis, *Hardhats, Hippies, and Hawks*, 102–15.

27. Sandra Scanlon, *The Pro-War Movement: Domestic Support for the Vietnam War and the Making of Modern American Conservatism* (Amherst: University of Massachusetts Press, 2013), 260.

28. DeBenedetti and Chatfield, *An American Ordeal*, 123, 211.

29. "Johnson's Rating on Vietnam Drops," *New York Times*, February 14, 1968.

30. Christian G. Appy, *American Reckoning: The Vietnam War and Our National Identity* (New York: Viking Press, 2015), xvi.

31. DeBenedetti and Chatfield, *An American Ordeal*, 162.

32. Jon Olsen to Bob, July 16, 1967, folder 1, box 1, WDRU, WHS; Henry E. Anderson, "The Folklore of Draft Resistance," *New York Folklore Quarterly* 28 (June 1972): 135–50; Sherry Gershorn Gottlieb, *Hell No, We Won't Go: Resisting the Draft during the Vietnam War* (New York: Viking Press, 1991), 102, 155.

33. Thomas J. Bray, "Young Men Dream Up Some Ingenious Ways to Avoid the Draft," *Wall Street Journal*, April 11, 1966; Drew Pearson, "Avoiding the Draft Is Becoming the Favorite Sport Among Youth," *Los Angeles Times*, Sept. 27, 1965.

34. "Evading the Draft: Who, How, and Why," *Life*, Dec. 9, 1966, 42.

35. Howard James, "Draft Dodging: Is it Growing?" *Christian Science Monitor*, Sept. 1, 1965.

36. "Bald Case in Point: Pro Football's Magical Immunity," *Life*, Dec. 9, 1966, 46.

37. Quoted in Michael Useem, *Conscription, Protest, and Social Conflict: The Life and Death of a Draft Resistance Movement* (New York: Wiley Press, 1973), 94.

38. United States Selective Service System, *Annual Report of the Director of Selective Service for the Fiscal Year 1966 to the Congress of the United States Pursuant to the Universal Military Training and Service Act as Amended* (Washington, D.C.: GPO, 1967), 17 [hereafter *Annual Report*, (year)].

39. Flynn, *Lewis B. Hershey*, 236–39.

40. Daniel O. Omer, "The Selective Service System Today," in *Dialogue on the Draft: Report of the National Conference on the Draft*, ed. June A. Willenz (Washington, D.C.: American Veterans Committee, 1966), 15.

41. Peter Henig, "On the Manpower Channelers," *New Left Notes*, Jan. 20, 1967: 1, 4–5; Michael S. Foley, *Confronting the War Machine: Draft Resistance during the Vietnam War* (Chapel Hill: University of North Carolina Press, 2003), 61.

42. "Selective Service Softens Policy of Channeling," *Washington Post*, Dec. 14, 1967.

43. United States Selective Service System, "Channeling," *Orientation Kit*, 1965, 3, 6, 8.

44. Rebecca E. Klatch, *A Generation Divided: The New Left, the New Right, and the 1960s* (Berkeley: University of California Press, 1999), 121, 211, 230, 361 note 32.

45. Gilbert Badillo and G. David Curry, "The Social Incidence of Vietnam Casualties: Social Class or Race?" *Armed Forces and Society* 2, no. 3 (May 1976): 397–406; Christian G. Appy, *Working-Class War: American Combat Soldiers and Vietnam* (Chapel Hill: University of North Carolina Press, 1993), 12; Michael Useem, "Conscription and Class," *Society* 18, no. 3 (March/April 1981): 28–30.

46. Baskir and Strauss, *Chance and Circumstance*, 9.

47. Appy, *Working-Class War*, 13.

48. Flynn, *The Draft*, 232.

49. Neil Fligstein, "Militarism, Not Service" *Society* 18, no. 3 (March/April 1981): 43–44; David R. Segal, "How Equal Is 'Equity?'" *Society* 18, no. 3 (March/April 1981): 31–33.

50. Neil Fligstein, "Who Served in the Military, 1940–1973?" *Armed Forces and Society* 6 (1980): 297–312, available at http://afs.sagepub.com/content/6/2/297, DOI: 10.1177/0095327X8000600210.

51. Baskir and Strauss, *Chance and Circumstance*, 9.

52. Beth J. Asch, et al., *Military Enlistment of Hispanic Youth: Obstacles and Opportunities* (Washington, D.C.: National Defense Institute, 2009), 1.

53. Flynn, *The Draft*, 234–35; Useem, "Conscription and Class," 30.

54. Roger Little, "For Choice, Not Chance," *Society* 18, no. 3 (March/April 1981): 49.

55. Charles C. Moskos Jr., "The American Dilemma in Uniform: Race in the Armed Forces," *The Annals of the American Academy of Political and Social Science* 406 (March 1973): 99; Appy, *Working-Class War*, 19.

56. Edward J. Drea, *McNamara, Clifford, and the Burdens of Vietnam, 1965–1969*, Secretaries of Defense Historical Series, vol. 6 (Washington, D.C.: Historical Office, Office of the Secretary of Defense, 2011), 268–70; Thomas G. Sticht et al., *Cast-Off Youth: Policy and Training Methods from the Military Experience* (Westport, Conn.: Praeger, 1987), 41; Janice H. Laurence and Peter F. Ramsberger, *Low-Aptitude Men in the Military: Who Profits? Who Pays?* (Westport, Conn.: Praeger, 1991), 29.

57. Fligstein, "Who Served in the Military," 303.

58. Kimberley L. Phillips, *War! What Is It Good For? Black Freedom Struggles and the U.S. Military from World War II to Iraq* (Chapel Hill: University of North Carolina Press, 2012), 206.

59. Moskos, "The American Dilemma in Uniform," 101.

60. Black Draft Counseling Center, n.d., Black Draft Counseling Center, box 6, Social Action Vertical File, WHS; Jack Frazier, "The Negro and the Draft," *The Catalyst*, July 18, 1966, Louisville Peace and Freedom Center, box 26, Social Action Vertical File, WHS.

61. "Hispanics in the Army," The Army and Diversity, U.S. Army Center of Military History, online at https://history.army.mil/html/faq/diversity.html (accessed Feb. 13, 2018); Charley Trujillo, *Soldados: Chicanos in Viet Nam* (San Jose, Calif.: Chusma House Publications, 1990), vii.

62. Marmion, *Selective Service*, 77. The conferences in Washington, D.C., and the University of Chicago published their proceedings. See June A. Willenz, ed., *Dialogue on the Draft: Report of the National Conference on the Draft* (Washington, D.C.: American Veterans Committee, 1966); and Sol Tax, ed., *The Draft: A Handbook of Facts and Alternatives* (Chicago: University of Chicago Press, 1967).

63. Additional academic studies included James W. Davis Jr. and Kenneth M. Dolbeare, *Little Groups of Neighbors: The Selective Service System* (Chicago: Markham Publishing Company, 1968); Roger W. Little, ed., *Selective Service and American Society* (New York: Russell Sage Foundation, 1969); David F. Bradford, *Deferment Policy in Selective Service*, Research Report Series No. 113, Industrial Relations Section, Department of Economics (Princeton, N.J.: Princeton, 1969). Works for a popular audience included Bruce Chapman, *The Wrong Man in Uniform: Our Unfair and Obsolete*

Draft—and How We Can Replace It (New York: Trident Press, 1967); Jean Carper, *Bitter Greetings* (New York: Grossman, 1967); George Walton, *Let's End This Draft Mess* (New York: David McKay, 1967); Peter Barnes, *Pawns: The Plight of the Citizen-Soldier* (New York: Alfred A. Knopf, 1971).

64. Flynn, *The Draft*, 189.

65. Jack Raymond, "Pentagon Finds Draft Must Stay; Urges Revision," *New York Times*, May 9, 1965.

66. Flynn, *The Draft*, 193; Useem, *Conscription, Protest, and Social Conflict*, 89–90.

67. Betty M. Vetter, "For a Selective Process: Critical Occupations and Deferments," in *Dialogue on the Draft: Report of the National Conference on the Draft*, ed. June A. Willenz (Washington, D.C.: American Veterans Committee, 1966), 49.

68. Flynn, *The Draft*, 192–95.

69. Flynn, *The Draft*, 192.

70. House Committee on Armed Services, *Review of the Administration and Operation of the Selective Service System: Hearings Before the House Committee on Armed Services*, 89th Cong., 2d sess., 1966, 9627, 9634, 9639.

71. National Advisory Commission on Selective Service, *In Pursuit of Equity: Who Serves When Not All Serve?* (Washington, D.C.: GPO, 1967).

72. Civilian Advisory Panel on Military Manpower Procurement, *Report to the Committee on Armed Services, House of Representatives*, 90th Cong., 1st sess., February 28, 1967, 20.

73. Senate Armed Services Committee, *Amending and Extending the Draft Law and Related Authorities: Hearings Before the Committee on Armed Services, United States Senate*, 90th Cong., 1st sess., April 1967, 3.

74. Senate Committee on Labor and Public Welfare, *Manpower Implications of Selective Service: Hearings Before the Subcommittee on Employment, Manpower, and Poverty of the Committee on Labor and Public Welfare*, 90th Cong., 1st sess., 1967, 1, 3, 5.

75. Flynn, *Lewis B. Hershey*, 252–53.

76. Lyndon B. Johnson, *Message from the President of the United States*, H. Rpt. 75, 90th Cong., 1st sess., March 6, 1967.

77. Flynn, *The Draft*, 215, 219.

78. Flynn, *The Draft*, 242.

79. Robert Semple Jr., "Nixon Abolishes Draft Deferment for Fatherhood," *New York Times*, April 24, 1970.

80. Trujillo, *Soldados*, 41–42.

81. Kyle Longley, *Grunts: The American Combat Soldier in Vietnam* (Armonk, N.Y.: M. E. Sharpe, 2008), xiv.

82. James R. Ebert, *A Life in a Year: The American Infantryman in Vietnam, 1965–1972* (Novato, Calif.: Presidio Press, 1993), 9.

83. Ebert, *A Life in a Year*, 22.

84. Stanley W. Beesley, *Vietnam: The Heartland Remembers* (Norman: University of Oklahoma Press, 1987), 5.

85. Charles Moskos Jr., *The American Enlisted Man: The Rank and File in Today's Military* (New York: Russell Sage Foundation, 1970), 116–17.

86. Trujillo, *Soldados*, 1.

87. Ebert, *A Life in a Year*, 7.

88. James R. Wilson, *Landing Zones: Southern Veterans Remember Vietnam* (Durham, N.C.: Duke University Press, 1990), 70.

89. Stanley Goff, Robert Sanders, and Clark Smith, *Brothers: Black Soldiers in the Nam* (Novato, Calif.: Presidio Press, 1982), xvi.

90. Ebert, *A Life in a Year*, 23.

91. Tom Weiner, *Called to Serve: Stories of Men and Women Confronted by the Vietnam War Draft* (Amherst, Mass.: Levellers Press, 2011), 23.

92. Appy, *Working-Class War*, 51.

93. Loren Baritz, *Backfire: Vietnam—The Myths That Made Us Fight, The Illusions That Helped Us Lose, The Legacy That Haunts Us Today* (New York: Ballantine Books, 1985), 278, quoted in Ebert, *A Life in a Year*, 19.

94. Trujillo, *Soldados*, 143.

95. Weiner, *Called to Serve*, 9; Baskir and Strauss, *Chance and Circumstance*, 86–87.

96. Gerald Robert Gill, "Afro-American Opposition to the United States' Wars of the Twentieth Century: Dissent, Discontent, and Disinterest" (PhD diss., Howard University, 1985), 218; Baskir and Strauss, *Chance and Circumstance*, 86.

97. United States Selective Service System, *Semiannual Report of the Director of Selective Service for the Period January 1 to June 30, 1970* (Washington, D.C.: GPO, 1970), 15.

98. Prosecutions during Fiscal Year 1969, n.d., folder 98, box 8, Midwest Committee for Military Counseling Collection, Special Collections, Richard J. Daley Library, UIC.

99. "Many Seek to Beat Deadline," *New York Times*, Aug. 27, 1965; "Marriage and the Draft," *The New Republic*, Sept. 11, 1965, 9.

100. Andrea Kutinova, "Paternity Deferments and the Timing of Births: U.S. Natality during the Vietnam War," *Economic Inquiry* 47, no. 2 (April 2009): 351–65; Baskir and Strauss, *Chance and Circumstance*, 33.

101. *Annual Report*, 1966, 17.

102. David Card and Thomas Lemieux, "Going to College to Avoid the Draft: The Unintended Legacy of the Vietnam War," *The American Economic Review* 91, no. 2 (May 2001): 101. See also Harvey Galper and Robert M. Dunn, "A Short-Run Demand Function for Higher Education in the United States," *Journal of Political Economy* 77, no. 5 (Sept./Oct. 1969): 765–77; and John Bishop, "The Effect of Public Policies on the Demand for Higher Education," *Journal of Human Resources* 12, no. 3 (Summer 1977): 285–307.

103. Lacey Fosburgh, "Teachers' Ranks Swollen by Men Avoiding Draft," *New York Times*, Jan. 7, 1969.

104. Baskir and Strauss, *Chance and Circumstance*, 32.

105. "Grad School Enrollment Up Report Shows," *Selective Service*, May 1969; Baskir and Strauss, *Chance and Circumstance*, 32.

106. James E. Westheider, *The African American Experience in Vietnam: Brothers in Arms* (New York: Rowman & Littlefield, 2008), 26.

107. Ebert, *A Life in a Year*, 15.

108. Westheider, *The African American Experience in Vietnam*, 34.

109. Ebert, *A Life in a Year*, 16; Robert Rawitch, "Salad Days Over for Army's Reserve," *Los Angeles Times*, March 2, 1970.

110. Westheider, *The African American Experience in Vietnam*, 34.

111. Westheider, *The African American Experience in Vietnam*, 35.

112. Michael S. Neiberg, *Making Citizen Soldiers: ROTC and the Ideology of American Military Service* (Cambridge, Mass.: Harvard University Press, 2000), 94, 101, 117, 118.

113. Bill Clinton to Colonel Holmes, Dec. 3, 1969, at *Frontline*, http://www.pbs.org/wgbh/pages/frontline/shows/clinton/etc/draftletter.html (accessed, December 3, 2018).

114. Paul Lyons, *Class of '66: Living in Suburban Middle America* (Philadelphia: Temple University Press, 1994), 76, 96.

115. Foley, *Confronting the War Machine*, 68–75.

116. Weiner, *Called to Serve*, 210–12; Gottlieb, *Hell No, We Won't Go*, 19–20.

117. Baskir and Strauss, *Chance and Circumstance*, 37. Donald Trump's history with the Selective Service remains murky. It is clear that he received a letter from a medical professional, although who that professional was and how they were acquainted with Trump has not been firmly established. See Steve Eder, "Did a Queens Podiatrist Help Donald Trump Avoid Vietnam?" *New York Times*, Dec. 26, 2018, available at *The New York Times* online, https://www.nytimes.com/2018/12/26/us/politics/trump-vietnam-draft-exemption.html, (Accessed Dec. 27, 2018).

118. See, for example, Samuel C. Brownstein, *Barron's How to Prepare for the Student Draft Deferment Test* (Woodbury, N.Y.: Barron's Educational Series, 1966); David Suttler, *IV-F: A Guide to Medical, Psychiatric, and Moral Unfitness Standards for Military Induction* (New York: Grove Press, 1970); Arlo Tatum and Joseph S. Tuchinsky, *Guide to the Draft* (Boston: Beacon Press, 1969); Tuli Kupferberg, *1001 Ways to Beat the Draft* (New York: Grove Press, 1967); Darrell Hatfield Nicholson, *You and the Draft Lottery, 1970* (Murfreesboro, N.C.: D. H. Nicholson and C. P. Stevens, 1970); Update Questionnaire, Draft Counseling Center, University of Hartford, Oct. 18, 1971, Mass., R.I., Conn., box 14, CCCO, SCPC; MADIC Monthly Report, n.d., Milwaukee Area Draft Info Center, box 28, Social Action Vertical File, WHS; "Dear General Marsbars," column, *Washington Free Press*; "The Draft Counselor," column, *Boston Globe*.

119. Baskir and Strauss, *Chance and Circumstance*, 37.

120. A Proposal to Develop Draft Counseling in Black Communities, n.d., Counselor Training Program, box 9, CCCO, SCPC.

121. Report for the Year Ending August 31, 1949, Annual Reports, 1949–1962, box 1, CCCO, SCPC.

122. Annual Report, September 1, 1952–August 31, 1953, Annual Reports, 1949–1962, box 1, CCCO, SCPC.

123. Annual Report of the Executive Secretary, September 1, 1959–August 31, 1960, Annual Reports, 1949–1962, box 1, CCCO, SCPC.

124. Annual Report of the Executive Secretary, September 1, 1960–August 31, 1961, Annual Reports, 1949–1962, box 1, CCCO, SCPC.

125. "25 Years—The Struggle for Conscience," n.d., Constitution (1969), box 1, CCCO, SCPC.

126. A Proposal Made to the Episcopal Church for Financial Assistance, n.d., Church Development (1969–1970), box 9, CCCO, SCPC.

127. Dan Swinney to Dear Friend, n.d., folder 3, box 1, WDRU, WHS.

128. List of Draft Counseling Centers, n.d., folder 2, box 3, WDRU, WHS. See also lists contained in box 14, CCCO, SCPC.

129. See pamphlets contained in folder 11, box 1, and folder 1, box 2, DCIC, WHS.

130. See, for example, Gottlieb, *Hell No, We Won't Go!*, 243–47.

131. See documents contained in folder 3, box 3, DCIC, WHS.

132. Seymour P. Lachman to Members of the Board, Jan. 5, 1970, folder 3, box 3, DCIC, WHS; Update Questionnaire, Interfaith Center for Draft Information, Worcester, Mass., Oct. 26, 1971, Mass., R.I., Conn., box 14, CCCO, SCPC.

133. No title, n.d., folder 5, box 1, WDRU, WHS.

134. See Account of Activity, New Orleans Draft Resisters Union, July 21, 1967, folder 1, box 1; Dan Swinney to Robert Maki, Feb. 19, 1968, folder 2, box 1, and Thomas Hammerly to Dear Sir, May 16, 1968, folder 2, box 1, all in WDRU, WHS.

135. Some Thoughts About CCCO, March 1972, Form Letters/Releases (1970–), box 3, CCCO, SCPC.

136. Dear Friend, n.d., folder 3, box 1, WDRU, WHS [emphasis in original].

137. By May 1972, the CCCO's list of relevant Supreme Court cases ran to six pages. See "Tools for Counselors, Attorneys, Libraries, Vol. 1," 1972, Tools for Counselors, Attorneys, Libraries, box 7, CCCO, SCPC.

138. See, for example, *DeRemer v. United States*, 340 F.2d 712, 715 (8th Cir., 1965). See also, Charles H. Wilson Jr., "The Selective Service System: An Administrative Obstacle Course," *California Law Review* 54, no. 5 (Dec. 1966): 2123–79.

139. W. D. to John Reints, March 15, 1967, W.D., Personal Files of COs, box 6, CCCO, SCPC.

140. *Oestereich v. Selective Service System Local Board No. 11*, 393 U.S. 233 (1968); *Gutknecht v. United States* 396 U.S. 295 (1970).

141. *United States v. Seeger*, 380 U.S. 163 (1965), Justia: U.S. Supreme Court, https://supreme.justia.com/cases/federal/us/380/163/case.html (accessed Dec. 3, 2018).

142. Quoted in Ann Fagan Ginger, *The New Draft Law: A Manual for Lawyers and Counselors*, National Lawyers Guild, 1972, 235, 47, in Atty's Guide, box 11, CCCO, SCPC.

143. *Welsh v. United States*, 398 U.S. 333 (1970), Justia: U.S. Supreme Court, https://supreme.justia.com/cases/federal/us/398/333/case.html (accessed Dec. 3, 2018).

144. *Gillette v. United States*, 401 U.S. 437 (1971).

145. Useem, *Conscription, Protest, and Social Conflict*, 131.

146. According to Baskir and Strauss, close to twenty-seven million men reached draft age during the Vietnam War. Of these, approximately 171,000, or approximately 0.63 percent, were certified as COs (Baskir and Strauss, *Chance and Circumstance*, 5, 30). Although this percentage is low, it is almost half again as great as the comparable proportion (0.45 percent) from World War II, assuming that one hundred thousand men were certified as COs out of a draftable pool of twenty-two million men between the ages of eighteen and thirty-seven (Flynn, *The Draft*, 63).

147. Chambers, "Conscientious Objectors and the American State," in *The New Conscientious Objection: From Sacred to Secular Resistance*, ed. Charles C. Moskos and John Whiteclay Chambers II (New York: Oxford University Press, 1993), 42.

148. Peter Elbow, "Who Is a Conscientious Objector?" August 7, 1968, Form Letters/Releases (1963–1969), box 3, CCCO, SCPC.

149. "The Left—View From Within," [Philadelphia] *Evening Bulletin*, March 10, 1966, in Newsclippings by Name of C.O., 1966–1970, box 8, CCCO, SCPC. See also Baskir and Strauss, *Chance and Circumstance*, 70–73.

150. Lee Lowenfish and Dan Swinney to Friend, March 21, 1967, folder 1, box 1, WDRU, WHS.

151. Flynn, *The Draft*, 180.

152. Flynn, *The Draft*, 205, 213.

153. Baskir and Strauss, *Chance and Circumstance*, 82; Flynn, *The Draft*, 214.

154. Letter, March 1, 1971, folder 58, box 5b, Midwest Committee for Military Counseling, UIC.

155. Quoted in Baskir and Strauss, *Chance and Circumstance*, 42–43.

156. See, for example, Answers to SS Form 150 and Later Amplification, n.d., and SS Form 150 (revised 8-30-68), attached to C.O. Statement, n.d., both in folder 2, box 2, DCIC, WHS.

157. Saul Braun, "From 1-A to 4-F and All Points in Between," *New York Times*, Nov. 29, 1970.

158. Gill, "Afro-American Opposition to the United States' Wars of the Twentieth Century," 134, 173; Ernie Alexander, "A Black Response to a White Draft Counseling Community," n.d., National Black Draft Counselors, box 31, Social Action Vertical File, WHS.

159. For more on Muhammad Ali, see B. T. Harrison, "Muhammad Ali Draft Case and Public Debate on Vietnam," *Peace Research* 33, no. 2 (2001): 69–86; Herman Graham III, *The Brothers' Vietnam War: Black Power, Manhood, and the Military Experience* (Gainesville: University Press of Florida, 2003), chap. 5.

160. Gill, "Afro-American Opposition to the United States' Wars of the Twentieth Century," 178.

161. Dear Friends, Oct. 8, 1969, folder 51, box 5a, Midwest Committee for Military Counseling, UIC.

162. Dear Folk, June 21, 1970, and Letter, Feb. 16, 1970, both in folder 51, box 5a, Midwest Committee for Military Counseling, UIC.

163. See Upstairs at Atwood C.H., n.d., folder 7, box 1, DCIC, WHS; SG to Rev. Ruetz, Nov. 22, 1967, and Rennie Davis to Friends, May 14, 1967, both in folder 2, box 1, WDRU, WHS; Why We Do Draft Counseling, n.d., Draft Counseling Misc., box 17, Social Action Vertical File, WHS; and A Proposal to Develop Draft Counseling in the Black Communities, n.d., Counselor Training Program, box 9; Update Questionnaire, Bristol-Washington Co. (Va.) Draft Information Center, Emory, VA, Oct. 18, 1971, folder 14, box 1, both in CCCO, SCPC.

164. Update Questionnaire, Celebrate Life—Draft Information Services, Alexandria, VA, Nov. 9, 1971, Wash. D.C., Del., Md., W.Va.,Va., box 14, CCCO, SCPC.

165. Upstairs at Atwood C.H.

166. Braun, "From 1-A to 4-F"; Baskir and Strauss, *Chance and Circumstance*, 48.

167. Lewis, *Hardhats, Hippies, and Hawks*, 75.

168. Frank Adams to Bob Seeley, Oct. 11, 1971, N. Carolina, S. Carolina, Tenn., box 14, CCCO, SCPC.

169. Update Questionnaire, Bristol-Washington Co. (Va.) Draft Information Service.

170. Hell No! We Won't Go, n.d., Black Anti-Draft Union, box 6; Black Draft Counseling Center, n.d., Black Draft Counseling Center, box 6; Press Release, n.d., Blacks Against the Draft, box 6; Press Release, Feb. 1, 1968, Kentucky Conference on the War and the Draft, box 24; Dear Brothers and Sisters, Feb. 22, 1972, National Black Draft Counselors, box 31; Progress Report on Black Draft Counseling in the Philadelphia Area, n.d., National Black Draft Counselors, box 31, all in Social Action Vertical File, WHS; National Black Draft Counselors: What We're About, n.d., folder 1, box 2, DCIC, WHS.

171. Remarks of Ralph Hendrix, n.d., Black Anti-Draft Union, box 6, Social Action Vertical File, WHS.

172. Westheider, *The African American Experience in Vietnam*, 26.

173. National Black Draft Counselors: What We're About, n.d., folder 1, box 2, DCIC, WHS.

174. Black Draft Counseling Center, n.d.; A Black Response to a White Draft Counseling Community, n.d., National Black Draft Counselors, box 31, Social Action Vertical File, WHS.

175. Gill, "Afro-American Opposition to the United States' Wars of the Twentieth Century," 227–28.

176. You and the Draft, n.d., box 4, CCCO, SCPC.

177. Braun, "From 1-A to 4-F"; Homosexuality and the Draft, n.d., folder 8, box 1, DCIC, WHS; Weiner, *Called to Serve*, 153, 192, 222–23; Quote from Autobiography of a Fort Knox Trainee, n.d., Kentucky Military and Draft Counseling Center, box 24, Social Action Vertical File, WHS.

178. Remarks of Ralph Hendrix, n.d.

179. You *Can* Keep This Leaflet, n.d., folder 10, box 1, DCIC, WHS; CADRE Personal Statement, June 30, 1967, folder 3, box 1, WDRU, WHS.

180. Resist: Five Personal Statements, n.d., Chicago Area Draft Resisters, box 8, Social Action Vertical File, WHS.

181. Dear Friend, n.d., folder 3, box 1, WDRU, WHS.

182. There is much still to be examined on the broad contours of gender during the Vietnam era, but for examples see Heather Marie Stur, *Beyond Combat: Women and Gender in the Vietnam Era* (New York: Cambridge University Press, 2011); Justin David Suran, "Coming Out Against the War: Antimilitarism and the Politicization of Homosexuality in the Era of Vietnam," *American Quarterly* 53, no. 3 (September 2001): 452–88; Tim Hodgdon, *Manhood in the Age of Aquarius: Masculinity in Two Countercultural Communities, 1965–1983* (New York: Columbia University Press, 2008). For an overview of second-wave feminism see Ruth Rosen, *The World Split Open: How the Modern Women's Movement Changed America* (New York: Penguin Books, 2001).

183. Lewis, *Hardhats, Hippies, and Hawks*; Joshua B. Freeman, "Hardhats: Construction Workers, Manliness, and the 1970 Pro-War Demonstrations," *Journal of Social History* 26, no. 4 (Summer 1993): 725–44.

184. On the Vietnam veteran's movement, see Andrew E. Hunt, *The Turning: A History of Vietnam Veterans against the War* (New York: New York University Press, 1999); Richard Moser, *The New Winter Soldiers: GI and Veteran Dissent during the Vietnam Era* (New Brunswick, N.J.: Rutgers University Press, 1996); Gerald Nicosia, *Home to War: A History of the Vietnam Veterans' Movement* (New York: Crown Publishers, 2001).

185. Gertrude Wilson, "I'm Not a Flag Waver, But I've Learned A Lot," in "Draft-Age Dilemma," *McCalls*, August 1967, 34.

Conclusion

1. Alfred A. Blum, "Work or Fight: The Use of the Draft as a Manpower Sanction during the Second World War," *ILR Review* 16, no. 3 (April 1963): 366–80.

2. Selective Service System, "Channeling," *Orientation Kit*, 1965, 6–7.

3. For more on the Army as a welfare institution, see Jennifer Mittelstadt, *The Rise of the Military Welfare State* (Cambridge, Mass.: Harvard University Press, 2015).

4. These men, along with Yale Brozen, an economics professor at the University of Chicago; Bruce K. Chapman, the author of *The Wrong Man in Uniform*, a work that publicized the problems of the draft; Richard C. Cornelle, the author of *Reclaiming the American Dream*, a book that promoted the libertarian vision of voluntarism to solve the nation's problems; David Franke, the editor of the *New Guard*, the organ of the Young Americans for Freedom; Sanford Gottlieb, political action adviser for the National Committee for a SANE Nuclear Policy; and Eugene Groves, president of the National Student Association, a student activist organization, all sponsored the University of Chicago–based Council for a Volunteer Military. See Thomas B. Curtis, "Conscription and Commitment," n.d., reprint, May 15 [1969] Meeting, box 1, Records of the President's Commission on an All-Volunteer Armed Force, 1969–1970, Records of Temporary Committees, Commissions, and Boards, RG 220, Papers of Richard Nixon, NACP. The reprint of the original article, which appears to have run in *Playboy*, was sponsored by the Council for a Volunteer Military.

5. See Bernard Rostker, *I Want You! The Evolution of the All-Volunteer Force* (Arlington, Va.: RAND Corporation, 2006); Beth Bailey, *America's Army: Making the All-Volunteer Force* (Cambridge, Mass: Harvard University Press, 2009); and Mittelstadt, *The Rise of the Military Welfare State*, chap. 1–3.

6. Bailey, *America's Army*, 2, 24.

7. See Rostker, *I Want You!* 32–36, 52–58.

8. For more on the Gates Commission, see Rostker, *I Want You!* 76–89; Thomas S. Gates, *Report of the President's Commission on an All-Volunteer Armed Force* (Washington, D.C.: GPO, 1970).

9. U.S. House of Representatives, *Draft Deferments: Message from the President of the United States Relative to Reforming the Draft System*, H. Doc. 91-324, 91st Cong., 2d sess., April 23, 1970.

10. T. Christopher Jespersen, "The Bitter End and the Lost Chance in Vietnam: Congress, the Ford Administration, and the Battle over Vietnam, 1975–76," *Diplomatic History* 24, no. 2 (Spring 2000): 265–93; Steven Hurst, *The Carter Administration and Vietnam* (New York: St. Martin's Press, 1996); Eric T. Dean Jr., "The Myth of the Troubled and Scorned Vietnam Veteran," *Journal of American Studies* 26, no. 1 (April 1992): 59–74; Jerry Lembcke, *The Spitting Image: Myth, Memory, and the Legacy of Vietnam* (New York: New York University Press, 1998), chap. 7.

11. Marjorie J. Spruill, *Divided We Stand: The Battle Over Women's Rights and Family Values that Polarized American Politics* (New York: Bloomsbury, 2017), 102; Michael Sherry, *In the Shadow of War: The United States Since the 1930s* (New Haven, Conn.: Yale University Press, 1995), 372–73.

12. Political attempts to renew the draft after the terrorist attacks of September 11, 2001, were met with derision. See, for example, William F. Buckley Jr., "Who's Fighting the War," *National Review*, May 5, 2003, 55; "Backdraft," *The Nation*, Dec. 1, 2003, 8; "Draft Dodge," *Wall Street Journal*, Jan. 6, 2003; Carl Hulse, "A New Tactic Against War: Renew Talk About the Draft," *New York Times*, Feb. 9, 2003; Clyde Haberman, "Draft Talk, But Source Is Antiwar," *New York Times*, Jan. 3, 2003.

13. Bailey, *America's Army*, esp. chap. 2; Mittelstadt, *The Rise of the Military Welfare State*, chap. 1–3.

14. Jeremy Varon, *Bringing the War Home: The Weather Underground, the Red Army Faction, and Revolutionary Violence in the Sixties and Seventies* (Berkeley: University of California Press, 2004); Robert O. Self, *All in the Family: The Realignment of American Democracy since the 1960s* (New York: Hill and Wang, 2010), chap. 10.

15. Sherry, *In the Shadow of War*, 337–40; Jefferson Cowie, *Stayin' Alive: The 1970s and the Last Days of the Working Class* (New York: The New Press, 2010); Andreas Killen, *1973 Nervous Breakdown: Watergate, Warhol, and the Birth of Post-Sixties America* (New York: Bloomsbury, 2006); Meg Jacobs, *Panic at the Pump: The Energy Crisis and the Transformation of American Politics in the 1970s* (New York: Hill and Wang, 2016).

16. Sherry, *In the Shadow of War*, 365–74. See also Self, *All in the Family*, esp. chap. 13; and Natasha Zaretsky, *No Direction Home: The American Family and the Fear of National Decline* (Chapel Hill: University of North Carolina Press, 2007).

17. Sherry, *In the Shadow of War*, 401.

18. George Bush, "Remarks to the American Legislative Exchange Council," March 1, 1991, reprinted at Gerhard Peters and John T. Woolley, *The American Presidency Project*, University of California–Santa Barbara, http://www.presidency.ucsb.edu/ws/?pid=19351 (accessed Feb. 13, 2018).

19. Lembcke, *The Spitting Image*, 25.

20. Susan Jeffords, *The Remasculinization of America: Gender and the Vietnam War* (Bloomington: Indiana University Press, 1989); Lembcke, *The Spitting Image*.

21. Susan Jeffords, "Debriding Vietnam: The Resurrection of the White American Male," *Feminist Studies* 14, no. 3 (Autumn 1988): 527.

22. New research indicates that the children of men who served in Vietnam were more likely to join the military than the children of men who did not. See Tim Johnson, et al., "Numbers Assigned in the Vietnam-Era Selective Service Lotteries Influence the Military Service Decisions of Children Born to Draft-Eligible Men: A Research Note," *Armed Forces and Society* 44, no. 2 (2018): 347–67.

Index

Page references in italics indicate a photograph.

Lightning Source UK Ltd.
Milton Keynes UK
UKHW011116090721
386819UK00013B/580